BEAUTIFUL BOTTOM, BEAUTIFUL SHAME

EDITED BY MICHÈLE AINA BARALE,

JONATHAN GOLDBERG, MICHAEL MOON,

AND EVE KOSOFSKY SEDGWICK

BEAUTIFUL BOTTOM, BEAUTIFUL SHAME

Where "Black" Meets "Queer"

KATHRYN BOND STOCKTON

DUKE UNIVERSITY PRESS

Durham and London

2006

2nd printing, 2007

© 2006 Duke University Press

All rights reserved

Printed in the United States of

America on acid-free paper ♾

Designed by Amy Ruth Buchanan

Typeset in Scala by Tseng

Information Systems, Inc.

Library of Congress Cataloging-

in-Publication Data appear on

the last printed page of this book.

For Shelley and Jake

CONTENTS

ACKNOWLEDGMENTS

I am embarrassed by how many people have been asked to read this book —in all or in part. I owe so much to attentive comments and smart suggestions made by Henry Abelove, Charles Berger, Karen Brennan, Gillian Brown, Lynn Butler, Mary Carpenter, Robert Caserio, Barbara Christian, Beth Clement, Bill Cohen, Stuart Culver, Richard Dellamora, Jane Garrity, Brooke Hopkins, Karen Jacobs, Dorothee Kocks, Karen Lawrence, Kim Lau, Brian Locke, Pamela Matthews, Colleen McDannell, David McWhirter, Constance Merritt, Mary Ann O'Farrell, Jackie Osherow, Stephanie Pace, Peggy Pascoe, Matt Potolsky, Wilfred Samuels, Grant Sperry, Sandra Kumamoto Stanley, Nicole Stansbury, Henry Staten, Steve Tatum, Michael Thomas, and Claudia Wright. Becky Horn and Melanee Cherry have offered a superb combination of humor and intellectual companionship throughout the length of this book's life. Martha Ertman has added her own charming wit and incisive suggestions (not to mention baked goods) in the crucial last stages of my deliberations. And Barry Weller, my most enduring interlocutor and unfailing advisor on these topics, has offered editorial wisdom at every turn in this process.

As for institutional support, the University of Utah's English Department (especially my chair, Stuart Culver), the College of Humanities (particularly my dean, Robert Newman), and the Associate Vice President for Diversity, Karen Dace, have offered material and intellectual assistance beyond compare. Utah's Tanner Humanities Center, along with the University of Utah's Faculty Fellowship Program, have provided me with generous grants for research leave, and in the early days of this project I spent a blissful semester as a senior research fellow at Wesleyan University's Humanities Center. Students in my courses—particularly in "The Semiotics of Race," "Queer Theory," "African-American Texts and Contexts," "The Color of Form and the Contents of Debasement," and "Canonical Perversions"—have added their support by making my research bend back to where it matters: live student bodies with skeptical views.

Particular, in-depth gratitude is due to my gender studies' "riot grrls": my first administrative partner, the remarkable Debra Burrington; my indispensable associate director, Gerda Saunders, whose readings of my work have been as precise, brilliant, and genuinely helpful as she is; the ever-perceptive Michelle Turner, who aided me generously and immeasurably when we worked together; the always elegant Tiffany Merrill, whose mental acuity graced my work for one short year; the fabulous kt farley (she of the faux-hawk), who has been an intellectual tiger for me in securing permissions and, more broadly, in keeping my book (and, more truly, me) on track down the stretch; and the endlessly surprising, wonderfully discerning Erin Menut, whose research assistance and academic friendship have made enormous contributions to my work.

Warmest thanks are also owed to the impressive people working with me on my book at Duke University Press: first and foremost, Ken Wissoker, whose patience, incisiveness, and kindness throughout the editorial process have literally made this book possible; and Christine Dahlin, Anitra Grisales, Kate Lothman, Katie Courtland, Fred Kameny, and Katharine Baker—all tremendously helpful and professional, and all such a pleasure to have on one's side. The readers who read my work for the Press—Eve Kosofsky Sedgwick and a second, anonymous reader—could not have been more crucial for the form this book now takes; uncompromising, trenchant, and encouraging suggestions have been offered to me, which I have admired and tried to enact.

Earlier, much different versions of a few of these chapters have appeared in other places and are reprinted here with kind permission from the publishers. A version of Chapter 1, "Cloth Wounds, or When Queers Are Martyred to Clothes: Debasements of a Fabricated Skin," was published in *Aesthetic Subjects*, edited by Pamela Matthews and David McWhirter (University of Minnesota Press, 2003); other versions appeared in John Schad's edited volume *Writing the Bodies of Christ: The Church from Carlyle to Derrida* (Ashgate, 2001) and *Women: A Cultural Review* (spring 2003), in a special issue on gender and fashion edited by Isobel Armstrong. A very early version of Chapter 2, "Bottom Values: Anal Economics in the History of Black Neighborhoods," appeared in *Cultural Critique* (spring 1993); it was then reprinted in *Other Sisterhoods: Literary Theory and U.S. Women of Color*, edited by Sandra Kumamoto Stanley (University of Illinois Press, 1998). "Prophylactics and Brains: Slavery in the Cybernetic Age of AIDS," my fifth chapter, was previously published in a special issue of *Studies in the Novel*, edited by Eve Kosofsky Sedgwick (fall 1996); it reappeared in Sedgwick's edited volume *Novel Gazing: Queer Readings in Fiction* (Duke University Press, 1997).

Finally, I carry some intimate debts that I am happy to acknowledge: to my brother's family (David, Judy, Adam, and Jon), whose constant care and intellectual engagement have held me close; to my parents, Ed and Marilyn, who are, quite simply, my closest friends; and to Shelley White—all love here to my book's best reader—whose wisdom and beauty put me to shame.

Introduction

EMBRACING SHAME

"BLACK" AND "QUEER" IN DEBASEMENT

The Eyes of the Times

In the same summer the TV sensation *Queer Eye for the Straight Guy* burst on the scene, making it seem as if every man who was hopelessly dense about housewares and clothes was now a happy mannequin to a group of queens, the *New York Times Magazine* was reporting, in a cover story, on AIDS and double lives in the black homosexual underground.[1]

Such an uncovering by the *Times*, linking black men to hide-outs and AIDS, was probably not pretty to conventional eyes: black men meeting in the basement of a bathhouse, trying to dress like "thugs," seeking sex from men who also seek "thugs," men who report that they are not gay, just black men seeking other black men on the secret circuit they call the Down Low. "Gays are the faggots who dress, talk and act like girls. That's not me," one man explains (32). Or, as the *Times* reporter put it: "Rejecting a gay culture they perceive as white and effeminate, many black men," who sleep with men, and come from many walks of life (professional, unemployed, working-class), "have settled on a new identity, with its own vocabulary . . . and its own name: Down Low" (30). Hypermasculinity is their calling card; "DLThugs," their online chat room.

True, said the *Times*, "there have always been men—black and white—who have had secret sexual lives with men. But the creation of an organized, underground subculture largely made up of black men who otherwise live straight lives is a phenomenon of the last decade" (30). A man on the DL glosses the term: "Being on the DL is about having fun. . . . The closet isn't fun. In the closet, you're lonely. . . . I think DL is just a new, sexier way to say you're in the closet" (31). "Still," said the *Times*, "for all the defiance that DL culture claims for itself, for all of the forcefulness of the 'never apologize, never explain' stance, a sense of shame can hover at the margins" (48). And whatever its intent, the article makes shame hover rather darkly by citing "grim statistics": "According to the Centers for Disease Control," the *Times* continues, "one-third of young urban black men who have sex with men in this country are HIV-positive, and 90 percent of those are unaware of their infection," "making [these men] an infectious bridge spreading HIV to unsuspecting wives and girlfriends" (30).

This new news for the *New York Times*, in 2003, was a form of old news in a different form: the strained relations between "black" and "gay" at the level of signs, even as ongoing struggles for rights and a health epidemic of epic proportions continued to connect black and gay people. Not much newer in the *Times*'s cover story was the dream of a bottom (here, the Down Low) as a sexual and economic social communion, more than any kind of economic condition—one ensuring pleasures, even if they come with shame. As I say, these dynamics—sensitive relations between two signs and embrace of bottom states—were hardly new, as I will amply show. But there has been too little intellectual curiosity applied to the ways these dynamics intersect.

I would like to take a newly curious look at bottom values for women and men; to understand why certain forms of shame are embraced by blacks and queers, and also black queers, in forceful ways. We are bound in this pursuit to probe the value of debasement as a central social action, even when debasement seems a private, lonely act. We are likewise bound to cut a path through strained relations (between groups of people and between their signs) to see how "queer" and "black" touch upon each other's meanings, no matter who or what would keep them apart. These two forms of social communion—through acts of debasement and the crossing of signs—are the focus of this book.

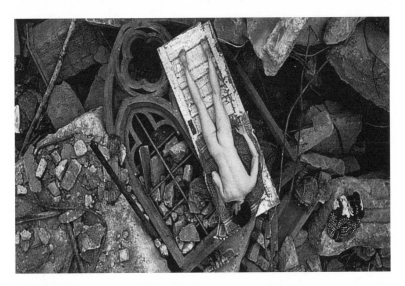

1. Hedwig bottom-up on door, *Hedwig and the Angry Inch* (2001).

Seductive Debasement and the Role of a Switchpoint

Let me introduce, provisionally here, how we might think about the crossing of signs in the context of debasement—and think about debasement in the context of seduction. Imagine a man's putting candy on some rubble, making a line, marked by candy, on top of the rubble, drawing you toward his beautiful body, parts of it covered in candy when you see it. The candy-covered body, with its candy-colored spread, leads you to find yourself carried away—by a seduction that you've never seen take this strange form.[2]

The seduction of our eyes (eye candy, indeed) takes place while we are seeing a seduction on its way to unfolding a debasement. In *Hedwig and the Angry Inch* (2001), an East German youth (effeminate, flamboyant, lying bottom up on the ruins of a door) meets a seductive and older black American army sergeant (a buff "Sugar Daddy," with a rich supply of candy) when the youth is tanning, in a bombed-out crater, by the Berlin Wall (see figures 1 and 2). The two hatch a plan to marry each other by unusual means, thereby pulling the German twenty-something across the wall: the youth will have a sex-change. As it turns out, the procedure is botched, leaving the young man not with a penis nor with a new vagina, but, instead, an "angry inch," as the movie's title puts it. His move to the States is simultaneous with the fall of the wall (ironically making his

2. Sugar Daddy with candy, *Hedwig and the Angry Inch* (2001).

great escape moot), along with the end of the lovers' relations, leaving the viewer at this point to wonder: the film needs a black American male (needs a specifically black Sugar Daddy) to indicate . . . what?

We can't fully tell, though any number of associations seem to rise up: freedom, false freedom, migration (of course), the cutting tone of irony, myths of castration and genital fullness, miscegenation. The black man's momentary passage through this text operates as a luxurious crossing, so voluptuous at the level of image that no one's political extraction of a point can sufficiently deliver the funk of his candy-covered form. And yet, in its fullness, this crossing also works as a fascinating switchpoint. By switchpoint here, I mean the point at which one sign's rich accumulations—those surrounding "American black"—lend themselves to another—"East German queer" (among other possible readings of these bodies). That is, through the figure of the black Sugar Daddy, numerous meanings attached to "black" (perhaps false freedom or myths of castration, to take two obvious associations) switch onto new tracks and signify in the field of "queerness" (whether his own queerness or that of the boy).

I think of a switchpoint, at least in part, in railroad terms, according to which a "switch" is "a movable section of railroad track" that is "used in transferring a train from one set of tracks to another"; or, in electrical terms: "a device used to open, close or divert an electric current"; or, in the general sense of a switch as "a shift or transference, especially if sudden or unexpected." My talk of switchpoints throughout this book will draw on all these possible meanings. Largely, I will use the term to refer to a point of connection between two signs (or two rather separate connotative fields) where something from one flows toward (is diverted in the direction of) the other, lending its connotative spread and signifying force to the other, illuminating it and intensifying it, but also sometimes shifting it or adulterating it. Indeed, the meaning of Hedwig's sex change—as a botched promise of happy migration—becomes more expansive (more textured and intense) by a series of connotative junctures with the history of the signifier "black," and with the layered meanings of a black Sugar Daddy. Not that we receive a precise and singular view from this switchpoint. We only know for sure that the film puts the sign of a black man (differently queer from the boy) at the origin of the "angry inch"—the start of a surprisingly tender debasement, which it is the viewer's troubled task to comprehend.

Comprehending Debasement and the Value of Shame

Exploring the conceptual contours of debasement, this book discovers switchpoints between black and queer, queer and black, with reference to such matters as the stigmatized "skin" of some queers' clothes (chapter 1), the anal iconography of black labor struggles (chapter 2), the visual power of interracial so-called same-sex rape (chapter 3), the pretzel logic of homosexual miscegenation (chapter 4), and the fluid, AIDS-like transmissions to blacks of memories of dead black American slaves (chapter 5).

Consider the following textual blocks that depict these debasements:

> The law said [women] had to be wearing [at least] three pieces of women's clothing. . . . I never told you what they did to us down there [in the jail]—queens in one tank, [we] stone butches [dressed like men] in the next—but you knew. . . . You gently rubbed the bloody places on my shirt and said, "I'll never get those stains out."
> —Leslie Feinberg, *Stone Butch Blues*

> [In the] darkness and freezing stench [of the outhouse], Eva turned [her] baby over on her knees, exposed his buttocks and shoved the last bit of food she had in the world (besides three beets) up his ass.
> —Toni Morrison, *Sula*

Butch cuts across traffic and dashes into a business with a sign that reads: MASON-DIXON PAWNSHOP. . . . Miserable, violated and looking like a rag doll, [black druglord] Marsellus [Wallace], red ball gag still in his mouth, opens his watery eyes to see Butch coming up behind [the redneck who just raped Marsellus].
—Quentin Tarantino, screenplay, *Pulp Fiction*

I saw suddenly the power in his thighs . . . and in his loosely curled fists. That body [Joey's body] suddenly seemed the black opening of a cavern . . . in which I would lose my manhood. Precisely, I wanted to know that mystery and feel that power. . . . A cavern opened in my mind, black, full of rumor, suggestion. . . . ["The incident" of sex with Joey] remained . . . at the bottom of my mind, as still . . . as a decomposing corpse.
—James Baldwin, *Giovanni's Room*

And, for some reason she could not immediately account for, the moment she got close enough to see [Beloved's] face, Sethe's bladder filled to capacity. . . . She never made the outhouse. Right in front of its door she had to lift her skirts, and the water she voided was endless. . . . [I]n front of her own privy [she was] making a mudhole too deep to be witnessed without shame.
—Toni Morrison, *Beloved*

Each of these blocks gives a view of shame that is unique conceptually and potent historically: a stigma attached to certain clothes akin to the stigma of colored skin (and a strange martyrdom to cloth that ensues), a woman's anal penetration of a male as a way of feeding and protecting him, a body's anal cut (through the act of anal rape) in which is tucked a history (a Mason-Dixon history) that is piercing to the eye, male-to-male miscegenation as the birthing of a corpse that is black in the mind, and the brain's prophylactic struggle with the dead, especially those voided who were beloved, who threaten to wash across the mind in the manner of a fluids exchange.

Before I return, later, to outlining these specific chapters, let me explain the definitions and intents that shape this book—and also, in a moment, offer my reader a critical genealogy of influential thinkers thinking through shame. Moving through Bataille, Kristeva, Taussig, Bersani, and Sedgwick—the latter most centrally—along with Edelman, Litvak, Kennedy, Muñoz, Holland, and also Reid-Pharr, I will join this genealogy. But first, some definitions. Obviously, shame is a common, forceful word for disgrace. By definition, shame is "a painful emotion caused by a strong sense of guilt, embarrassment, [or] unworthiness." For example, in the textual blocks above, we clearly encounter guilt over sex (rendered in the image of a decomposing corpse), obvious embarrassment over voiding (Sethe's making of "a mudhole too deep to be witnessed without shame"), and two attempted enforcements of unworthiness through police brutality and redneck rape. We also encounter a seemingly more matter-of-fact description of an anal feeding by a mother in an outhouse—a scene likely to risk a reader's attribution of embarrassment, an attribution that Morrison both goads and refuses in her uniquely uncensorious relation to anality in *Sula*. In fact, it will be a constant question in this study: who attributes shame to any feeling or action? A character, a narrator, a literary critic? And what wide-ranging tonalities are evident (including a kind of matter-of-factness) in the ways these different texts take on (potential matters of) embarrassment, guilt, or unworthiness?

Although I will speak of shame in these contexts, I will also gravitate to shame's synonym, "debasement," in this book. I like its relation, the seeming misfit of debasement, to the concept of "value." I like its association with "adulteration." I enjoy as well its propensity to be misheard by a hearer as "the basement." According to the dictionary, "to debase" means "to lower in quality, character, or value." Debasement, by this definition, would seem opposed to value, since "to value" means "to esteem highly." So what would the value of debasement look like? My book probes this issue. Secondly, "to debase" means "to adulterate": "to make impure . . . by adding extraneous or improper ingredients." This definition suits my mixing of black and queer signs and associations in this study (an adulteration, perhaps, to some readers) along with my specific interest in mixing (miscegenation). Finally, I have found that whenever I tell people what I am writing—a book about debasement—almost to a person, they think I am writing on "the basement." This misperception accords, of course, with debasement's "lowering." It also agrees with the physical, material lowering I discuss in reference to the "bottom": the body's bottom (two chapters are about queer anality), but also just as centrally the bottom of one's mind, and, by economic reference, the lowest end (the bottom, that is) of an economic scale. For all of these reasons, "debasement" is one of my terms of choice, along with "abjection" and "humiliation," which I ask the reader to keep close at hand. "Abject" (listed in its adjectival form) adds the sense of "cast away" (from the Latin *abjectus, abjicere*, to throw away) and means "of the most contemptible kind." "Humiliation" lends the important sense of "religious mortification"—illustrated, in *American Heritage*, by Donne's line: "Humiliation is the beginning of sanctification." This sense will figure in my book's first chapter on a martyrdom to clothes, and in several other chapters in more subtle ways.

For all of this, debasement should not be seen as a theme in this book—though anyone wanting to theorize shame or historicize shame (as some might put it) should read on. Debasement is a fully indispensable informant. It is a key to understanding the ties, bold and subtle, between two signs that would seem linguistically, historically separate. The strangeness of queerness would not seem particularly destined to meet the darkness of blackness, except in the bodies of dark queer folk. We will see this is not so. Shame is an equal-opportunity meeting-place for these signs. In fact, I believe we cannot grasp certain complicated cultural, historical entanglements between "black" and "queer" without, at the same time, interrogating shame—its beautiful, generative, sorrowful debasements that make bottom pleasures so dark and so strange.

Before I continue with this book's plan, and take up more fully the crossing of signs in the context of debasement, I want to offer a short genealogy of influential thinkers who have thought about embracing shame, or something like it. Intriguing patterns of thought emerge across this group (which is not exhaustive) and raise the question of certain asymmetries clinging to studies of blacks and queers.

Who Thinks About Embracing Shame? A Critical Genealogy

At first glance, embracing shame would seem to be anathema to (overlapping) groups like queers and blacks, who have been so publicly marked as degraded and debased. In fact, famous voices such as those of Frantz Fanon, writing in the 1950s, and bell hooks, writing in 2004, have tirelessly and carefully championed dignity.

Fanon, in his classic *Black Skin, White Masks*, opens his book with an epigraph taken from Aimé Césaire: "I am talking of millions of men who have been skillfully injected with fear, inferiority complexes, trepidation, servility, despair, abasement."[4] He starts his chapter "The Fact of Blackness" with the stinging lines, " 'Dirty nigger!' Or simply, 'Look a Negro!' . . . I found . . . I was an object in the midst of other objects. . . . I was indignant. . . . I burst apart" (109). A few pages later: "Shame. Shame and self-contempt. Nausea. . . . The evidence was there, unalterable. My blackness was there, dark and unarguable. And it tormented me, pursued me, disturbed me, angered me" (116–17). And so, he tells us, he is writing his book to address black peoples' "internalization—or, better, the epidermalization—of this inferiority" (11). "I hope by analyzing it to destroy it," Fanon says succinctly. "I seriously hope to persuade my brother, whether black or white, to tear off with all his strength the shameful livery put together by centuries of incomprehension" (12). Shame is like a garment, then ("a shameful livery")—but also like a skin (an "epidermalization")— that can be taken off, and put on. ("Willy-nilly, the Negro has to wear the livery that the white man has sewed for him," 34.)

Half a century past Fanon, and writing not in a French psychoanalytic vein like his (with its stress on an "inferiority complex") but in a more American idiom, bell hooks, in a recent book, *Salvation: Black People and Love* (2004), speaks in terms of "self-esteem." In a chapter entitled "Moving Beyond Shame," hooks addresses "the negative impact of the color caste system . . . as a major impediment to healthy self-esteem," which, she states, is a bigger problem now, post–civil rights, than it used to be for black Americans.[5] "Since television has primarily exploited stereotypical images of blackness," hooks writes, "small children held captive by these screen images from birth . . . absorb the message that black is inferior, unworthy, dumb, evil, and criminal" (77). What hooks refers to as "racialized shaming," which may result from standards of beauty, forms of humor, or verbal attacks, "has been a central component of racial assault," she writes, and "leads . . . to significant breakdowns in [black people's] mental health" (81–82). hooks concludes her chapter: "There should be books that do nothing but accentuate the positive, sharing theories and strategies of decolonization that enable self-love" (92).

I give these examples from Fanon and hooks to beg an uncomfortable question from the start. Is the conception of valuable shame something only a queer would consider (a white queer at that)? Throughout this book, I will say it is not. First of all, we should note that homosexuals, gays, and lesbians, from the early homophile movements of the fifties (when Fanon is writing) to gay public advocates as diverse as Larry Kramer, Urvashi Vaid, Jonathan Ned Katz, Audre Lorde, and the changing heads of the Human Rights Campaign (all of whom are active when hooks is writing), also speak to dignity. Second, though surely strange and perverse, this embracing shame (as I am calling it) in cultural criticism and social commentary does not begin with queer theory—a phenomenon under way in the United States only by the 1980s. This embrace, that is, is not homosexual in its inception. Moreover, when queers do take it up, it is furthered by blacks as well as whites. Thus, to the extent that thoughts about embracing shame seem weighted toward the field of queer theory, this weighting may result from the greater embrace inside queer theory of the thinkers I will mention. As regards fiction, not expository prose, and this particular distinction is crucial, I hope to show dramatically that Baldwin, Genet, Tarantino, and Morrison, among other writers discussed in this book, are intensely engaged in embracing certain generative aspects of shame. The beautiful bottom as imaginative resource is a well-traveled crossroads for "black" and "queer."

Charmingly, the reason for this is the toe—at least according to Georges Bataille, a highly influential and original critical voice who speaks to embracing debasement. Someone seen as perverse by surrealists (which is not as contradictory as it sounds), someone deemed an "excremental philosopher" by André Breton (the chief surrealist in the twenties and thirties when Bataille is writing), and someone who wrote a novel entitled W.C. (with its heroine Dirty), Bataille is known for attacking dignity. Of course, he might say that (ideas of) dignity jumped him first and assaulted his humanity. This is where the human toe enters in. The big toe, specifically—an equal opportunity organ, we might note— "is the most *human* part of the human body," Bataille asserts, since it differentiates people from apes and allows human beings to stand erect.[6] "But whatever the role played in the erection by his foot," Bataille writes, "man . . . sees it as spit, on the pretext that he has this foot in the mud"— "mud and darkness being the *principles* of evil," he reminds us (his emphasis) (20). Bataille continues: "Human life entails, in fact, the rage of seeing oneself as a back and forth movement from refuse to the ideal, and from the ideal to refuse—a rage that is easily directed against an organ as *base* as the foot" (his emphasis) (21). Moreover, "man willingly imagines himself to be like the god Neptune, stilling his own waves, with majesty; nevertheless, the bellowing waves of the viscera . . . put an end to his dignity" (22).

Two points clearly emerge from this essay (called "The Big Toe"): debasement is within us and defines our humanity; debasement is seductive. On this latter point, Bataille reminds us of the "sacrilegious charm" of something as revered as the queen's foot: "Here one submits to a seduction radically opposed to that caused by light and ideal beauty; the two orders of seduction are often confused because a person constantly moves from one to the other, and . . . seduction is all the more acute when the movement is more brutal" (23).

Bataille's aggression against standard beauty is seen with the flower as well as the foot. In "The Language of Flowers," beauty is a cover that distracts us from debasement. "The interior of a rose," Bataille asserts, "does not at all correspond to its exterior beauty; if one tears off all of the corolla's petals, all that remains is a rather sordid tuft"; and, furthermore, even in an intact flower "after a very short period of glory the marvelous corolla rots . . . in the sun." "For flowers," Bataille writes lyrically (and comically), "do not age honestly like leaves, which lose none of their beauty, even after they have died; flowers wither like old and overly made-up dowagers, and they die ridiculously on stems that seemed to carry them to the clouds" (12). And then there are roots, which take us more dramatically back toward the toe. For "in order to destroy" the "favorable impression" made by the flower, "nothing less is necessary than the impossible and fantastic vision of roots swarming under the surface of the soil, nauseating and naked like vermin." More to the point, Bataille suggests that "the incontestable moral value of the term *base* conforms to this systematic interpretation of the meaning of roots: what is evil is necessarily represented . . . by a movement from high to low." This question of value can only be explained, in Bataille's estimation, by the fact that we have customarily assigned "moral meaning to natural phenomena"—mistakenly so (13).

Sometimes these assignments are not just distractions. They are ways of not seeing. In his essay "Rotten Sun," Bataille tells us that the sun *not* looked at is "the most elevated conception," "spiritual," "poetic," "perfectly beautiful"; whereas the sun "scrutinized" is "horribly ugly," leading to blindness, madness, combustion (57). Again, for Bataille, conventional beauty is incompatible with the debasement that interests him, though in its concealments and its timidity beauty is, for him, "emasculation" (a point I engage rather early in this book). Certainly, "Rotten Sun," along with "The Big Toe" and "The Language of Flowers," illustrates a point that cannot be missed when one is reading the full text of each. That point is this: debasement is strange and strangely funny—a kind of black comedy, if you will, a form of dark camp such as we will encounter many times throughout this book. Or, as Bataille himself confesses: "I arrived at reductions that were extremely simple . . . but at the same time monstrously comic" (75). (One thinks of those dowagers.)

Finally, it is critical to realize that Bataille finds political meaning—not moral meaning—in natural phenomena. Drawing on volcanoes, not just on flowers ("the terrestrial globe is covered with volcanoes, which serve as its anus, . . . [and this globe] often violently ejects the contents of its entrails," 8), Bataille imagines that an "eruptive force accumulates in those who are necessarily situated below." More specifically, "communist workers appear to the bourgeois to be as ugly and dirty as hairy sexual organs, or lower parts; sooner or later there will be a scandalous eruption" (8). Bataille, to be sure, welcomes this purge.

Julia Kristeva, in psychoanalysis, and Michael Taussig in anthropology, follow in unique ways on this kind of thinking, and on Bataille specifically. Both Kristeva and Taussig make debasement a more complex matter than a sheer negative.[7] And both repeat the axioms Bataille quite eccentrically lays out for us: debasement is within us, debasement is seductive, debasement is political, debasement is comical (though in seriously consequential ways). In her treatise *Powers of Horror: An Essay on Abjection* (1980; 1982), Kristeva makes "abjection" her great term of choice. Abjection is for her a state of being thrown away—cast out or aside. The abject is what is thrown out from oneself or from a group of others. Or, as the dictionary helps us to know, "abject" is "of the lowest degree," "lacking in self-respect; degraded." Its synonym is "base." Kristeva even calls abjection "that perverse interspace."[8] Reminiscent of Bataille in her explorations, Kristeva begins with the body's "abject others," what we deem debased and filthy: food in some cases, refuse, corpses. Kristeva explains: "Food loathing is perhaps the most elementary and most archaic form of abjection. When the eyes see or the lips touch that skin on the surface of milk . . . I experience a gagging sensation. . . . 'I' do not assimilate it, 'I' expel it" (2–3). "Refuse and corpses," furthermore, "*show me* what I permanently thrust aside in order to live. The corpse . . . is the utmost of abjection. It is death infecting life" (3–4; her emphasis). Kristeva, unsurprisingly, offers an epigraph from Bataille in her chapter "From Filth to Defilement," as she draws on *Purity and Danger* by the British anthropologist Mary Douglas (56).

Yet if Kristeva makes abjection exclusion (as the word itself insists), she also makes abjection a form of challenge and frightening seduction. "That leap [through abjection] is drawn toward an elsewhere as tempting as it is condemned"; "from its place of banishment, the abject does not cease challenging its master" (1–2). Even the corpse "beckons to us and ends up engulfing us" (4). The abject "beseeches us," offering a "*jouis-*

sance" that "swallows" us (5). "One thus understands," Kristeva writes, "why so many victims of the abject are its fascinated victims—if not its submissive and willing ones" (9). Famously so, "mystical Christendom," cites Kristeva, "turned this abjection of self into the ultimate proof of humility before God"; "witness Elizabeth of Hungary who 'though a great princess, delighted in nothing so much as in abasing herself'" (5). Building toward more political overtones, or at least toward something subsequent critics have made political, Kristeva deems the abject "what disturbs identity, system, order"; "what does not respect borders, positions, rules" (4). In fact, "filth is not a quality in itself," Kristeva informs us, "but applies to what relates to a boundary" (69). Here are the seeds of that now-familiar slide (seen in many critics at the time of her book and long afterward) from identity-subversion to political subversiveness (a slide I am going to critique in this book). Hence, her analytic formulations turn political. She claims the "abject or demoniacal potential of the feminine," since it "does not succeed in differentiating itself as *other* but threatens one's *own and clean* self, which is the underpinning of any organization constituted by exclusions and hierarchies" (65; her emphases). More directly implying her embrace of abjection, Kristeva states at one point: "abjection, which modernity has learned to repress, dodge, or fake, appears fundamental once the analytic point of view is assumed. Lacan says so when he links that word to the saintliness of the analyst, a linkage in which the only aspect of humor that remains is blackness" (27). Black humor, again.

As for Michael Taussig, his embrace of debasement takes the form of touting the wonder of "defacement"—his specific focus in the book by that name: "Defacement works on objects the way jokes work on language, bringing out their inherent magic."[9] Bataille's fingerprints are everywhere here. Sacred destruction, perverse attraction, and valuable baseness all make their appearance in Taussig's work. He begins: "When the human body... is *defaced*, a strange surplus of negative energy is likely to be aroused from within the defaced thing itself. It is now in a state of desecration, the closest many of us are going to get to the sacred in this modern world"—"the Latin root *sacer* meaning both accursed and holy," he writes later on (1; 52; his emphasis). "This I call *the law of the base*," says Taussig, sounding very much like Bataille, "playing on the doubleness of the word 'base' as both substantial support and as obscene or abject which, in a cavalier gesture, I regard as the base of holiness itself" (53; his emphasis). He even paraphrases (what he calls) Bataille's "astonishing fable of the ape's anus": "It all began as a frightening scene at the zoo, the ten-der faces of children exposed to the blossoming bottom of the ape swing-ing its scarlet self into focus to dominate the visual field like a gorgeous flower" (5). In this paraphrase, Taussig implies, though he doesn't quite state, that beauty *is* a feature of Bataille's imagination, albeit beauty of a rather new sort, a beauty tied to a "blossoming bottom." Earlier, indeed, Taussig writes of the moment of defacement: "beauty has been waiting for this incendiary moment . . . at the moment of its self-destruction, its illuminating power is greatest . . . beautiful in its own right" (2). Bottom line for Taussig, in his general theories and in his ethnography (a study of unmasking in primitive societies, as they are called): "defacement exerts its curious property of magnifying, not destroying, value, drawing out the sacred from the habitual-mundane" (54).

It is not hard to find traces of these thoughts among queer theorists. One thinks immediately of Leo Bersani and Eve Kosofsky Sedgwick, both writing out of the depths of theory, in its psychoanalytic and deconstruc-tive forms, and also out of the bowels of public animus against "homo-sexuals." For all of what they share, they take distinct paths toward de-basement and shame. Bersani, avowedly thinking through Bataille (and always through Freud), supremely embraces debasement in his essay "Is the Rectum a Grave?" (1987). The purpose of this essay, written at the height of the American AIDS crisis (at least at the height for white gay men), appears to be twofold. First, Bersani's essay explores a malignant aversion to gay male sexuality—and thus he explores a shaming of gay men—in public discourse at the time he is writing. Second, he explores the debasement fundamental to sexual pleasure, as odd as that notion may sound to some ears. On the first score, Bersani explains that pub-lic discourse, with denigration as its purpose, closely associates gay men with women by associating gay men with anal penetration—and thus with feminine sexual passivity, since "to be penetrated," even going back to the days of the Greeks, "is to abdicate power," Bersani reminds us, citing Foucault.[10] More precisely, public discourse about gay men, in the 1980s age of AIDS, resembles the public depictions of prostitutes in the nineteenth century, presenting them as contaminated vessels of sexual disease and, thus, as the sign of "an unquenchable appetite for destruc-tion" (211).

Rather than counter these extraordinary views, which make the rec-tum a literal grave, Bersani finds a more extraordinary aversion—to sex itself—in this invective. And this aversion, this unwillingness to embrace debasement, we might say, Bersani discovers in all kinds of thinkers, along the spectrum from homophobic moralists to radical theorists of sexuality. Never mind the homophobes, the problem with the sexuality theorists (from Catherine MacKinnon and Andrea Dworkin to Michel Foucault—unlikely bedfellows, as he notes) is that they all seek "to alleviate" "the problem" of the passive role in sex as "demeaning" (though in quite different ways, to say the least). Bersani, by contrast, wants to affirm both the passive and demeaning aspects of sex, to stop denying the "equally strong appeal of powerlessness . . . in both men and women," and to recognize the "self-debasement" fundamental to sexual "ecstasy" —what he deems a "*jouissance* of exploded limits." In other words, the act of sexual pleasure (for either penetrator or penetrated—or, presumably, someone reaching climax by other means) is a "self-shattering," "a kind of . . . self-debasement," "a radical disintegration and humiliation of the self," in which "the sexual itself [is] the risk of self-dismissal," since "the self" is psychically overwhelmed at climax (217). This example of sexual pleasure interests me for at least two reasons. First, it is a pleasurable debasement that is often willingly pursued, and, in some measure, practiced. Secondly, Bersani never clearly tells us whether sexual pleasure causes or simply reveals self-dismissal. I suspect he means the latter: that sex is a kind of intensification or a mode of revelation of an always-already shattering self. Because the self is shattered, says Bersani, so, also, the supposed relationality or community of the couple (which depends on selfhood) is undone. Sex, in this way, Bersani claims, might be seen as an odd "ascetic" practice, a sexual instead of a religious self-denial (222). All of which leads Bersani, especially when reading Jean Genet, to praise "solitude" ("a movement out of everything") as the proper goal of the "anticommunal, antiegalitarian, antinurturing" nature of sex.[11] I will have cause, in the context of Toni Morrison's fiction, to return to the political import of these views, to see where they might take us.

Eve Kosofsky Sedgwick takes us deeper into shame—and more broadly so. Less the student of Bataille and Kristeva in this matter than the pupil of Henry James, on the one hand, and the reader of Silvan Tomkins, on the other, Sedgwick is the theorist most down-to-earth *and* refined on this topic. And she seems to have thought about it more, and more creatively, and for longer, than any other queer theorist on the scene—especially in essays as distinct as "Shame, Theatricality, and Queer Performativity: Henry James's *The Art of the Novel*" and (with Adam Frank) "Shame in the Cybernetic Fold: Reading Silvan Tomkins." Regarding James, Sedgwick finds shame to be a highly animating feature of his life—perhaps as much an "organizing" feature of his life as she professes it is of her own. For example, she refers to James's "exhibitionistic enjoyment and performance of a sexuality organized around shame."[12] But not just his sexuality—also his work. Speaking of James's New York Edition prefaces and his relation to his "younger self" and his "younger fictions" in these prefaces, Sedgwick nearly evokes embrace: "[His] attempt is to love them . . . both in spite of shame and, more remarkably, through it" (40).

Sedgwick's suggestions here stem from several engaging convictions. First of all, through Tomkins, and her reading of him, she views shame as centrally bound to "interest," or even "fascination." Sedgwick quotes Tomkins: "'Like disgust, [shame] operates only after interest or enjoyment has been activated, and inhibits one or the other or both'" (97). Or, as Sedgwick puts it, "without positive affect, there can be no shame: only a scene that offers you enjoyment or engages your interest can make you blush" (116). Second, shame is not tied just to interest but to "communication." "Like a stigma, shame is itself a form of communication"; "blazons of shame, the 'fallen face' with eyes down averted . . . are semaphores of trouble and at the same time of a desire to reconstitute the interpersonal bridge" (36). These dynamics make shame both a personal, "individuating" experience and an odd form of reaching out, of "uncontrollable relationality"—"the place where the *question* of identity arises" (37; her emphasis). It is the "most mercurial of emotions," Sedgwick states (97).

Not surprisingly, when she recontextualizes both of these essays in her volume *Touching Feeling: Affect, Pedagogy, Performativity* (2003), she implicitly offers a research agenda, at least part of one, to future theorists. Linking the by-now old theoretical chestnut "performativity" to the much-less-talked-about old word "shame," Sedgwick asserts: "I suggest that to view performativity in terms of habitual shame and its transformations opens a lot of new doors for thinking about identity politics"— especially given what she later calls shame's "protean susceptibility to new expressive grammars" (62; 64). In a statement I take particularly to heart, and that appears borne out by other theorists' mention of humor, as we've seen—black humor or monstrous comedy—Sedgwick briefly mentions that "shame/performativity may [even] get us a lot further with the cluster of phenomena generally called 'camp'" (64).

The legacies of Sedgwick and Bersani on these issues (he speaking of debasement and humiliation, she more commonly speaking of shame) continue to surface among queer theorists (even when they are pursuing other topics), as do (in)direct links to Bataille, Kristeva, and Taussig. To cite just two important examples, one could look to the work of Lee Edelman and Joseph Litvak. In his famous essay on cold war politics and its public discourse, "Tearooms and Sympathy: The Epistemology of the Water Closet" (1994), with its titular nod to Sedgwick's *Epistemology of the Closet*, Edelman implicitly affirms debasement of a certain sort. Specifically, his densely woven accusations against the heteronormative male's inability to recognize the fact of his "hole" (in both psychic and bodily senses) builds rather elegantly, and originally, on Bersani (also, directly, on Kristevan abjection). As Edelman words it:

> [T]he "urinary" function in the institutional men's room customarily takes place within view of others—as if to indicate its status as an act of definitional display; but the private enclosure of the toilet stall signals the potential anxiety at issue in the West when the men's room becomes the locus . . . of intestinal relief. For the satisfaction that such relief affords abuts dangerously on homophobically abjectified desires . . . and overlaps too extensively with the Kristevan abjection that recoils from such evidence of the body's inescapable implication in its death.[13]

These are thoughts that lead, in other contexts, to his smartly piercing revelations of Alfred Hitchcock's sublimated anal fascination with the camera and its cutting capacity (*"Rear Window*'s Glasshole"); and thoughts, indebted to Bersani and Lacan, that lead to Edelman's daring embrace of the death drive itself in "*Sinthom*-osexuality," and now in his *No Future: Queer Theory and the Death Drive* (2004).[14]

In his remarkable volume *Strange Gourmets: Sophistication, Theory, and the Novel* (1997), Litvak is writing more in Sedgwick territory. Here, in relation to canonical novelists of James's ilk (Austen, Thackeray, and Proust), Litvak appears determined (says D. A. Miller) "not to disown but parade" the "embarrassing" "intimacy between sophistication and rawer forms of taste"—and also "to make visible a value . . . regarded as too frivolously 'aesthetic.' "[15] That is, sophistication is a gay-inflected shame. The word itself—"sophistication"—means perversion, corruption, adulteration, according to the OED, which, as Litvak surprisingly discovers, "lists not a single positive definition"; moreover, sophistication "arouses the suspicion that it is *impure*, contaminated from the outset by the desiring, and thus disgusting, body" (4; 6; his emphasis). What partially explains "sophistophobia" (which is "typically but not necessarily exclusively middle class") is the fact that "gay people function as subjects of sophistication," as if there were something powerfully homosexualizing about it (3–4). There is, insofar as sophistication is linked to both artificiality (unnaturalness) and excess (excessive aesthetic and culinary pleasure). Thus, in his own move to embrace debasement (the embarrassment and perversion of sophistication, but also its fascinating tangles with naiveté), Litvak says that his "book aims to help gay, queer, and other would-be adversarial critics make the most of our bad publicity," not to overturn it (5).

As I have said, this embrace of debasement, with its "labor of the negative" (to use Taussig's term), is not often found in African American social, political, or literary commentary—though I will demonstrate how richly it appears in certain African American novels. Even so, there are exceptions in expository prose. *Nigger* (2002) is one of them. This best-selling book by Randall Kennedy, a Harvard law professor, attempts to track "the strange career of a troublesome word," as his subtitle puts it. Or, as the back of the paperback touts: "It's 'the nuclear bomb of racial epithets,' a word that whites have employed to wound and degrade African Americans for three centuries. Paradoxically, among many black people it has become a term of affection and even empowerment." By no means does Kennedy, or his book, come neatly down on the side of lovingly adopting "nigger" as some kind of valuable slap in the face. But in his unblinking, open explorations of the "protean n-word," Kennedy elucidates how such "an ugly, evil, irredeemable word" has long served a complicated role, one might say a communal role, inside African American communities.[16] This is so even for those who, like Kennedy, thought they had "decided to condemn 'nigger' wholesale" (xv). And Kennedy admits there is much to condemn. "Nigger" is a "debasing slur," often seen in the locution "dirty nigger," used for the purposes of "denigration," "racial abasement," "injury," even "self-abnegation"—the latter when blacks use it as "a shorthand way of reminding themselves . . . where they perceive themselves as standing": " 'ofays on top, niggers on the bottom' " (xvi). Put succinctly, the "nigger seat" is "a place of shame" (5).

But there are other sides and shades to this word. Quoting from Helen Jackson Lee's autobiographical *Nigger in the Window*, Kennedy cites how this word " 'could be opened like an umbrella to cover a dozen different moods, or stretched like a rubber band to wrap up our families with other colored families. . . . Nigger was a piece-of-clay word that you could shape . . . to express your feelings' " (30). This elasticity makes its appearance in "black folk humor"—and, much later on, in the routines of Lenny Bruce (who "recommended a strategy of subversion through overuse") and, most memorably and most potently, in the comic work of Richard Pryor—especially in his Grammy-award-winning album *That Nigger's Crazy* (1974) (31). Now, particularly among younger people, there is much "experimenting with nonderogatory versions" of the n-word: for example, the use of "nigga" (a different form of the word) for affection or respect (xvii). Through artists like Ice-T, Tupac Shakur, comic Chris Rock, and NWA (Niggaz Wit Attitude), the term "nigger" (sometimes "nigga") has "new currency" and "cachet." For Professor Clarence Major, when "nigger" is "used by black people among themselves, [it] is a racial term with undertones of warmth and good will—reflecting . . . a tragicomic sensibility that is aware of black history" (29).

And there's the catch. Who can say "nigger" with warmth and affection? Largely, black people. Anyone else tries it on with risk. As Kennedy states, "many people, white and black alike, disapprove of a white person saying 'nigger' under virtually any circumstance" (41). Eminem obeys this rule—though I point out in the course of this book that Tarantino does not. Kennedy puts all these dynamics into question, leaving us to ponder whether the new currency of "nigger" is alarmingly diminishing "a stigma" that should stand (stand as a testament to its racist history), or is robbing racists, helpfully so, of their linguistic power.

Queers of color are also showing signs of directly or subtly affirming certain modes of abjection and shame. Like Lee Edelman and Joseph Litvak, they may not formulate their moves in this way, since this is not their focus, but one can see the outlines of such an endeavor emerging in these works. This is true, it seems to me, in the work of José Esteban Muñoz, in his book *Disidentifications: Queers of Color and the Performance of Politics* (1999). As his title states, "disidentification" is his topic—a term he takes from the French linguist Michel Pecheux, which refers to "a mode of dealing with dominant ideology, one that neither opts to assimilate within such a structure nor strictly opposes it."[17] "Destabilization" of "normative" identities and political "resistance" are the heart of what he claims for "disidentification." But a decided embrace of shame lurks around the edges of his considerations. Since his focus is "performance" by various queers of color—the kind that often takes place in a basement, on a stage—Muñoz discusses the engagement of (what he terms) "gaudy and toxic stereotypes," "rendered in all their abjection," by performers such as Jack Smith, Carmelita Tropicana, and Marga Gomez, among others (xiv; 3). In each case, Muñoz finds performances "inflected with disidentificatory difference that helped toxic images expand and become much more than quaint racisms," "enabling me," he later states, "to somehow understand the power and shame of queerness" (x; 5). This link of a toxic image to shame—but also to power—is made more direct when he briefly quotes Sedgwick: " 'The forms taken by shame are not distinct "toxic" parts of a group or individual identity that can be excised' "; " 'they are instead integral to and residual in the process in which identity is formed' " (12). Muñoz keeps these thoughts close at hand as he explores the potent combination of "comedy" and "rage" in colored queer performances.

As for Sharon Patricia Holland, in *Raising the Dead: Readings of Death and (Black) Subjectivity* (2000), she takes Taussig, among other thinkers, as an animating force, as she explores the indignities of death, especially those surrounding the signifier "black." She cites Taussig as stating that " 'the space of death is important in the creation of meaning and consciousness, nowhere more so than in societies where torture is endemic and where the culture of terror flourishes. We may think of the space of death as a threshold that allows for illumination as well as extinction.' "[18] In this same paragraph, Holland states her aim: "discovering who resides in the nation's imaginary 'space of death' and why we strive to keep such subjects there"; but giving more scope to Taussig's claims for death's illuminations, she proceeds to add: "embracing the subjectivity of death allows marginalized peoples to speak about the unspoken," since, she later offers, "there might be useful material in the new subjectivities that the dead bring to life" (8–9). In her epilogue Holland, citing Muñoz, calls these matters a "disidentification with life" (179). Here she looks at queer dancer/choreographer Bill T. Jones and rapper Tupac Shakur, side by side, stating that "when black artists flirt with the culture of death, or the 'space of death,' to borrow again from Taussig, they claim . . . kinship with the dead"—this while "each performing the event of his own death and packaging it as art" (176).

Intriguingly, a fragmented picture of a black man in a crucifixion pose, though a man without holes in his hands and feet, graces the cover of Robert Reid-Pharr's *Black Gay Man*, his book of essays from 2001. And though Reid-Pharr, in his introduction, asserts "our need to produce images of community in which all of us might find some discrete sense of dignity," he also claims, on an earlier page, that "there is no way to arrive at the beloved community except through the sullied byways we ourselves have produced."[19] For example, it is "within [the] intellectual tradition [of black nationalism] that one sees the question of the essential impurity, the perversity if you will, of the Black American community" (14). Further, Reid-Pharr, taking us back in a direction shared by Kennedy, would like us to remember "that black and gay identities have been creatively crafted out of the basest of insults" (101). This is not a matter for unqualified embrace. Speaking candidly and personally, Reid-Pharr explains: "I still have to resist the impulse to flinch when someone refers to me as a queer and to positively run for cover when someone refers to me as a black queer, as I have not yet rid myself of the suspicion, left over from my childhood, that I am being politely hailed as a nigger and a faggot" (103). Perhaps in order to grasp this "slippage in meaning," as he calls it, using a familiar postmodern phrase, Reid-Pharr conducts what he calls his own "slippage in my writing between the academic and the pornographic" (10). Indeed, he at times launches us swiftly into talk of his sex play—first with Rick, "an ugly, poor, white trash southerner": "what attracts me to Rick," Reid-Pharr writes, "is precisely how ugly he is"; "[he] reminds me of white boys from my youth, the ones so ugly and country that they seemed somehow to exist in another arena of whiteness" (9).

Such fleeting inserts, especially surrounding cross-racial desire, come to a head in his chapter entitled "The Shock of Gary Fisher," on the "ugly, unsettling, if strangely erotic effect of poetry and prose [in *Gary in Your Pocket*] written by an already dead writer"—the thirty-two-year-old Gary Fisher, who died of complications from AIDS (135). Here, in academic mode, Reid-Pharr sounds Fisher's pornographic musings, his fascination with "erotics of slavery," and explains: "Even as we express the most positive articulations of black and gay identity, we are nonetheless referencing the ugly historical and ideological realities out of which those identities have been formed" (137). Trying not to solve "the shock of Gary Fisher," but only to present it, Reid-Pharr states that it "turns squarely on his fierce articulation of what lies just beneath the surface of polite, 'civil' American race talk"; "the life of the nigger is so caught up in the debauchery of the white master that even when 'nigger' is translated to 'black' it is still possible to sense the faintest hint of the raw milk smell of cum on his breath" (148).

Hints of Kristeva in this phrase carry over to the literary critical essay Reid-Pharr also includes in his collection: "Tearing the Goat's Flesh" (originally subtitled, in its journal form, "Homosexuality, Abjection and the Production of a Late Twentieth-Century Black Masculinity"). Reid-

Pharr's essay investigates, through the lens of Eldridge Cleaver, Piri Thomas, and James Baldwin, how the black homosexual has functioned as a "scapegoat"—as the excluded and the abjected, that, once stricken, "return[s] the community to normality, to create boundaries around blackness." Kristeva's political sense of challenge and resistance, and perhaps of seduction, remains in these dynamics (though, in his revision, Reid-Pharr never mentions Kristeva; he discusses her only in his journal version), for "even as the profligate subject is destroyed, we retain 'him' within the national consciousness, always on the brink of renewal" (104). The black (abject) homosexual allows a kind of contact with the boundary-breakage that the community, at least on some level, actually seeks.

I have been presenting only a sketch of lines of thought (some extensive, some contained, some direct, some submerged) about shame, debasement, humiliation, and abjection, especially about their attractive twists. I myself have written directly on these matters, from 1989 to the present time, alongside many of the thinkers I have mentioned. Taking these thinkers as a group, as I do now, I can say that they are my "retrospective manifesto" (in the phrase of the architect Rem Koolhaas).[20] That is, although fictions have driven my theories in this book, I can see, looking back, how my study seems to fit in a line of thought that I admire. I think it is time for a study devoted to valuable, generative, beautiful shame—a research agenda implicitly set by Eve Kosofsky Sedgwick, from the side of queer theory, and, differently so, by books like Randall Kennedy's *Nigger* in black studies. I will add my own twist by looking at this issue inside the crossing of "black" and "queer." Again, this crossing has been called for and deemed remarkably under-theorized. Sedgwick, in *Touching Feeling*, refers to the "almost genocidally underrepresented topic of black gay men in the United States," and "the apparently unrepresentably dangerous and endangered conjunction, queer and black" in the public domain—a danger just being spoken to now by recent books on the Down Low.[21] José Muñoz, speaking for many frustrated theorists, offers this critique:

> Most of the cornerstones of queer theory that are taught, cited, and canonized in gay and lesbian studies classrooms, publications and conferences are decidedly directed toward analyzing white lesbians and gay men. . . . When race is discussed by most white queer theorists, it is usually a contained reading of an artist of color that does not factor

questions of race into the entirety of their project. . . . [They] continue to treat race as an addendum.[22]

I would further add that there is much to learn about "black" and "queer" by asking how these signs even outside of black gay people—maybe especially outside of gay blacks—have congress with each other. Debasement, I claim, supremely informs us of this conjunction. And fictions help us to theorize both the social communion of shameful states and the social communion of crossing signs.

Fictionalizing, Historicizing, and Socializing Shame

✳To this end, I offer a book that builds conceptually, not chronologically. From the work of shame at the body's surface (in chapter 1) to its penetrations of the depths of the brain (in chapter 5), I explore each conceptual block in a certain historical context (or an interlocking set of contexts). I do so while using fictions to conceptualize shame in ways that (established forms of) theories seem unable to conceptualize.[23] In these respects, this book is a composite form. It can be read for historical logics that emerged at certain times and may still circulate in critical ways. It can be read for its speculative theories on shame's surprising operations and values: shame's significant relation to adornment, communal consolation, visual fascination, sexual attraction, and acts of mourning. And it can be read for engagements of artists rarely, if ever, read together in a study (Toni Morrison with Jean Genet, for instance—even with Quentin Tarantino).

Shame itself proves exceptionally composite, as I am going to show. There is no purely black form of debasement—nor a queer one. Only blended forms of shame. A circuitry of switchpoints keeps associations sparking between "black" and "queer" and the signs attached to them: between cloth and skin, between sexual dirtiness and the filth of neighborhoods, between tabooed attractions and acts of racial punishment, between miscegenation and sexual sameness, and between the autoimmunities of memory and those of the body. If we would have a feel for the shame in play for those who wear these signs, queer and black, we may need to pull on the possibly unfathomable roots of these debasements. These long roots are sunk in a social field of values and are simultaneously lied about, cherished, spurned, held in secret, or sacrificed for, in public view.

Moreover, we cannot grasp how shame moves—goes to work on people—without comprehending its composite operations. More often than not, debasements attach to a person's body, highlighting attributes of some kind of surface or calling attention to a dirty bottom depth. Even in the case of dirty surroundings, shame paints place as part of one's intimate physical sphere. Debasement, that is, takes (its) place: in a body, in a neighborhood, or in a human brain. We will see that many debasements that lodge in a mind, or spread throughout the brain, still enter through the body—the eye, ear, gullet, vagina, or anal cavity. Mental operations have bodily channels, just as the anus, in several of our texts, swings open to the brain. The multiform operations of debasement are apparent in each of the texts considered here, though this book is arranged to build conceptually from key historical logics of shame's operations at a surface (clothing as beautiful, stigmatized skin in chapter 1), to debasement's operations through anal penetrations (even if they operate to solace a neighborhood in chapter 2), to the force of shame at the level of the eye (chapter 3) or in the workings of the mind (mental operations such as tabooed attractions—homosexuality and miscegenation in chapter 4—but also to AIDS-like invasions of the brain by the well-beloved dead in chapter 5). For all these reasons, shame is a highly indispensable informant for queer theoretical work and black studies. It can be seen to have swallowed a host of critical issues on which it may inform us, pointing us to an archive of depictions that force a range of valuable questions on these fields (black studies, queer theory). Debasement informs us of hidden connections, cultural logics, and histories of fantasies, pain, and attractions far more telling than the weak conceptions of oppression and subversion.

Thus, I intend to throw a monkey off our backs. The monkey I mean is the limiting question, seldom asked by novelists, though often posed by theorists, of whether some phenomenon (debasement, in this case) serves to "subvert" "dominant structures." In the hands of Foucault's many followers, this question often fills the frame of any study, limiting the other kinds of questions we might ask. This is not my question.[24] Rather, I want to ask of my texts what they imagine debasement produces, at certain moments, for those people who actually undergo it, who, in a manner of speaking, practice it. How does debasement foster attractions? How is it used for aesthetic delight? What does it offer for projects of sorrow and ways of creative historical knowing? These kinds of questions raise the issue of value. And "value" carries several meanings in this study: "an amount considered to be a suitable equivalent for something else" (what does any given debasement cost or lend, and in what terms?); "monetary or material worth" (how is shame in conversation with money and class position?); "utility" (to what use or uses may a given debasement be put?); and "precise meaning or import, as of a carefully considered word" (what does debasement mean to its practitioners, and how is it spoken?). (Value also happens to mean "the relative darkness or lightness of a color in a picture," "value correspond[ing] to lightness of the perceived color.") "Beautiful Bottom, Beautiful Shame" is a phrase that captures not only a topsy-turvy of value but, more dramatically, an angle of attraction. It can be asked: what is so attractive about bottom states, and by what logic does beauty find itself wed to shame?

From these kinds of questions, I plan to show how queer theory and black studies are together far from over their academic moments. Perhaps, especially conceived as joint ventures, they can be invigorated and redirected—if we theorize from deep within their fictions. Aesthetic attention is a way to expand the political curiosity—and, finally, the investigative force—of these domains. The task is to draw from aesthetic details fascinating theoretical, speculative fields more than subversions or political points. Such a move would reverse the usual flow of theory "down" to fiction. Instead of seeing fictions in need of theories' explanatory moves, I would show how theory (that strangely reified, ossified term) needs new fictions. We need to demonstrate not only how to use literary fictions to engage the heuristic potential still apparent in several key theories but also to debase these theories themselves—to show their stunning limits. This task requires us avidly to follow the attractions of fictions, both in their fullness and their force.

As must be obvious, this is not a book built to answer one specific historical question. Instead, I interrogate imaginative understandings of several select historical contexts—by artists as diverse as Genet, Morrison, Tarantino, and Baldwin—to build a way toward unexpected critical conversations. To put the matter mildly, there are odd turns to the ways these texts go about their thinking through historical issues. In chapter 2, to take one example, 1970s unemployment blues for black Americans are a backdrop to Morrison's fictional neighborhood called "the Bottom" (indeed, to its stunning scenes of anality) from 1919 to 1965 (the year of the infamous Moynihan Report) when, according to *Sula* (Morrison's novel), this beautiful black Bottom collapsed—collapsed because it traded its richly enacted communal debasements for a new stake in a much more demoralizing (Moynihan?) tale of conventional progress. Similarly, in chapter 5, 1987 is the year of publication for Morrison's *Beloved*, and the year of the AIDS quilt, making us wonder whether a novel about early death and transmissions from the beloved dead (through a model of viral memory) is offering 1873 (the novel's setting just after slavery) as passed through the sieve of contemporary ills, ills that make remembering chain-linked deaths such a necessary trauma for blacks and queers. This same vein of intersecting histories, of highly different periods speaking to each other, informs chapter 1. Here, in a kind of triple layer, 1990s feminist longing (à la Feinberg's *Stone Butch Blues*) to embrace the bar raids of 1960s Buffalo, New York (when lesbian butches were beaten by cops for wearing men's clothes) is a highly unexpected way of soothing a long-standing loneliness sharply expressed, in 1928, through the British aristocracy (via Radclyffe Hall's *The Well of Loneliness*). Each of these renderings, as it emerges from imaginative meditations on multiple, interlocking moments in history, shows its own peculiarities, which I will unfold. And yet an intriguing pattern arises among these texts. They investigate shame (and shameful states) as an invaluable if also painful form of sociality, even when debasement seems lonely and interior.

This sociality may be precisely why we need to free debasement from its command performance as either oppression or subversion, or, in the now familiar critical sense, both-at-once.[25] One man's attraction to the mystery of another man's loosely curled fists—this attraction, as Baldwin conceives it, opening a cavern that is "black" in the mind—is not best examined as either oppression or subversion. Nor are the fascinating features of a mother-daughter reunion, set amid a mother's "endless voiding," best perused along these lines. The thrust of the debasements I will be exploring is a turning toward forms of sociality (attractions, reunions, lovemaking, even acts of clothing) that use humiliation for their own designs. Taking a hint from Sedgwick that shame is itself a kind of communication (though what kind, exactly?), my stress on a social embrace of debasement makes a different kind of move than Bersani's celebration of anticommunal acts of a self-demeaning nature.[26]

In contrast to Bersani, I will scrutinize the social nature of self-debasing acts, as I plumb the structures (convivial, communal) that make debasements possible, bearable, pleasurable, creative, even in their darkness. Not that I would drop from view the anticommunal slant of these debasements. Only, I would counter that it sometimes takes a village to produce a solitude (a sense of seclusion or perhaps insulation from the general social field). In fact, on the evidence of texts selected here, it often takes at least two people (think of sex) to debase a self. And then, even so, according to these texts, this shattering self is socially braced *as* it shaves the edge of the anticommunal. One thinks of how even Sethe's distant neighbors, in the novel *Beloved*, keep her in mind (and later act to brace her), while she's locked inside her house, declining in her dignity as much as in immunity, as she's locked in debasement with Beloved.

These social actions (these self-debasements) do not create harmonious communities of like-minded blacks or similarly identified same-sex queers. They create, instead, a kind of social solitude of people who are set, in some deep measure, apart from each other—but in an apartness they create together and in which they are held (sometimes sexually by a lover, sometimes mentally in someone else's mind). I suggest a phrase —"social holdings"—to capture this range of people holding people in their arms and in their minds, even in astonishing scenes of debasement. "Holdings" also points to this study's ongoing question of value, insofar as the word can also mean such material gains as "land" and "property."

The Surprising Life of Signs

As I explore this range of conceptions of shame and debasement, I will be engaging the linguistic markers "black" and "queer" in the social field of signs. In this study, black and queer (with or without quotation marks) carry the status of labels worn by people (sometimes willingly, sometimes not, sometimes habitually, sometimes intermittently) and written on the surface of cloth, skin, genders, economies, and locations in ways that (de)form them.

And yet, one could ask, why engage black and queer in this study? Isn't the more relevant comparison between the signs "queer" and "nigger"? Are not these latter signs more symmetrical? Actually, they are not. In fact, each pairing ("black" with "queer," "queer" with "nigger") is uniquely asymmetrical—and that interests me. (It is also the case that "nigger" comes from the Latin *niger*, meaning black, and only became a slur over time—by 1830, Kennedy tells us.) Admittedly, "nigger" and "queer" seem to be, at least on the surface, matching invectives. Both have been, and still can be, dramatically offensive. Both, moreover, in spite of such offensiveness, are having revivals. There are now people willing to call themselves niggers and queers (and some, nigger queers). However, parallels such as these are thrown out of kilter by the different histories surrounding each word.

Kennedy's book is careful to trace why so many people would claim special negative status for "nigger," or the n-word, as it is called. "Is it," asks Kennedy, "a more hurtful racial epithet than insults such as *kike, wop, wetback, mick, chink,* and *gook*?" Kennedy answers: in the minds of many Americans, yes. Nigger is "the paradigmatic slur," "'the all-American trump card, the nuclear bomb of racial epithets,'" "'the most noxious racial epithet in the contemporary American lexicon,'" and "'the filthiest, dirtiest, nastiest word in the English language.'" Kennedy concludes: "In the aggregate . . . nigger is and has long been the most socially consequential racial insult" (22; 25). As evidence of consequence, Kennedy points to the frequency of the n-word's appearance in federal and state court cases: it "appears in 4,219 reported decisions," far outweighing any other racial slurs. And sexual slurs? Kennedy never offers us this comparison. As for revivals, "queer" and "nigger," I would suggest, are having different rebirths. With the advent of *Queer Eye for the Straight Guy,* "queer" has entered the public domain as a word that straights can use for gays — and as an adjective for gay ways. There is no need for a "q-word," for instance. "Nigger," by contrast, as Kennedy states, is a trickier move for whites on blacks. Go there at your peril would seem to be the maxim. (In fact, spell check will not let me go there; it lets me use "queers," but tells me "niggers" is not in its dictionary.)

So there is no clear, mirrored relation between these terms. But nor is there a neat, untrammeled comparison between "black" and "queer." Indeed, I would argue, the near-parallels and asymmetries here are much more fraught and thus even richer than they are with "queer" and "nigger." Dictionaries indicate "queer" and "black" are linguistically elastic and historically narrow. "Black" is an adjective (designating color, mood, degree of hope) that may potentially apply to any noun; "queer" in its general signification (meaning "strange") may append itself to anything. Yet, in what we might call their congealed forms, these fluid terms, which might seem to flow in so many directions, have been hardened by historical use into nouns (blacks and queers) that trail debasements powerfully behind them.

To be more precise, they trail contaminations. "Black" and "queer" could easily illustrate a basic feature of any meaning-making: the "contamination" of any word's meaning by other meanings it also allows. I suspect that it is harder now (say, than it was in the 1920s) to use the word "queer" to mean simply and only "strange," without a listener's or reader's thinking "homosexual." The word's most group-specific definition ("[Slang for] homosexual: term of contempt or derision") contaminates, and sometimes overtakes, its more general spread, giving the term the feel of congealment, as if it freezes in the form of "homosexual." Many queer activists, along with queer theorists, have fought this freezing—but not, intriguingly, its contaminations. In a by now well-known move, queer activists and theorists (one thinks of central writings by Eve Kosofsky Sedgwick, Lee Edelman, Joseph Litvak, Lauren Berlant, Michael Warner, Carolyn Dinshaw, and Judith Butler) have tried to reinstate "queer" as "strange," to break against any scripted identities for "gays" or "homosexuals"—to break with congealment, as it were. And yet, in a sense, they would willingly, gladly, spread contamination. They would make supposedly "normal" sexualities confess their strangeness and, therefore, their queerness, lending "normal" sex a whiff of their slang. (The phrase "straight queers" illustrates this point.)

As for "black," there's a different dynamic. A dynamic nearly opposite. It is as if the word's more general meanings—"totally without light," "soiled," "dirty," "disgraceful," "harmful," "full of sorrow or suffering," "disastrous," "sullen or angry," and "without hope"—threaten to swamp its group-specific definitions, which sound, by comparison, more benign: "designating . . . any of the dark-skinned traditional inhabitants of sub-Saharan Africa, Australia, or Melanesia or their descendants in other parts of the world; by, for, or about black people as a group." (Nothing sounds particularly menacing or disgraceful in this definition.) The range of contaminating significations sticking to "black," even so, has led, in rather remarkable fashion, to politically sensitive forms of congealment on the part of some anti-racist advocates. I am referring to the urge not to use —indeed, to stop using—any negative general meanings of "black" altogether ("this is a black day," "the outlook is black," something "soiled black"), so as to cleanse the sign. The urge, in this case, is to foster freezing without contamination—to foster the use of a pure group sign for a people's identity.

Granted, there are now black queer theorists whom we might interpret as pushing to read "black" as a sign for loss of boundaries or the queerness of death. But if "black" spreads in these studies—I am not sure it actually does—it does so on the back of "queer." Holland, in her epilogue (" 'I'm in the Zone': Bill T. Jones, Tupac Shakur, and the (Queer)

Art of Death") to *Raising the Dead* argues that "our proximity to death as human beings . . . might mark the queer space in us all because the possibility of an impending death is something we all share"; one page later, she states that "the space of death is marked by blackness and is therefore always already queer" (179–80). However, it is not entirely clear whether "blackness" retains a narrow application in this claim (applied specifically to Bill T. Jones and Tupac Shakur) or whether it slides along with "queer" into "something we all share." Just above this claim, Holland cautiously approaches even the spread of "queer": "If we are to expand the definition of queer to encompass other bodies, then we will need to do some hard work here. We will need to focus on what we really mean when we equate the queer body/subject with liminal spaces. . . . It represents an apocalyptic moment for queer studies and a challenge to read 'race' into the equation of its origins" (180). Similarly, in *Black Gay Man*, Reid-Pharr suggests that "the homosexual, like the Jew, becomes in late-twentieth-century Black American writing a vehicle by which to express the omnipresence of black boundarylessness" (15). He later adds: "I argue in this work that the black gay stands in for the border crossing and boundarylessness that has so preoccupied contemporary Black American intellectuals. In particular, I argue that black gay men represent in modern American literature the reality that there is no normal blackness, no normal masculinity to which the black subject, American or otherwise, might refer" (103). To be sure, "gay," in Reid-Pharr's thinking, is making "black" spread beyond the bounds of normativity.[27] But what is the range of black border crossing? Just how far does "black boundarylessness" extend itself? Whatever the answer, aside from such thinkers working both terms ("queer" with "black"), there has not been an obvious move within black American or black Atlantic studies to spread the sign "black," with its contaminations, over the general social field. True, whiteness studies have forced recognition of white as a color, as a racial specificity, but not as a form of blackness per se.

Debasement clings to these matters even so. Clearly, that is, for all their distinctions, the congealed forms of "black" and "queer" are importantly part of a story of debasement. The varied histories surrounding "black pride," in the American idiom, and self-named queer activist groups (Queer Nation, most famously) actually share an initial logic. They share the logic of a social self-debasement. Here is what I mean. Early political adherents of these moves (to embrace these signs "black" and "queer," much like those who would now embrace "nigger") had to risk demeaning themselves with the sign's contaminated history as an insult (as adherents, perhaps, still do)—in an attempt to renegotiate its terms. And though no one has suggested this conception, nor do I imagine that it would catch on, blacks and queers (and, surely, "niggers") who consent to wear these terms could be conceived of as social clubs of self-debasers with a purpose (though these purposes, I would emphasize, might dramatically differ from one self-debaser to the next). It is largely our incuriosity surrounding self-debasement (its complex attractions) that makes this suggested conception ("self-debasers with a purpose") sound offensive—sound incompatible with what swiftly, in these diverse histories, has been linguistically converted into pride ("I'm black and I'm proud"; "we're queer, we're here"; Niggaz Wit Attitude . . .).

In fact, to wound oneself with an insult-trailing tag ("queer," "black," or the n-word) may be a way, bluntly so, to "out" the violent side of mainstream, normalized America (what Butler calls the "regulatory regime") —goading it to hit you with an insult in order to reveal its coiled abuse.[28] Or, once again to turn from subversion, those who elect to wear the sign that trails abuse may attempt to say, "You gave me regulations, I made something else. . . . Read it if you can (though I don't fully care if you do or you don't)." Such a gambit might then gesture in the direction of a "nonce taxonomy": a kind of one-time classification. The phrase is Sedgwick's (from her *Epistemology of the Closet*) and seems to be meant precisely in this sense of a one-time naming.[29] (In the dictionary, "nonce": "for the one [purpose or occasion].") Late in his career, Roland Barthes found himself "bearing witness to the only sure thing that [is] in me . . . a desperate resistance to any reductive system." "For each time, having resorted to any such language [the sociological, the semiological, or the psychoanalytic] . . . each time I felt it hardening and thereby tending to reduction and reprimand, I would gently leave it and seek elsewhere. . . . why mightn't there be, somehow, a new science for each object?"[30] This "new science" would be a nonce taxonomy—perhaps a description, with vivid details—that would serve a one-time use. (Consider the sergeant's, the black Sugar Daddy's, candied seduction.) Still, this one-time use would itself be a making, or a doing, that could be filed, one might say, under the sign "black" or "queer," or perhaps under both. It would stand for a historical instance (even if it happens in a film or a novel) of what can be done, sometimes quite imaginatively, with that sign.

These examples—their potential mix of interest and offense—suggest the surprising life of signs, even of the congealed variety. And this surprising "life," fully articulated by my final chapter (where I consider the viral life of signs), is very much at the heart of this book. A cautionary note: if I refer at any point to black or queer texts, I am designating novels, essays, films, or theories that engage, in substantial ways, with these signs and their associations—regardless of authors' purported backgrounds, though these backgrounds are intriguing signs as well. Overall, I examine unforeseen switchpoints between the markers "black" and "queer." I say "switchpoints," as I earlier explained, since I wish to explore how seemingly definitive associations attached to each, "black" and "queer," might be taken up, or crossed through, by the other.

The law comes in to sharpen my point. Critical legal theorist Janet Halley has brilliantly assessed the conceptual problems surrounding certain instances of "like race" argumentation undertaken by gay and lesbian legal advocates. Stressing the "analytic incommensurability" between key concepts in these arguments, Halley notes the tendency, among well-meaning gay-affirmative advocates, on the one hand, and sometimes by anti–affirmative action advocates, on the other, to smooth over quickly conceptual dilemmas in their analogies. "The danger" of these arguments, Halley writes, "arises not because blacks and gays are alike or different, but because they can be flashed as signs of each other in a discourse [sometimes conservative, sometimes liberal] that operates so smoothly it can remain virtually silent."[31] This particular problem interests me: that the possible mismatch between race and sexual orientation (in the eyes of critical legal theorists) does not stop blacks and gays from being "flashed as signs of each other" by liberals or conservatives.

Halley's flashpoint is my "switchpoint"—with one important difference. The switchpoints in the texts I examine in this book may act to elucidate incommensurabilities, not cover over them. I emphasize the obvious switching of signifying tracks that occurs when a sign that is generally attached to blacks, let's say, flashes in the signifying field of "queer"; when, for example, the sign of stigmatized skin flashes in the domain of queer clothing, or, to flip directions, the sign of anality flashes along the track of blacks' economic burdens. Each switchpoint is a kind of off-rhyme (to employ a different metaphor): a point at which we intellectually sense how one sign (the stigma attached to the surface of skin, especially its color) lends its force to another (the stigma attached to the surface of cloth), which we know to be distinct. (An off-rhyme, as a term from poetics, means a near or partial rhyme—for example, the rhyme between "laws" and "because" or "down" and "own." The reader's ear hears something similar but distinct in these sounds that are not identical.) In chapter 1, for instance, a queer person's deeply wished-for clothes (say, a lesbian's longed-for suit, a gay man's close-fitting sweater and pants) are not much like a black person's skin, though as "stigmas" that are worn on the bone, which may also quite strongly delight, they seem to create an intriguing off-rhyme between those stigmas, impressed on the surface, of blacks and queers. In my second chapter, I explain how, in a Morrison novel, the anal penetrations and bottom stimulations our culture quite readily links to gay men intersect black women's negotiations with their (and their men's) positions in the economic basement of a neighborhood Morrison names the Bottom. These switchpoints—or off-rhymes, even—make us understand the ways in which "black" and "queer" miss each other as they meet each other on a signifying plane (even on the body of a single individual). Switchpoints also make us think about shame in ways that literary critics might now usefully pursue.

There may be a reason for our collective slowness to approach this particular life of signs, which would require us to think through congealments, switchpoints, and what we may still wish to refer to as textual "details" (more on these in chapter 3). I believe this slowness has to do with a focus once so generative but now too familiar and too imprecise: that much more watery and indistinct form of meaning-redirection, going under the name of "instability." It appears that "instability" (of meanings and identities) remains a mantra. Indeed, instability is building a home. I think it is time now to shift from this focus—shift from its status as destination—so that we may explore more specific collisions, collusions, and borrowings between the signs that identities, however unstable, may be fond of, or even despise.[32]

I have said my goal in this book is to follow the skeins of thought surrounding debasement (surrounding the signs black and queer) that emerge from different timeframes. Many of these texts end in an impasse, without a clear message or political program, unable to solve all the problems they have posed. That is to say, they encompass instabilities. Yet it is the lines of thinking-through that capture me, the provocative switchpoints, historical congealments, and fresh sets of details that make debasement intensely informative about hidden values.

P. 34 - 40

I want now to sketch the plan of this book.

A woman hating, in relation to herself, the beautiful garments her girlfriend wears; another woman even willing to be beaten for refusing women's clothes; a beautiful sailor in beautiful clothes as the sign of a man calling "arms" upon himself. Chapter 1, "Cloth Wounds, or When Queers Are Martyred to Clothes: Debasements of a Fabricated Skin," is an exploration of sartorial shame. It explores bodily and psychic wounds sticking to the surface of certain clothes, and mines the value of these very wounds. Clothes, as we know, may function as the sign of a sexual prefer-ence. More to the point, they are part of this preference. Both at the level of object choice and at the level of sexual subjectivity, most of us strongly prefer some clothes over other kinds of clothes. I want to show how, in certain key depictions of queers (in certain novels from the 1920s, '50s, and '90s), sartorial preference makes for scenes of self-betrayal (of a com-plex sort), as if lesbians and male homosexuals are showing their own true colors when they seek certain people and clothes. Doing so, queers betray themselves. They offer up to public view (and condemnation) their pre-ferred selves. In fact, in a twist, self-betraying sacrifice finds itself joined to sexual fantasy, and the mark of martyrdom turns out to sit on cloth. There is nothing more telling of debasement in these fictions than a beau-tiful garment. And nothing more attractive than a beautiful shame.

This is a forceful kind of social self-debasement, as I will unfold it. It forms as well an off-rhyme with skin—the stigma attached to the color of skin, to be more precise. General Colin Powell, when he was the Chair-man of the Joint Chiefs of Staff, went on record officially reminding us that "Homosexuality is not a benign . . . characteristic, such as skin color. . . . It goes to one of the most fundamental aspects of human behavior."[33] This first chapter responds to Powell's claim. Powell himself understands little about the mismatch he is citing. The more intriguing definitional prejudice informing homophobia (in certain specific historical ways) con-cerns not sexual but sartorial behavior: prejudice against a sexual prefer-ence for a certain kind of clothes. This sort of prejudice reveals something crucial that Powell is ignoring, which makes the issue of benign char-acteristics a bit more dazzling. Not the benign surface of skin, but the surface of cloth. Is the color or cut of clothes, one may ask, any less be-nign than the color of skin? Admittedly, the act of clothing oneself is still a behavior-based consideration (even a "fundamental aspect of human behavior," to use General Powell's terms). A stigma, however, attached to cloth (an object arguably more like skin than it is like sex) raises the stakes for Powell's kind of claim. I will show this chapter to be haunted by skin.

Chapter 2 flips the direction of transfer ("Bottom Values: Anal Economics in the History of Black Neighborhoods"). Here key associations with queerness track onto "black." Moving from the body's surface to its hidden, genital depths, I will investigate how the Bottom in Morrison's *Sula* (the Bottom, her fictional black neighborhood, exemplary of black economic binds from 1919 to 1965) is haunted by the prejudice—the kind of prejudice—surrounding the general public's resistance to queer anality. This specific shadowing, made more direct by a chain of anal reference in Morrison's novel, colors the historical placement of blacks in the bottom of America's capitalist system. It also highlights the powerful mixture of value and stigma attaching to unusual communal behaviors in the novel's neighborhood. Mothers "freeing" their children's stools so that children can eat; women piercing, with a sense of pleasure, but also with a sense of sad renewal, their lovers' "soil"; two young girls building a "bottom" (clearly figured as a grave) in which to bury a young black boy; black men finding their faces in reflections from a toilet bowl's waters. The title of this chapter relates quite directly to the title of my book. (A version of this chapter was written at a time—1989—when very little had been written on anality either from a queer or black studies angle.) Exceedingly rich in its panoply of details, rendering a neighborhood called the Bottom, *Sula* raises the quandaries surrounding black folks' historical upendings of established economic values and thus their embrace of the value of debasement. Nevertheless, putting other values (sex, food, protection, and sorrow) in conversation with those attached to money (as Freud did before her), Morrison boldly rivals Freud as an anal historian and reveals the limits to his bottom theorizations.

Chapter 3 cuts a different angle on debasement. Here the question of shame turns toward the reader's eye, ear, and mind, even as we stay rather fixed on something we read at the anus. In "When Are Dirty Details and Scenes Compelling?: Tucked in the Cuts of Interracial Anal Rape," I propose we read Tarantino's *Pulp Fiction* (1994) against the backdrop of work by Toni Morrison, Robert Mapplethorpe, and Roland Barthes—as well as in relation to black gay male cultural productions of the late 1980s and early 1990s, especially Isaac Julien's *Looking for Langston* (1989). I want to ask about our attraction—sometimes admitted, often denied or left unexamined—to details and scenes on a cinema screen that, in common parlance, would be tagged as "dirty": grimy, contemptible, obscene, or scatological. What is their relation to generative shame, to humiliations that produce social holdings? What kinds of value, to make matters tricky, cling to a scene of an anal rape, a black man's rape by redneck whites? And what kind of author, of such a scene as this one, would viewers likely trust to offer something other than gratuitous, unthinking violent shame? In answering these questions, I show the importance of queer sexualities to pulp fictions generally (also how Tarantino draws on gay pornography) and argue that images central to America's Jim Crow history of sexual assault against black Americans serve as pulp fictions in Tarantino's film. To understand why this particular switchpoint—between gay pornography and American racialized pulp fictions—might offer viewers a range of attractions that also wound them (with crisscrossing tones), I discuss debates surrounding Robert Mapplethorpe. Especially pertinent, as I show, are stinging critiques by black gay critics (of Mapplethorpe's photos of black gay men), critiques that later turn toward confessions of their pleasure intermingled with sorrow and aesthetic admiration for Mapplethorpe's experiments. Complicating Barthes's formulations of visual attraction as a form of violence, I suggest that even Tarantino's scene of rape may attract us and cut us, in ways I will explain. Tucked in these cuts are such diverse matters as our aesthetic interest, our complicated fantasies, and entire histories of pain and attraction invoked by suggestion.

My book's fourth chapter, "Erotic Corpse: Homosexual Miscegenation and the Decomposition of Attraction," takes the issue of shameful attractions even further, especially as they penetrate and burrow in the mind. Chapter 4 considers historical logics surrounding a social self-debasement rarely studied: miscegenation between two men. This miscegenation is even definitionally indecorous, since, by definition, "miscegenation" cannot be "homosexual." ("Miscegenation": "The interbreeding of what are presumed to be distinct human races, especially marriage between white and nonwhite persons.") Men, it would seem, cannot mix in such ways as to "interbreed" or (in most times and places) "intermarry." For this reason, the markers black and queer (more precisely, black and homosexual) come together in this chapter to show what "homosexual miscegenation" could be conceived to mean. And what it cannot mean. It can't mean relations of a typical, presumed homosexual sameness. Something, to be sure, breaks down "homo" in the mix of light and dark. Nor can homosexual miscegenation be conceived as conceiving, in the usual sense, a mixed offspring. There is no baby. Only attraction—and something perilous it produces in the mind. For two opposing writers, James Baldwin and his unforgiving critic Eldridge Cleaver, writing in the 1950s and '60s alongside Norman Mailer, homosexual miscegenation is grounded in their shared conviction that, when it comes to sexual magnetism, "opposites attract": most potently, apparently, white men and black men. Particularly, white men's obsessions with black men—most dramatically, sometimes slavishly, in their minds—lead to something beyond but including mental breakdowns. I will limn the breakdown one could refer to as the mind's "decomposition." I will also examine, through the mental image of a decomposing corpse, the surprising social holdings of men's keeping men, so sorrowfully, in mind.

A kind of mental holding, owing to memory's invasive force, is the trauma of *Beloved* and the central focus of Chapter 5, "Prophylactics and Brains: Slavery in the Cybernetic Age of AIDS." The trauma of memory is the usual understanding of *Beloved*'s focus. But *Beloved* as a novel also bears the trace of AIDS, as I propose to show. As we move deeper into the mind and the circuits of the brain (in this fifth chapter) to follow another form of debasement, the kind that comes with remembering unshakeable forms of shame, we discover a remarkable switchpoint—between the signs of the holocaust of slavery and the signs of AIDS. For here, in *Beloved* (published 1987), we find a viral model of memory—a viral gothic—as a result of uncontrollable transmissions from the dead; dead ones invading through fluids exchange; the dead reproducing themselves in the brain; and mothers, through their memories, suffering dramatic collapses in immunity. Canny echoes of AIDS infections seem to haunt *Beloved*, with its scenes of socially formed self-debasements. These surprising echoes are made more telling when we consider developments in cyberspace and the world of cloning, which offer hauntings through virtual futures and the aggressively viral spread of signs. Chapter 5, then, addresses the shame of taming the dead, of learning how to hold, in the mind's secluded space, your own beloved, who you fear is going to spread to every corner of your thoughts—and consume your life.

My conclusion, "Dark Camp: Behind and Ahead," looks at the thread of camp sensibilities running through many of the thinkers I engage. Here I explore important historical links between the artifice and playfulness of camp and the seemingly darker shades of shame for queers and blacks. In this way, I argue that a history of dark camp needs to be written (at some point in the future), which would include many figures and concepts from my book. Such a camp history would explore the central contributions of violence, cruelty, shameful attractions, and sorrow to camp's unnaturalness and exaggerations. Such a history would also make a place for writers not usually "in" the camp canon—for instance, Toni Morrison and Eldridge Cleaver—who conceptually add so much to camp anger, outrage, and flamboyance. As a way to indicate more recent permutations of this concept, "dark camp," and to test the informative nature of my arguments here, in this study, I end my conclusion by looking briefly at two important films: Todd Haynes's *Far From Heaven* (2002) and David Fincher's *Fight Club* (1999). Each film incorporates several (if not nearly all) of the forms of debasement I tackle throughout this book, showing our need to grasp these crucial conceptual blocks.

Chapter One

CLOTH WOUNDS, OR WHEN QUEERS

ARE MARTYRED TO CLOTHES

DEBASEMENTS OF A FABRICATED SKIN

Cloth and Skin

Clothing is the problem from which I launch my book and my book's specific aims: to scout debasement's surprising values, to understand debasement as crucial to the crossings between "black" and "queer," and to focus squarely on fictions' theoretical/speculative force. In a book that moves from debasements attached to the actions of clothing, to anal penetration, to interracial rape, to decomposition, to hauntings by the dead, a look at clothing comprises this book's first layer for a reason. Clothing raises the question of a surface to which shame attaches.

One such familiar surface is skin. Civil rights activists, black student radicals, and black studies scholars, among many other readers of race, have made us familiar with the prejudicial hate attaching to a surface— nonwhite skin—that people of color don't choose for themselves.[1] But I want to ask about an unexamined switchpoint between "black" and "queer": the switchpoint between these nonelective skins and what are for some queer women and men the highly preferred, habitually chosen, strongly valued, almost sewn-to-the-bone cloth skins that we call clothes.

At this switchpoint, a reading of queer cloth wounds might function as a study within a larger field of wounded surface and denigrated skins. Not because cloth and skin are identical, but because they lend associations to each other, in certain key contexts, as they track along their own specific logics.

Cloth and skin touch on each other's meanings since each is a surface —with intense, complex, and variable codings attached to it—that may be the object of prejudice, violence, attraction, and invective. Each may be physically marked with a wound (torn cloth, torn skin) and each can elicit psychic wounds (self-loathing, for example) because of the shame it seems to carry. Each can also, in certain contexts, elicit pride—or sexual attraction and aesthetic delight.[2] That is, there is beauty. But here there is a specific dynamic that adheres more closely to cloth than to skin: shame, in certain historical cases involving clothes, attaches to a surface (for example, women's clothes) generally and openly admitted to be beautiful. Though it is possible nonwhite skin is secretly seen as beautiful by racists, it would be unusual for racists to confess that they shame blacks *because* black skin is beautiful.[3]

Where skin and cloth more obviously and dramatically diverge from each other as forms of surface is in their perceived degrees of permanence.[4] Given that a person can more easily remove her clothes than her skin and can change kinds of clothes (from feminine to masculine, from glamorous to plainstyle), certain cultural imperatives that ask for a person's compliance—you must wear this, you can't wear that—are hard to duplicate with skin.[5] As a result, if a man can be told he must dress like a man, not a woman—it is after all physically possible for him to dress as either gender—his defiance of this order can be a self-debasement. Such defiance can even lead to martyrdom: "a sacrifice" or "extreme suffering," "endured in order to further a belief, cause, or principle."[6]

How it has happened that a culture's investment in gendered clothes (along with clothing's relation to beauty) makes for cloth wounds (which touch on skin) is the topic of this chapter. Martyrs to clothes can illuminate the logics surrounding elective but intensely worn (or spurned) cloth skins. Such acts of martyrdom are bold self-debasements, revealing the social holdings of shame.[7]

Martyrs to Their Clothes

It is surprising that shame can adhere to forms of beauty, especially to the contours of beautiful cloth. Women wrapped in beautiful clothes may betray the vanity said to be their shame. Men who rush to their own cloth beauty may also suffer a woman's vain shame. These are dynamics this chapter will engage. From the outset, one should consider their narrowness—for all their broad and sweeping generality. That is to say, these cultural dynamics involve predilections for plainstyle clothing among Euro-American men, of largely white and nonethnic cultures, primarily beginning in the nineteenth century. They also presume a bourgeois, middlebrow preference for plainstyle—one still in force in American contexts at least at the end of the 1990s, according to Malcolm Gladwell's essay for *The New Yorker*, "Listening to Khakis: What America's Most Popular Pants Tell Us about the Way Guys Think" (1997).

Gladwell's essay reminds us of just how fraught clothes are for straight, white, middle-class men, never mind for the queer men and women I will focus on here. In fact, in his article Gladwell explores "the roundabout way [required] to sell a man a pair of pants," since "the man in the middle [of the economic spectrum] . . . probably isn't comfortable buying clothes at all." Taking a look at the Dockers campaign, beginning in the fall of 1987, along with other spinoffs (Haggar ads, for instance), Gladwell examines "the notion of khakis as nonfashion-guy fashion," which "lure[s] men . . . with the promise of a uniform," "so as not to scare them." The point of these ads was "to talk about [fashion] in such a coded, cautious way that no man would ever think Dockers was suggesting that he wear khakis in order to look *pretty*," since if a man "knows he is attractive and is beautifully dressed—then he's not a man anymore. He's a fop. He's effeminate."[8] He's deemed vain. Perhaps unwittingly, phenomena such as metrosexuality and the TV show *Queer Eye for the Straight Guy* (first appearing in 2003) may be confirming while also changing these stereotypes. The label "metrosexual" indicates a need to signify, and also make more acceptable, a new breed of straight, noneffeminate men who like (their) clothes. The reality show known as *Queer Eye* offers straight "guys" a more roundabout fantasy. Five gay men (who make over straight men) give them permission to care about fashion and beautiful clothes—while, through it all, the straight men still get to pose as fully clueless (helpless and hopeless) about clothes and beauty, thereby confirming their obvious straightness. All of the know-how, and all of the action, rests in the hands, not to mention the eyes, of five gay men ("the Fabulous Five") who hold themselves responsible for all that transpires.

These are the contortions required for some straight men's relations to even moderately beautiful men's clothes. There are still more startling dynamics in store for their relations to womanly clothes. In an article for the *New York Times*, a reporter tells of being asked by the paper to wear, as an experiment, a tasteful Jean Paul Gaultier skirt "intended for men" on his daily rounds. "The neuroses quickly set in," says the journalist. "I went through a phase not unlike the stages of grieving." "I called my wife, who helped by laughing uncontrollably." She even asked: " '[Won't] you feel like a total idiot?' " The reporter continues, "I was sure I could walk around East New York in the skirt without being beaten up. But no way could I hope to interview witnesses to a shoot-out and be taken seriously. . . . Out in the street I found myself trying to hide between telephone booths and cars. As people stared, it occurred to me that, when you are a guy in a skirt, pretty much any abuse that anyone heaps on you seems fair."[9]

It is striking to hear this phrase, and so to grasp the shame attached to beauty, especially to beauty attached to clothes. It is more striking to learn, from certain novels, that this debasement clinging to beauty can make the wearer of beautiful garments a martyr to clothes. What can it mean to be martyred for clothes—to believe in your clothes as you suffer from clothes, to bear the wounds that come with clothes, even to give up your very self (but what would that mean?) for the cause of your clothes? So-called homosexual fictions—from fictional lesbian autobiographies (without any claim to aesthetic density) to the high modernist camp of the novels of Jean Genet (aesthetic texts of such dense weave, such lyric sheen)—lend a range of intricate answers.

As an initial foray into martyrdoms, I will sample novels from three distinct histories, offering twentieth-century martyrs as diverse as those of the mannish lesbian of Great Britain's '20s, American butches and femmes of the '60s, and even the sailors of postwar France. These remarkably various fictions specify, remarkably, not entirely various logics.[10] Taking up the cause of clothes, as if clothing were a dangerous rite that they would defend, all three novels imagine scenes of sacrifice. However, in ways we might not expect, sacrifice is joined to sexual fantasy. As we will see, the throwing of one's self outward in sacrifice merges with the goal of being caught by other arms—a sexy pietà. This odd motion of throwing and being caught calls our attention to something odder still.

Clothing, in these novels, is a throwing and a catching, a centrifugal force. In the act of clothing, one is thrown outward, body and skin, into cloth arms (the arms of one's clothes), caught and held as a public gesture, in the social field. Clothing is this act of public self-betrayal, by which one seems to reveal oneself, to show one's colors.[11] But could clothing also be a kind of social holding, a social self-hoarding, as odd as that may seem, of one's humiliation at the hands of something loved? What are the features of this social self-debasement? According to our novels, from three different histories, that depends dramatically on how one negotiates the wounds that come with cloth.

Cloth of Woundedness

There are many ways to be hurt by one's clothes. A psychic wound may emerge from wearing certain clothes, as if one's thoughts show a certain cut of cloth. A woman's genital "wound" (à la Freud) may be announced or dismissed by one's clothes, calling out on "every woman's" garment a vagina; on "every man's" unadorned, masculine garment escape from this sorrow. Some may hand out bodily wounds to those who wear "unnatural" clothes, wounds which themselves may be worn as clothes: a bruise, for example, as a kind of purple cloth. Finally, perhaps most intriguing of all: one may suffer the divine humiliation of devotion to . . . fabric: a sailor, in his fantasy, may feel a blackening "coat" of "coal dust on his body, as women feel, on their arms . . . the folds of a material that transforms them into queens."[12]

These are cloth wounds. Which makes both Freud and the dictionary wrong, or simply defensive, when it comes to cloth. The dictionary tells us clothes are designed to cover, protect, or adorn the body (in a sense, to function as superior skin), slyly saying nothing of their flagrant penchant for revealing, wounding, or debasing the body that they pretend to cover.[13] Moreover, we are told that "cloth" is related to the Old English *clitha*, meaning "a poultice": a soft moist mass, of flour or herbs, applied to a sore or inflamed body part. By this rendering, cloth is seen as a solace for sufferings, soothing skin, not as an agent, as cloth also is, for a stigmatized appearance.

Freud, for his part, adheres to a covering. In his essay "Femininity" (1933), Freud imagines pubic hair as a natural model for human clothing, since it covers and conceals a woman's genitals. Here is the "unconscious motive," Freud tells us, for women's contribution (their only contribution) to civilized development: plaiting and weaving, which, of course, only "imitates" nature's invention of the pubes.[14] "The step that remained to be taken," says Freud, in the passage from pubic hair to clothes, "lay in making the threads adhere to one another, [since] on the body they stick into the skin and are only matted together." In other words, as it solves the problem of sticking, cloth adds a greater adhesion to a covering.

But what is being covered? Not a person's body in any simple sense. Not, even more particularly, the genitals. Freud is more specific still. What is being covered, in Freud's own phrase, is "genital deficiency"—his essay is on "Femininity," after all. Indeed, what has led Freud to pubic hair and cloth is his last, rushed, rag-bag discussion of "a few more psychic peculiarities of mature femininity": "vanity" and "shame." Peculiar, indeed, is the feminine adherence of one to the other, shame to vanity, vanity to shame, so that they would appear to wear each other's clothes. As it happens, one is a cover for the other. "The vanity of women," Freud famously informs us, is "a late compensation for . . . original sexual inferiority." Vanity, in other words, is fancy-pants shame, which "has as its purpose," says Freud, ". . . concealment of genital deficiency." Yet this is no concealment at all. Vanity is calling out: "look at my cover." By Freud's rendering, in spite of what he claims, clothing is not primarily concealment; it is not primarily a more attractive version of its model, pubic hair. Clothing, rather, is bold revelation; a revelatory, fabricated, secondary skin, a cover turning inside out: it reveals the *category* (male or female) of the person's genitals it purports to cover. On "every woman's" sweater, a vaginal wound.

If I have offered the fictions of Freud—lacking in all subtlety and cloaking historicity, when it comes to clothes—it has been to dramatize how Freud, in this case, gets something right even when he is wrong. He stresses clothing's concealments, unconvincingly, even as he rightfully points to its displays. Additionally, whether rightly or wrongly, Freud, by implication, fingers display of genital shame as "civilization's" strong investment in gendered clothes (different clothes for women and men). Yet his lack of historical regard (stressing clothing's universal operations) does not keep Freud, in 1933, just five years past Radclyffe Hall's *The Well of Loneliness* (1928), from exemplifying his own peculiar timeliness. For I think it would be fair to say that Freud and Radclyffe Hall were voicing something in much stronger terms than were their contemporaries: not just the sociopolitical disadvantage attached to women's clothes but the bodily and psychic wounding that may powerfully adhere to them.[15]

Even the psychoanalyst J. C. Flugel did not put the matter of clothes so starkly in his famous treatise, *The Psychology of Clothes* (1930), launched from a series of talks he gave for the BBC in 1928 — the year in which *The Well* was banned.[16] Flugel had no theory of wounding. True, he argued to abolish fashion in favor of some kind of uniform dress (which would level differences), and he himself theorized clothes (in a move Freud intensified) as satisfying two "contradictory tendencies" (those of "decoration" and "modesty"). This duality makes clothes mimic, according to Flugel, the neurotic symptoms of people who suffer "attacks of . . . blushing" as they negotiate between the states of "shame" and "exhibitionism," so that "clothes resemble a perpetual blush upon the surface of humanity." Yet, in spite of this theory of blushing — which, we might notice, makes clothing into a coloring skin — Flugel had no theory of wounding.[17]

Nor exactly did the New Woman writers have any theory of clothes wounding women, though they were grappling with what women's clothes mean and limit.[18] (Constraints on women's freedom of movement, the fit of women's clothes to their jobs, and sartorial limitations to cultural authority were central issues here.) Rather, it was when debates about the New Woman got replayed, in the so-called second wave of feminism, especially and most clearly among historians of the 1980s, that feminist talk about some of the New Woman's cloth wounds emerged.[19] Feminist historians, at that moment, sought to grasp the various motives and stakes attached to the New Woman's frequent refusal of standard women's clothes. Some historians largely explored the kind of New Woman who they imagined "adopted male dress as a self-conscious political statement," believing that "clothes are cultural artifacts, lightly donned or doffed."[20] They explained with less ease (what they referred to as) the "mannish lesbian" of the 1920s, a New Woman whose costume change was not so easy, and whose "symbols [thus] acquired a second, darker message. . . . public condemnation, social ostracism, and legal censorship" (279). It was left to those more sympathetic to this figure to explain the mannish lesbian's bold refusal of women's clothes as a sign that she symbolized "the stigma of lesbianism (just as the effeminate man is the stigma-bearer for gay men)."[21]

What interests me is this mention of "stigma." Notice the assumption that a woman *refusing* women's clothes would find herself still bound to a wound — more pointedly, a stigma. (Stigma: "a distinguishing mark burned or cut into the flesh, as of a slave or criminal"; "marks resembling the crucifixion wounds of Jesus"; "a mark, sign, etc. indicating that something is not considered normal or standard.") This sort of stigma would seem to be the sign of "lesbianism" pure and simple: refusing women's clothes may publicly reveal one's sexual preference for other women's bodies. But can we put the emphasis the other way around? One's public preference for other women sexually can make the public see—and see, perhaps, in a whole new way—something about some women's refusal of women's clothes. What might the reading public never have had put before them, in any large way, before the public banning of Hall's *The Well of Loneliness* (a banning that so dramatically publicized Hall and her protagonist as "the mannish lesbian")?[22] Something perhaps deeply known by many women. A different kind of shame from the presumed "stigma" of "lesbianism" (though there was surely that). What *Well's* readers might have confronted is the shame some women have historically felt (not the discomfort, not the displeasure, but, really, the shame) in having to wear women's clothes, a kind of psychic debasement that runs so deep it seems in excess of a simple preference for wearing men's clothes. Moreover, this shame could eerily match, and therefore newly emphasize, the psychic debasement that men in Hall's time were asked to feel in relation to women's clothes on themselves. ("Imagine a man in a dress like that," says Captain Ramsey in *The Well of Loneliness*, "too awful to think of—.") Without this psychic stigma, Stephen, the novel's mannish lesbian, could not feel such shame in women's dresses. Discomfort, yes. Even a sense of diminished pleasure. But not the humiliation she feels.

What might this psychic debasement—as shown in *The Well of Loneliness*—say about a deep-seated stain on the meanings attached to "normal" women's clothes, even to their acknowledged beauty? This strong reaction to women's adornment—expressed through a character who must contemplate these clothes upon herself—amounts to a hate for what she also loves, for what she would admit is beautiful but also both wounding and debasing. What may be alluring when held at arm's length—women's clothes and their acknowledged beauty—may be debasing if put upon oneself, even for "normal" men who love women. Beauty, in this way, may be seen to be a wound. Or, to put it differently, what *The Well of Loneliness* suggests appears distinctively in *Stone Butch Blues* (1993) and Genet's *Querelle* (1947): it is queer to know a cloth wound when you see one.

It is even stranger to negotiate cloth wounds through the act of martyrdom. This is something we have yet to understand. In the novels I examine here, in this chapter, there are full-scale scenes of sacrifice, all involving clothes. These scenes of martyrdom clearly offer something beyond a symbol for queers' social stigma in the obvious sense. The question is, what, exactly, do they offer? Here another writer comes into view—Georges Bataille—one likely thoroughly read by Genet, though he was also writing at the same time as Hall (and, like Genet and Hall, writing from a background steeped in Catholic thought).[23] Bataille is heuristically interesting on sacrifice; his essays make us see what questions we could ask of a martyrdom to clothes, and further how this sacrifice goes hand-in-hand with fantasy.

Sacrifice, at times, can sound in common talk like a dour religious act, mired in resignation to a bad reality. Not so for Bataille. Briefly, Bataille, in *Theory of Religion*, deems "religion's essence . . . the search for lost intimacy."[24] Lest this "intimacy" sound too immediately relational or sexual, we should realize that this is a call to "the intimacy of the divine world," whose chief feature is its "unreality," its separation from "real relations" and the "world of things" (44). Religion, one could say, is a search for the intimacy of unreality. In fact, it is the main function of sacrifice to destroy "an object's real ties," by drawing "the victim out of the world of utility," while delivering her or him to a world of "unintelligible caprice," thus giving sacrifice "an appearance of puerile gratuitousness" (43; 45). Question one: Could sacrifice surrounding clothes, whatever that might look like, be depicted as destroying, at least in some respects, a person's "real ties" to the "world of utility"?

I have said that sacrificial destruction has a rather fanciful nature, in Bataille's view, taking one toward both caprice and unreality. Now we must see that sacrifice is also tied to a movement, in Bataille's rendering, so often linked to fantasy: a casting of oneself outside oneself (in fantasy, a mental leap) so as to break not just with one's reality but also with one's "individuality" (51). (Think of how in fantasy you mentally leap past material limits and beyond the confines of your life and self.) With the act of sacrifice, according to Bataille, such casting turns physical and, of course, violent. In fact, this break with one's individuality lies at the heart of the sacrificial urge, according to Bataille, and constitutes the intimacy of sacrificial violence. In his lurid essay "Sacrificial Mutilation and the Severed Ear of Vincent Van Gogh" (1930), Bataille proclaims that automutilation (the chopping off of one's finger, for example) reveals what's at stake in religious sacrifice: the need to externalize the self, to throw oneself out of oneself, to disrupt the homogeneity of the self, whether by the sacrifice of animal proxies (a religious cop-out) or the madman's chopping off of his ear.[25] Question two: Could clothing be creatively rendered as *both* an act of

fantasy and an act of sacrifice, allowing one to throw oneself, to feel oneself as a kind of thrown self? Our selected fictions, to be sure, are going
to show that a martyrdom to clothes is a striking self-betrayal. For when
you give up loneliness to make yourself a character, by means of either
fantasy or cloth, you give yourself away. But are you caught and held?[26]

Cloth of Loneliness

Arguably the most famous "lesbian" novel, Hall's *The Well of Loneliness*,
answers no: one is not embraced in a martyrdom to clothes. Sadly, in *The
Well*, fantasy fails. Sacrifice fails. The novel's martyr, as we are going to
see, is left in the singular posture of refusing her women's clothes, an act
that connects her to "Negro" laments.

As any reader of the novel will remember, *Well* begins and ends with
sacrificial scenes. The novel's heroine, Stephen Mary Gordon, carries in
her name a gendered cross between a famous church martyr—the figure
St. Stephen—and the Virgin Mary who wraps her martyred son in her
arms. Stephen is born on Christmas Eve and bears, as another character
puts it, the "outward stigmata of the abnormal—verily the wounds of One
nailed to a cross."[27] Yet, in what seems a cross-dressing pun, Stephen, the
novel's most loyal cross-dresser, wears a martyr's "cross" on her clothes,
as we will see. Whether she dresses as a woman or a man, Stephen is
unable to shake cloth wounds.

To begin, one notes that, for all its pains, the novel is actually shockingly flat—at the level of the sentence (no sentence is transporting) and
even at the larger level of its plot (which is, more or less, a story of impasse). This very flatness has clearly aided those who, since 1928, have
wished to read the novel as fairly factual—to find in *The Well* a historically accurate portrait of a second-generation New Woman (her lesbian
lust announced by her clothes) or to find a fiction "still true" to butch
women, and thus one easily altered on spec.[28] Consider, for example,
that, according to a recent oral history of a lesbian community (*Boots of
Leather, Slippers of Gold*), Hall's French twist on 1920s British aristocracy
was stretched by readers to cover their lives in the American 1950s factory town of Buffalo, New York.[29] Truly, *Well* has proved a crossover text
of vast proportions, only rivaled now by *Stone Butch Blues* (1993), through
which many readers universalize the lives of 1960s Buffalo lesbians.

None of this intrigue surrounding historicity is beside the point. The
power of *Well*'s sentimental realism, its relentless portrait of a cross-

dressing Christ, is for me its "clothemes" (to coin a comic word from Roland Barthes's "mythemes"): its myths surrounding clothes. I believe these clothemes are somewhat detachable from the specific plotlines that engage them; but, as they emerge in different plots and other histories, they are largely altered. Here is what I mean. In *The Well of Loneliness*, strutting, deflating, tearing cloth, and shedding tears (all involving clothes) are the central clothemes, one might say, all of which resurface in *Stone Butch Blues* to a similar logic but different effect. For here in *Well*, at the dawning of these clothemes (at least in novel form), fantasy sputters; sacrifice fails. There is, finally, only loneliness. Especially at the novel's start, other than her clothes, there are no arms of a public sort to catch a humiliated Stephen in embrace. Further in *Well*, there are no social holdings (no public structures), at least of the sort that Stephen can trust, to make her self-humiliation into a social solitude. This communal void, as Hall represents it, even in some ways goes smack against Hall's own experience of communal supports that she herself knew.[30] One has to wonder whether the large persecution Hall seemed determined to depict, along with her gothic, sentimental borrowings from nineteenth-century literature, drove her portrait of communal vacancy. In fact, the void intensifies, even when communities seem to be invoked: "As long as she lived Stephen never forgot her first impression of the bar known as Alec's— that meeting-place of the most miserable of all those who comprised the miserable army. . . . who, despised of the world, must despise themselves beyond all hope, it seemed, of salvation" (387). Even early on, the heroine's martyrdom looks like a sacrifice gone awry.

I refer, of course, to the tragicomic scenes at the start of the novel in which first love, first clothes, and first wounds all stick together in a first plot block. Stephen has fallen for her housemaid, Collins, as nursery stories have "stirred her ambition":

> She, Stephen, [age seven], now longed to be William Tell, or [Lord] Nelson, or the whole charge of Balaclava; and this led to much foraging in the nursery rag-bag, much hunting up of garments once used for charades, much swagger and noise, much strutting and posing. . . . Once dressed, she would walk away grandly . . . going, as always, in search of Collins, who might have to be stalked to the basement. (19)

Stephen courts Collins dressed as a boy—Lord Nelson, in particular, that famous martyr from the Battle of Trafalgar. Collins, for her part, laughs at Stephen and appears distracted, since she is suffering from "housemaid's knee." Seeing, perhaps, that masculine clothes cannot bear any comedy, that they shrink from laughter and suggestions of vanity, Stephen finds herself "thoroughly deflated," dressing up "as Nelson in vain," "and must tear off the clothes she dearly loved donning, to replace them by the garments she hated" (20).

Before we return to this scene's fascination—Stephen's bid for martyrdom—we should notice that sartorial beauty is perfectly seductive on someone else, as is a "soft" "dress" (which Stephen "very much wanted to remember") that a beloved of Stephen's later wears (a dress "so soft that it had easily torn," 141). The kind of beauty that Stephen herself is forced to wear ("the garments she hated") is a different matter altogether. Stephen takes what she feels in her clothes remarkably hard, beginning in this scene: "How she hated soft dresses and sashes, and ribbons, and small coral beads, and openwork stockings! Her legs felt so free and comfortable in breeches" (20). This motif of comfortable freedom fades from later passages, giving way to stronger laments: "I *hate* this white dress and I'm going to burn it—it makes me feel idiotic!" (37). "She stood there an enraged and ridiculous figure in her Liberty smock. . . . the bow [in her hair] sagged down limply, crooked, and foolish" (52). All of which comes to a head in a passage that shows cloth shame (her own humiliation) turning Stephen toward prayer:

> She wrenched off the dress and hurled it from her, longing intensely to rend it, to hurt it, longing to hurt herself in the process, yet filled all the while with that sense of injustice. But this mood changed abruptly to one of self-pity; she wanted to sit down and weep over Stephen; on a sudden impulse she wanted to pray over Stephen as though she were someone apart, yet terribly personal too in her trouble. Going over to the dress she smoothed it out slowly; it seemed to have acquired an enormous importance; it seemed to have acquired the importance of prayer, the poor, crumpled thing lying crushed and dejected. . . . She donned the new dress with infinite precaution, pulling out its bows and arranging its ruffles. Her large hands were clumsy but now they were willing, very penitent hands full of deep resignation. (74)

Later in the novel, this prayerful resignation, once again mixed with wrenching lament and deep-seated shame, shows up—in a startling scene—on black skin. With a large dose of racism, Hall describes "two Negro brothers" who mournfully, wrenchingly, sing their spirituals to Stephen and her friends:

Lincoln, the elder, was paler in colour. . . . His eyes had the patient, questioning expression common to the eye of most animals and to those of all slowly evolving races. . . . Henry was tall and as black as a coal; a fine, upstanding, but coarse-lipped Negro. . . . 'Deep river, my home is over Jordan. Deep river — Lord, I want to cross over into camp ground. . . . Didn't my Lord deliver Daniel, then why not every man? . . . Oh, my, what a shame, I ain't nobody's baby.' All the hope of the utterly hopeless of this world . . . all the terrible, aching . . . hope . . . seemed to break from this man and shake those who listened . . . [T]hey who were also among the hopeless sat with bent heads and clasped hands. . . . stirred to the depths by that queer, half defiant, half supplicating music. . . . Lincoln's deep bass voice kept up a low sobbing. . . . They were just two men with black skins and foreheads beaded with perspiration. Henry sidled away to the whiskey, while Lincoln rubbed his pinkish palms on an elegant white silk handkerchief. (362–65)

The sign of black skin and all that is attached to it — hopeless, queer half-defiance, and insoluble loneliness — makes this arresting, significant cut through Hall's text. For here, in the midst of depicting remarkably different stigmas, Hall cannot resist transferring something — some kind of meaning — from these black skins onto white silk cloth.[31]

Returning now to the earlier scene of Collins's knee, we see how striking it is that Stephen, dressed as a girl (in her "hated" girls' clothes), starts acting like a martyr. Stephen even tries, in her martyr-like fashion, to take on a wound that is not her own. It's a funny scene (a martyr seducing at the tender age of seven) in a novel hardly noted for either camp or wit. Nightly she cries in "an orgy of prayer":

Please, Jesus, give me a housemaid's knee instead of Collins. . . . Please, Jesus, I would like to bear all Collins' pain the way You did. . . . I would like to wash Collins in my blood. . . . This petition she repeated until she fell asleep, to dream that in some queer way she was Jesus, and that Collins was kneeling and kissing her hand, because she, Stephen, had managed to cure her by cutting off her knee, with a bone paper-knife and grafting it onto her own. The dream was a mixture of rapture and discomfort, and it stayed quite a long time with Stephen. (21–22)

For all these elaborate dreams of sacrifice, Stephen's fantasy of grafting Collins's damaged knee onto her own is not a sacrifice she can perform.

Just as sadly, this fantasy collapses into Stephen's loneliness instead of solving it. And so, since she cannot come to wear Collins's knee in this way, Stephen, yet again, changes strategy. Getting mad at Jesus ("'You don't love Collins, Jesus, but I do,'" 22), Stephen cries: "'I've got to get housemaid's knee my own way—I can't wait any longer for Jesus!'" (23). However, this bid for attaching her heart to a wounded knee makes a cloth wound more than anything else, which redounds upon herself:

> The nursery floor was covered with carpet, which was obviously rather unfortunate for Stephen. . . . All the same it was hard if she knelt long enough. . . . Nelson helped her a little. She would think: 'Now I'm Nelson. I'm in the middle of the Battle of Trafalgar—I've got shots in my knees!' But then she would remember that Nelson had been spared such torment. . . . [Still] there were endless spots on the . . . carpet, and these spots Stephen could pretend to be cleaning. . . . Enormous new holes appeared in her stockings, through which she could examine her aching knees, and this led to rebuke: 'Stop your nonsense, Miss Stephen! It's scandalous the way you're tearing your stockings!' (22, 23)

Earlier, Stephen had failed to extract the needed power from "Nelson's" clothes, which had led to Stephen's tearing them. Now her failure to elicit any wound from him (somehow he's a martyr without a wound to lend her) leads to different rips as she comically copies the movements of her servant, making her the figure of a carpet-cleaning Christ. As this savior, Stephen only succeeds in revealing, metaphorically and literally, the wound that sits on her women's clothes ("enormous new holes appeared in her stockings"). Moreover, because the invert child has "scandalously" torn her feminine garments, and has succeeded in tearing her skin, the head servant orders Collins to lie, to tell the child her knee is getting better from these efforts so that Stephen will stop them. This fabrication, which even Stephen questions, is emblematic for the book as a whole. Nothing is solved by the logic of wounding. Collins, according to conventional rhythms, consorts with a footman, while Stephen's martyr-doms are mainly productive of exile and tears:

> She sobbed as she ran . . . tearing her clothes on the shrubs in passing, tearing her stockings and the skin of her legs. . . . But suddenly the child was caught in strong arms, and her face was pressing against her father. . . . [S]he crouched here like a dumb creature that had somehow got itself wounded. . . . 'I'm going to send Collins away tomorrow; do

3. "St. Stephen," Beresford Egan's cartoon of *The Well of Loneliness*, courtesy of Stanford University Library, Special Collections Department.

you understand, Stephen?' . . . Bending down, [her father] kissed her in absolute silence—it was like the sealing of a sorrowful pact. (28, 29)

Gone is the purpose behind her wish for sacrifice: to be held by Collins and her own boy's clothes; really, to be held in her masculine clothes. Even this final wrapping by her father is no solution. Her father later dies; her lover, Mary, leaves, when Stephen sends her away to a man. It only closes off this first plot block, which repeats in different fashions throughout Hall's *Well*, recycling unmistakable clothemes of loneliness.[32]

One last cross. In a famous cartoon (Figure 3), joined to a satire called *The Sink of Solitude*, Beresford Egan applies his own sense of a wound to cloth. Nailing Hall to the banning of her book (hence the book and official in the foreground) and nailing both to the metaphor of martyrdom, Egan supplies "St. Stephen" with a wound that Freud could well appreciate. A naked dancing girl, with a single dancing shoe and an unmistakable genital cleft (not to mention a breast), is circling the martyr at the level of her genitals. "Hall" may be covered, but, by this rendering, she is not positioned to refuse anyone, or, indeed, anything, attached to her clothes.

Cloth of Communal Adherence

Out of the 1990s there arises a solace for this loneliness. In Leslie Feinberg's *Stone Butch Blues*, loneliness seems taken up and transformed in the space that Stephen Mary Gordon never trusted: the lesbian bar. Shot through with its nostalgia for community—1960s lesbian bar life in Buffalo, along with labor struggles in a string of city factories—*Stone Butch Blues* begins, even so, with a lonely letter. It has been written at the story's end, to a lover lost at the story's middle, though it is placed at the story's start: "Dear Theresa, I'm lying on my bed tonight missing you . . . hot tears running down my face. . . . as I have each night of this lonely exile."[33] *Stone Butch Blues* almost seems to pick up where *Well* left off; as if, years after sending her away, Stephen were writing to her great love, Mary, to reminisce about a lost community.[34]

And yet, what has changed between these novels' settings, between the loneliness of *Well*'s late twenties and the bracing sociality of *Stone*'s 1960s, is something very 1990s. Call it feminist-butch relations. Here I refer to the unforeseen phenomenon, still underway, of a feminist affirmation of the once dirty secret of a lesbian history: femme-butch relations, which relied on gender roles later so heavily critiqued by many feminists. Feinberg's acknowledgments to her novel are quite revealing on this score. From how she thanks the femmes in her life, we are asked to recognize the femme as rather powerful: demanding, critical, political, protecting, and even seminal: "You demanded that I write this novel"; "if I couldn't take criticism from a femme I wouldn't be here today telling this story"; "[you] consistently spoke up to defend butch lives as well as [your] own when voices like mine could not be heard"; "the thoughtfulness you brought to the editing was an extension of your political sensitivity"; "your commitment to this book—from planting the seed to midwifing its birth ('Push, push!')—flowed not only from your passionate beliefs but from your long history of political organizing." This is the voice of a feminist butch, thanking her femmes in a feminist way.

This affirmation in the larger sphere of feminist thought takes many forms; among them, as one can readily imagine, is a reading of these couples as deconstructing pairs.[35] But I am more struck by Feinberg's sense of sacrifice: the way in which her butch, who is physically wounded because of her clothes, wears her resultant gashes and burns, on her skin, for the sake of her femme, who wears women's clothes. This is a social working out of women's wounds, as we are going to see, and one in which the presence of the femme (even as the letter's worshipped ghost) makes all the difference. True, gone is Hall's Catholic discourse, but not its sense of martyrdom. And now, unlike the setting in *Well*, there are social structures—an erotic system, even—that can turn debasements toward a social self-enclosure (of a sacrificing self). This is even a fantastic self-betrayal: a feminist fantasy of *inequality*, a fantastic embrace of differential roles. Indeed, as if to underscore its fantasy structure, the novel's lonely letter is a form of pillow talk to a lost great love, but this pillow talk includes a remembrance of the (good old) raids of the 1960s when butches were beaten up by the cops. Here is a memory of a raid on a bar:

> That's when I remember your hand on my belt, up under my suit jacket. . . . where your hand stayed the whole time the cops were there. . . . "Stay with me baby, cool off," you'd be cooing . . . like a special lover's song sung to warriors. . . . The law said we had to be wearing three pieces of women's clothing. . . . I never told you what they did to us down there [in the jail]—queens in one tank, stone butches in the next—but you knew. . . . We never cried in front of the cops. . . . Did I survive? . . . only because I knew I might get home to you. . . . You bailed me out. . . . You gently rubbed the bloody places on my shirt and said, "I'll never get these stains out." (8–10)

> You laid out a fresh pair of white BVD's and a T-shirt for me and left me alone to wash off the first layer of shame. I remember it was always the same. . . . you would find some reason to come into the bathroom. . . . In a glance you would memorize the wounds on my body like a road map—the gashes, bruises, cigarette burns. Later, in bed, you held me gently. . . . You didn't flirt with me right away, knowing I wasn't confident enough to feel sexy. But slowly you coaxed my pride back out . . . You knew it would take you weeks again to melt the stone. . . . You treated my stone self as a wound that needed loving healing. (9)

Here again are *Well*'s recognizable sentiments: pride, swift deflation, sorrow, and a palpable longing for embrace. And again, we as readers are held to the novel by an intricate chain of interlocking clothemes. Overall, we see how the members of this couple reveal their culture's violent investment in an arbitrary surface: gender-differential clothes for men and women ("The law said we had to be wearing three pieces of women's clothing").[36] In the face of this investment, we see how this couple wears sexual deviance. They even wear it as something shared between them — a deviance that neither can sustain on her own. In unequal ways, they are marked by the discipline and punishments of gender.

The femme's deviance is strangely unmarked when she's on her own. Dressed as a woman, she can't be seen for the deviant she is, since she passes by wearing the "wound" of women's gender, as is expected, on her clothes. The butch, by contrast, looks to be refusing the women's clothes that, for herself, she feels as a wound (even though she clearly loves her lover to wear them).[37] Yet it is by this act of refusal that she gives herself away to her lover and the law. For when, sartorially, she throws herself from her woman's wound in her fantasy dress-up as a "man" (or, more precisely, as a masculine woman), she is seen by the law but is also lit up for her femme's attractions to gender clichés (warriors wearing BVDS as their heroics turn them into stone).

The femme herself, through these very clichés, also crosses expectations. The fabricated "man" she is choosing to love is a "failed" authenticity busted by authorities. Perhaps even to the butch's embarrassment and dismay, it is *for* this "failure," we are led to believe, the butch's position as a not-man, that the femme loves the butch.[38] This is in part because this "failure" allows the femme to be demanding, political, and protecting (she "bailed," she "rubbed," she "laid," she "held" — the bulk of the verbs belong to her). And indeed, it is the femme who springs the butch from jail and supports the butch financially when, because of her appearance, she loses employment. The femme advocates for the one who would not like to walk in her shoes.

Just as literally, the law becomes a character in these scenes of sacrifice — the cops invading, intruding, and forcing the butch to wear the surface signs — in this case, clothing — that signal the "normally feminine" wound that women (are asked to) wear as cloth. If the butch refuses (refuses women's clothes), she is sent to jail and beaten — made to wear on the surface of her skin (gashes, bruises) the wound she refuses to allude to with her clothes.

As if she were a macho Christ, the butch embraces the role of wearing these wounds on her skin. Around these wounds she forms a "stone." This is the mark of emotional hardening that is a monument to felt humilia-

tion. The femme's vocation, in relation to these wounds (which, complexly, mirror her own), is to catch a thrown self, a self thrown in sacrifice, a self dramatically externalized and ruptured, and then to "melt the
stone"—in essence to be the holder and dispenser of tears. The femme
melts the stone so the butch can decide not to take it anymore—but not to
take it anymore "again and again" (8). For here's the rub: the femme melts
the stone so the butch can go back, again and again, to encounter the law
("it was always the same," 9). Together, what they advocate is a repetition
of wounding and refusal at the hands of their clothes (the femme wears
the cloth wound, the butch fights the cloth wound, the cops intervene,
the butch wears the skin wound). All of which puts them about the business of holding, as a couple, a psychic wound they never would have made
each other wear.

One last cross for this text, too. From a cross-comparison with *Boots
of Leather, Slippers of Gold*, the oral history of this same community (also
published in 1993), the fictional work of *Stone Butch Blues* perhaps becomes apparent: particularly its wonderfully worked-out investment in
wounds as communal refusal of the cops. For it appears, if *Boots* is accurate, that there were very few raids in the 1950s and very few bars in the
1960s. I don't want to ride this point too strongly and thus appear to correct a novel with an oral history; and it may be that the bars in the late
1960s or the bars in Canada (where at least one raid takes place) showed
a different picture than the Buffalo bars of the 1950s. However, the difference between these accounts points, intriguingly, to one of my switchpoints. Police harassment, according to *Boots*, was largely directed at black
lesbians and cross-dressing men of various races. White lesbians, according to these sources, took their beatings mostly from each other or from
their attempts to "expand their territory" into other bars.[39]

Thus we are left with some tantalizing questions not meant to be
disparaging. What kinds of stories—those of cloth and colored skin—is
Leslie Feinberg creatively mixing? Or is she documenting how, in this
city, for the police, two hates crossed?

Cloth of Curve

Stone Butch Blues may offer a rather unimaginable lesson in how to have
a feminist fantasy—how to imagine two women addressing the shame
of their clothes by returning, in sacrificial cycles, to a beating that marks
one's skin. Genet's *Querelle* (1947; 1953[40]) is more circular still, propos-

ing the queer's devotion to fabric (his wish to be held, as it were, by his clothes) as an elegant, self-embracing shame—one that will dramatically show up as blackened skin.

This devotion to fabric is shame, not just because it resembles women's vanity, but because it points towards other men's arms. The wish to be held by your own clothes is a wish to be held by arms that both are and are not your own. Wrap-around shame that comes from the thrill of men's tightly wrapped clothes is tightly tied, moreover, to sacrificial scenes. Sacrifice is a kind of wrapping in *Querelle*. It mimes the act of clothing by being a throwing of oneself from oneself that allows the subject to touch back upon himself as if he had a different set of arms from his own.

Amazingly, the fighting in *Querelle* is as oddly self-reflexive as the clothing. In this novel about the sea and sailors, sailors in port, workmen and sailors, the dark circuitry between cops and criminals, who are sailors—set in the seaside city of Brest, destroyed by bombs in World War II—fighting is a way of calling arms upon oneself. (One sees these relations in David Fincher's *Fight Club*.)[41] Even the act of murder in the novel, performed by a sailor in glamorous clothes, is revealed to be self-sacrifice. This is hinted at by the title *Querelle*, which, the novel itself directly hints, is taken from the self-reflexive French verb *se quereller*, "to pick a fight," as if one's fight is with oneself. Killing can be self-reflexive in war: a soldier's state-sanctioned murder of other soldiers like himself may, at any time, turn back on himself as his state-ordered death (the command that he sacrifice himself for his brothers).

In Genet's novel, the link between this turn-around (from killing to sacrifice) and clothing's wrap-around is forged by fantasy. In *Querelle*, fantasy is central to narration, as is always the case in Genet. (The novel is narrated by a "we," who address themselves to "inverts.")[42] Here, in fact, sexual fantasy is fabrication of the most communal and literal sort: the actual filling of an outfit by the narrators. Counter to what novel readers might expect (starting with a character, who is then gradually described by a narrator), Genet's storytellers begin with clothes. They fantasize a fighting man in clothes they wish to wear. They launch him as a character in what they start to tell. They sacrifice their insides (their thoughts, their desires) in order to throw themselves outside themselves in this act of clothing. Indeed, we begin on the edge of their fantasy: the sailor's uniform "cradles the criminal, it enfolds him," "envelops him in clouds," "in the tight fit of his sweater, in the amplitude of his bell-bottoms" (4). This is an outfit the narrating "we" would like to fill out, ideally, with themselves. And so they do. They fabricate a sailor from themselves:

> Little by little, we saw how Querelle—already contained in our flesh—
> was beginning to grow in our soul, to feed on what is best in us, above
> all on our despair at not being in any way inside him, while having him
> inside ourselves. . . . (We are still referring to that ideal and heroic per-
> sonage, the fruit of our secret loves.). . . . [T]o become visible to you,
> to become a character in a novel, Querelle must be shown apart from
> ourselves. (17, 18)

Querelle is not just sweater and pants. As a walking fantasy, Querelle is a state of mind that gets externalized.[43] Indeed, by making narration fabrication, the filling of a sailor's suit, the narrators ostentatiously betray themselves. They reveal hidden desires inside themselves, in order to throw themselves outside themselves, making Querelle a desire they can cling to, and a concept to "get inside." That they imagine their fantasy man to be a murderer seems only right, for this lets him take a more virile route to their own self-sacrificial position, as if virility bends to their fantasy. For when Querelle's murders turn into sacrifice, he can be seen to put his virility at the service of their wish for passivity, to share with the narrators a longing to be caught in glamorous arms: those of a body or a dangerous weapon or a beautiful cape.

It is this very concept of the wrap-around that grounds the narrators' devotion to fabric, their interest in tightly fitting sweaters as a social self-enclosure. The novel's only invert, Lieutenant Seblon, even wears their fantasies on his sleeve, for the cops to see:

> [B]efore the two police officers had left [his] cabin, the Lieutenant
> wanted to put on his cloak of navy blue, and then did so with such
> coquetry—which he at once, and clumsily, corrected—that the total
> effect was not of just "putting it on,"—that would have been far too
> manly, but rather that of "wrapping himself in it"—which, indeed, was
> the way he thought of it himself. Again, he expected embarrassment,
> and he made up his mind (once more) never to touch a piece of ma-
> terial again in public. (92)

But, of course, he does. In fact, he becomes the novel's poster-boy for divine humiliation, betraying (in the sense of revealing) that the fantasy filling up Querelle is a man's secret wish to be surrounded. Here is the

Lieutenant on the subject of protection, blowing vanity's cool cover to uncover sacred shame:

> When I became an officer, it wasn't so much in order to be a warrior, but rather to be a precious object, guarded by soldiers. Which they would protect with their lives until they died for me, or I offered up my life in the same manner to save them. It is thanks to Jesus that we can praise humility, for he made it into the very characteristic of divinity. . . . Humility can only be born out of humiliation. Any other kind is a vain simulacrum. (265)

The Lieutenant knows that just as he and his soldiers wrap around to meet each other, playing, interchangeably, savior and saved, the soldier's protection is a social embrace, now making weaponry, like his cloak of navy blue, a sign of erotic self-revelation: a dead giveaway.

So we read that the Lieutenant, who "took care never to be caught counting the stitches of any imaginary needlework . . . [n]evertheless . . . betrayed himself in the eyes of all men whenever he gave the order to pick up arms, for he pronounced the word 'arms' with such grace that his whole person seemed to be kneeling at the grave of some beautiful lover" (24). Here, in the graceful lining of the sentence, lies the Lieutenant's wish for embrace, betraying both his loneliness and his longing for a lover-at-arms. Earlier, he mused:

> After having been so overwhelmed by the loneliness to which my inversion condemns me, is it really possible that I may some day hold naked in my arms . . . those young men whose courage and hardness place them so high in my esteem? . . . My tears make me feel soft. I melt. (8, 9)

No wonder the narrators' fantasy man, Querelle, feels depressed when he contemplates faggots. For he must be seen to shun such softness so that he can be hard for the narrators' fantasy. Yet, he is made to wear his shunning as a shawl:

> [This] quite depressing thought [about faggots] generated up his spine, an immediate and rapid series of vibrations which quickly spread out over the entire surface of his black shoulders and covered them with a shawl woven out of shivers. (88)

For the narrators who have crafted it, Querelle's "depressing thought" about faggots is their own self-debasement, as if they are wrapping themselves in a shawl of delicious shame, going both fabric soft and orgasmic in a quick spread of shivers, over "black shoulders."

There is clearly a skin dimension to their fantasy. They make their sailorboy, lovely Querelle, wear a "coat" of beautiful blackness: "When Querelle emerged from the coal bunkers and came up on deck . . . he was black from head to toe. A thick but soft layer of coal dust covered his hair, stiffening it, petrifying every curl, powdering his face and naked torso, [and] the material of his pants. . . . [The coal dust] was obviously just a veil, and Querelle raised it now and again by . . . coquettishly . . . blowing on his arms" (80, 85). "He was a black among the whites" (90). Somewhere between black cloth and black skin, between a "veil" and a "blackface act" (90), and quite in keeping with the novel's love of stigma, "the coat of coal" is beautiful dirt: "What was the substance covering these things? . . . nothing but a little coal dust . . . that simple ordinary stuff, so capable of making a face, a pair of hands, appear coarse and dirty. . . . [And so] Querelle felt certain that his surprisingly black face . . . would appear beautiful enough for the Lieutenant to lose his cool" (87, 84). The goal is accomplished: "What secret thought [wonders the Lieutenant], what startling confession, what dazzling display of light was concealed under those bell-bottoms, blacker now than any pair ever known to man?" (87).

The "secret thoughts" and "startling confessions" hiding there are those of the narrators, who, we know, wish to be surrounded by (and, therefore, be inside) Querelle and his beautifully blackened bell-bottoms. Hence, they think up murder. Their self-wrapping via Querelle, their sense of being dangerously surrounded, is even more fluid after his homicides. Here is Querelle flowing out of himself, then flowing back to fill himself, after killing a sailor like himself:

> Querelle grabbed [Vic] by the throat. . . . and severed the sailor's carotid artery. As Vic had the collar of his peacoat turned up, the blood . . . ran down the inside of his coat and over his jersey. . . . The murderer straightened his back. He was a thing. . . . Beautiful, immobile, dark thing, within whose cavities, the void becoming vocal, Querelle could hear it [himself as a thing] surge forth to escape with the sound, to surround him and to protect him. (61)

Here, of course, is that all-important wrapping: a kind of surround-sound. Then, Querelle, after a pause, "snorted twice . . . moved his lips so that Querelle might enter [himself], flow into [his own] mouth, rise to the eyes, seep down to the fingers, fill the thing [himself] again" (62). Beautiful, immobile, dark Querelle is doing what the narrators do, in fantasy and in clothing: flowing out of themselves to surround themselves. He is how they hear themselves. He is even how the narrators see themselves — see themselves sexually surrounded and sacrificed.

In fact, unexpectedly, Querelle seeks sexually to sacrifice himself after killing Vic. The murder is his alibi for this act of martyrdom. To "wash him[self] clean," he seeks to be buggered by the owner of a brothel (a man named Nono). "This would be capital punishment," we read, a "sacrificial rite" (68). "It came . . . from an imperative that had issued from within himself"; "his own strength and vitality were ordering him to bend over" (72). Odder still, this sacrifice commences with a curious act of clothing. At the moment of Querelle's "self-execution," Querelle and Nono surprise each other by performing "a perfectly synchronized" gesture which indicates their mutual experience of wearing sailors' belts that buckle at the back — a sign of "their submission," say the narrators, "to the glamour of the naval uniform" (73). Submitting to this "glamour" in the sacrificial act, Querelle receives a genital wound. He is opened, like a sailor's belt, at the back.

But there are fanciful terms to this sacrifice. Nono, penetrating, "was holding Querelle with seemingly the same passion a female animal shows when holding the dead body of her young offspring — the attitude by which we comprehend what love is: consciousness of the division of what previously was one . . . while you yourself are watching yourself" (75). Here in the strangeness of the animal metaphor are those breaks from real relations and from individuality that Bataille predicts. Nono, as a mother in an animal pietà, is watching how, in sacrifice, an animal proxy is thrown from oneself (as part of oneself) in loving division. Then, as if the figure of the cop is required for this fantasy, too, making this holding (Nono's holding) a public display, we read next: "Querelle felt floored by the full weight of the French Police Force: . . . [a cop's] face was attempting to substitute itself for that of the man who was screwing him. Querelle ejaculated onto the velvet" (76). In *Querelle*, this kind of layered sociality — the fantasy of French police, held in the face of a singular cop, superimposed on a brothel-owner's visage — makes debasement possible. By this eccentric setup, sacrifice passes through the martyr onto cloth. This is a gorgeous giving up of the ghost, as if, at the height of his crucifixion, Christ had climaxed on a lush altar cloth (and lived to tell the tale).

Strikingly, importantly, the novel ends by returning to a pietà, one in which Querelle, then the Lieutenant, plays the role of Christ. Actually, by a set of intricate ploys, Querelle bequeaths martyrdom to the Lieutenant. With Querelle's help, the Lieutenant accuses himself of a crime in order to aid a young man in jail.[44] This (self-)arrest allows Lieutenant Seblon to wrap himself in the humility that he believes defines divinity. Cloth is required to mark this shame, largely because any wound to the cloth (even a stain) makes one aware of a uniform's glamour, thus showing outwardly how humility can point to divinity. So the Lieutenant, on a tryst, in a thicket, happens to lie belly down on some waste, staining his uniform coat in the process:

> Shame went right to work on him. . . . In the mist . . . he still glimpsed the gold of the braids on his cuffs. As pride is humiliation's child, the officer now felt prouder than ever. . . . From this particular spot in Brest . . . a light breeze, gentler and lovelier than the petals of Saadi's roses, spread the humility of Lieutenant Seblon over the . . . world. (265–66)

Fittingly, this staining is the prelude to an ending, joining the Lieutenant to the fantasy, Querelle. Their farewell is a scene of embrace, such as the Lieutenant and the narrators have longed for. Now the fantasy hands his legacy back to his creators so they can possess it. In fact, Querelle, almost playing the faggot, is sending the Lieutenant off to sacrifice himself:

> [T]he officer pulled the sailor's head toward him, and Querelle rested his cheek on Seblon's thigh. . . . Then [Querelle] got up, throwing his arms round the officer's neck, and . . . riding the crest of a wave of femininity from god knows where, this gesture became a masterpiece of manly grace. . . . Querelle smiled at the thought of drawing so close to that shame from which there is no return, and in which one might well discover peace. . . . [T]his phrase formed in his mind, saddening in all that it evoked of autumn, of stains, of delicate and mortal wounds: 'Here's the one [Lieutenant Seblon] who will follow in my footsteps.' (274)

Then the Lieutenant, as if he is answering, though this is later and he is in custody: "I shall not know peace until he makes love to me, but only when he enters me and then lets me stretch out on my side across his thighs, holding me the way the dead Jesus is held in a Pietà" (275). This imagined wrapping in arms (the Lieutenant, finally, getting held) forms the obvious climax of a fantasy: the narrators' fashioning of an animated garment. It forms as well Genet's fantastic fusion of the novel's divine humiliation with the humiliation of devotion to fabric. By this juncture, fantasy has turned the invert reader away from persecution toward a pietà that insulates, as does a cloak, the strangely self-embracing queer. This is a betrayal that reveals a secret grace:

> Thus Lieutenant Seblon dreamt of wearing a wide black cape, in which he could wrap himself. . . . Such a garment would set him apart, give him a hieratic and mysterious appearance. . . . To wear a pelerine, a cape. . . . In such a garment I would feel rolled up inside a wave, carried by it, curled up in its curve. The world and its incidents would cease at my door. (191–92)

In the last analysis, the character and novel "Querelle" are akin to Seblon's black cape: something any invert, to assuage her loneliness, can crawl inside and read like a book.

Conclusion: Curve of Cloth

These are claims these novels make about the curve of cloth. Actually, recent critics of fashion—many of them feminists—seem to understand that clothes can operate debasement aesthetics. Material meant to decorate, seen as aesthetic enrichment for the body, can visit debasement upon the wearer, even as the wearer may think she's being praised. Perhaps unbeknown to the one who wears it, a beautiful black cape, for instance, may be read as a stigmatizing skin. In other words, there is a reason that blackness (in the form of characters and/or signs) appears in these novels. It is a hint of the dangers of clothes that are highly complicated, highly specific, not so benign, semiotic cloth skins.

Queers rip the veil from this game of cloth. At least according to the logic of these novels, rushing to or from their clothes, queers unveil some unspoken agreements. "Men" (of the middle-class plainstyle variety) may not, by definition, have wounds on their clothes, but, still, they cannot wish too strongly to be held by them. Clothes harm them least when they cease to behold them. Aesthetic recognition of even manly garments (one thinks of the Lieutenant) may turn men toward the dangers of debasement. "Women," by contrast, who turn from cloth beauty, may be supplied with substitute wounds (a skinned knee and formidable loneliness in Hall's *Well*; in *Stone Butch Blues*, gashes, burns, and pursuit by police). Only by such supplied debasements, often marked directly on the skin, can these women be let off the hook of aesthetics in these novels. Such is the shame at times attached to beauty. But, as I say, fashion theorists know this much. What they don't know is a martyrdom to clothes—what I have termed a pietà, a certain social holding of one's humiliation at the hands of something loved.

By these novel portraits we can ask ourselves why sacrifice appears in queer aesthetics. One reason must be obvious: a queer aesthetic that uncovers the shame that is so attached to beauty is likely to seem sacrificial if it wishes to hold onto beauty. The effort boldly to value shame (always a curve) is central to the legacy of a martyred god (as Hall knows and Genet lampoons, in his serious way). Shame, theologically, but so, too, aesthetically, can be a blush in the face of beauty. Shame can be a way of pointing at the "glamour" (by definition, "a seemingly mysterious and elusive fascination") that must in part escape us; even, by definition, must amaze us, causing, in Genet, a "submission to the glamour of the naval uniform."

More importantly, at least for my take on these novels, clothing mimics the action of sacrifice; it is the site of a social sacrifice. The subject-in-clothes is cast to a realm outside of itself, to a kind of "unreality," according to Bataille. Clothing, of course, would seem to contradict this; and, in some respects, it does. The subject-in-clothes seems thrown to a public all too real, caught and held by a social world that, traditionally, has been devoid of caprice in its gender prescriptions. Here, however, is the insight of our novels: if the act of clothing is this public self-betrayal, in a known social field, clothing can also be a move toward self-enclosure inside the wrap of fantasy. When certain clothes seem inappropriate for their wearers—when women wholesale adopt men's clothes—they seem to signal a body broken from established versions of "real relations." As a result, the social field must hold, and behold, this wearer as one humiliated, cast beyond its reach. The question then arises of how the subject bears humiliation and her seeming break from the larger social field, even as she's held on public display.

This is where the contexts of our novels are so telling. Well's negativity over social shame seems to stem from its Catholic groundings—ironically, the very source of Stephen's martyrdom—and its suggestion that the lesbian establishments of the 1920s (particularly for members of the British aristocracy) were sad places of humiliated loneliness. Consequently, there can be no holding of humiliation that is anything but loneliness. There is no pietà for Stephen in her clothes. This sad circumstance makes her resemble two lonely Negroes who are, in the novel's curious phrase, "just two men with black skins." In contrast to Well, Stone

Butch Blues, which may also build on the pain of colored skin, yet which views the lesbian bar and the labor union as sites of productive failure and shame, shows a pietà of a striking sort. The couple, sartorially split from itself, is a fascinating figure for the holding by one's clothes. Each reads her shame from the other one's arms, so that their holding becomes humiliation at the hands of something loved.

Beyond the enclosure of something like Feinberg's fantasy of bar life, Genet, in *Querelle*, concocts the dreamscape of a military fog. Here, as we have seen, in the narrators' fantasy of beautiful Querelle, black Querelle, or in something simpler, something like an officer's wide black cape, public self-betrayal of a dangerous sort is what the martyr risks. But this is a gamble for very large stakes, as I have been arguing all along. This is a wager for a kind of a social holding that begs no pity: the social solitude of a beautiful shame.

Chapter Two

BOTTOM VALUES

The Bottom and the bottom

. . . that part of town where the Negroes lived, the part they called the Bottom . . .
—Toni Morrison, *Sula*

The painfully familiar prejudice against black skin was the backdrop against which we looked at queer cloth wounds in chapter 1. Debasements attached to the surface of cloth made for a switchpoint between queer clothes and black-colored skin. Now we move from shameful wounds on beautiful cloth to the penetrations of bodily depths. In this way, we are poised to move from the unexpected shame attached to beauty to the more predictable shame of the bottom. General Colin Powell, in making his stand against gay troops (something rather comical in light of Genet), warned against comparing "benign" skin color (in the case of troops of color) to the evidently malignant "behavior" of homosexuals.[1] One could well conclude, using the comments of General Powell and others, that if benign skin color seems to be the most immediate focus for racial hatred, then the behavior of homosexuals—probably first and foremost anal penetration—is a central focus for homophobic hate.[2]

This is not surprising. But is there a switchpoint, again, hiding here? Does Powell's anxiety about dissociating black from queer hint at a hidden switchpoint already linking the two on the level of submerged prejudicial discourse? We found a switchpoint between cloth and skin, in chapter 1, through their partial similarities as surface. This time the switchpoint comes through a naming, and through its layered associations: "that part of town where the Negroes lived, the part they called the Bottom." As it turns out, the word "bottom," which Morrison plays on in so many ways, while she depicts a range of anal penetrations, was a common nickname for black slave quarters and black neighborhoods in small Southern towns. Is the Bottom, then, a benign naming in Morrison's *Sula*, meaning, geographically, "a low-lying alluvial land adjacent to a river; bottom land"?[3] Or is it a more aggressive exploration of historical patterns in black neighborhoods north of the Mason-Dixon line? I suggest the latter. And here, quite importantly, through Toni Morrison's thoughts on shame, the penetrations of bodily depths in a place called the Bottom make a new switchpoint. The bias against queer anality (and against its pleasures) oddly speaks to the stigma of people who live at the bottom of an economic scale.

How can these radically different stigmas be linked to each other through anything other than a mere pun—the fact that "bottom" is a well-established metaphor for economic hardship? At least in part, all punning aside, they link through dirt. The presumed physical and moral dirtiness of anal sexuality offends sensibilities in a way not entirely distinct from that dirtiness (physical and moral) that is presumed to attend (black) life on the economic bottom. Freud, to take one famous example, which I will explore, spelled out the "civilized" assumption that moral and economic progress together require one to leave one's attachment to the bottom behind.[4] As strange as it sounds, then, just as my chapter "Cloth Wounds" could function as a study in the larger field of wounded surface (which would include "benign" skin color), this chapter on a history of black bottom values, and on Morrison as an anal historian, could function as a study in the field of anality (which would include homosexual "behavior"). To be sure, these anal studies, in the hands of Toni Morrison, as I show here, open onto major patterns in black history, black labor history, black folks' migrations, signs of black gender, and the tender matter of racial castration.

Still at issue here—as it was in chapter 1—is the process of negotiating wounds that come with shame. In "Cloth Wounds," martyrdom, with frankly Christian roots, was the startling "method" of negotiating shame for unchurched queers. In this second chapter, I argue that a less recognizable but no less stunning method of addressing the wounds of debasement makes a showing in Morrison's novel. Crucially, it is again a social method we would not immediately associate with the sign attached to the people who undertake it. For something on the order of anal penetrations—linked to questions of feeding, pleasuring, burying, and mourning—is the *way* of working out wounds in *Sula*. It is unexpected, to say the least, that one group's trumpeted social crime (anal penetrations) should become another group's social address to its debasement. Such penetrations get entangled, as they do in Genet as well, in the sacrificial urge; there is no discourse on martyrdom in *Sula*, but a theological thread runs through it, even so. Moreover, we will find echoes of the butch's vulnerability in portraits of black men's predicaments and find an analogue to the femme's capacities in the depictions of black women's coping skills.

Strangely, Toni Morrison has more in common with Jean Genet, in aesthetic terms, than she does with her contemporary Leslie Feinberg, who historicizes femme/butch pain in a straightforwardly political manner. *Sula*, like Genet's *Querelle*, is lyrical, campy, over-the-top, and committed to the wedding of violence and beauty. Cruelty, murder, and fantasy are central to some of the novel's most beautiful scenes. And *Sula*'s eponymous character, like Querelle in the novel *Querelle*, is herself an icon of self-embracing shame and a figure, like Querelle, intimately in contact with beautiful dirt (he with the beautiful coat of blackness made of coal dust). The phrase "unintelligible caprice"—George Bataille's unusual phrase for sacrifice, which befits Querelle—could also define Sula's disturbing social actions, as she turns a metaphor for economic hardship toward a different bottom.

But this is getting ahead of ourselves. Since this chapter also moves from engaging theory as heuristically interesting (as I engage Bataille in chapter 1) to debasing theories (here Freudian theories) by the force of fictions, we must start with details. From these Bottom details will emerge significant, speculative questions about black labor history and the values of black neighborhoods.

*Details of the Bottom: "Good Taste [Is] Out of Place
in the Company of Death"*

The Bottom—"a nigger joke"—"that part of town where the Negroes lived, the part they called the Bottom in spite of the fact that it was up in the hills."[5]

"In the toilet water [Shadrack] saw [his] grave black face." (13)

The toilets for COLORED WOMEN were not in the stationhouse but in "a field of high grass." (23–24)

Nel's mother "gazed at her daughter's wet buttocks." (27)

In the "darkness and freezing stench" of the outhouse, Eva "turned [her] baby over on her knees, exposed his buttocks and shoved the last bit of food she had in the world (besides three beets) up his ass." (34)

"Even from the rear Nel could tell that it was Sula and that she was smiling." (85)

After catching Sula making love with her husband, Nel sought out the bathroom and "sank to the tile floor next to the toilet." (107)

Sula making love: " 'I will put my hand deep into your soil, lift it, sift it with my fingers, feel its warm surface and dewy chill below. . . . [T]hrough the breaks I will see the loam, fertile. . . . For it is the loam that is giving you that smell.' " (131, 130)

By 1965, "the Bottom had collapsed"; black people "who had made money during the war moved as close as they could to the valley" while moneyed whites moved up into the hills to build their television stations and a golf course; the blacks who moved down could not afford to move back up the Bottom. (165–66)

Sadistic Truth Telling: "Tucked Up There in the Bottom"

Every immigrant knew he would not come as the very bottom. He had to come above at least one group—and that was us.
—Morrison, "The Pain of Being Black"

Here is the surprising life of a sign: simply put, in *Sula*, the Bottom is a neighborhood; the Bottom is a metaphor. It tells where blacks live, up in the hills, in a place called "the Bottom." It says where they are placed, in relation to whites, on the bottom of an economic ladder or scale.[6] How they are placed, via economic metaphor and economic circumstance, seems banal, a root too familiar from which to spring a narrative, or so one would think. Yet, geographically, where they live surprises, since one does not imagine a Bottom that is up. Which leads us to ask: what if a neighborhood could unhinge a metaphor, at least for a time? What if the surprises attached to its location, as a Bottom in the hills, could partly redirect the meaning of its pun, as an economic basement? Could the very meaning of an economic jeopardy slide at times toward ecstasy? What kind of beauty or odd communal tenderness might spring up around financial sorrows?[7]

Despite the temptations of such metaphoric play, nothing works this sweetly, or easily, in *Sula*. Something more shocking is needed to show how a neighborhood restlessly stirs alongside (and partly aside from) its economic fate. To be sure, this is a book, like Morrison's other books, in which cruel events are lyrically rendered, as if the most violent moments of the narrative laid plans to give pleasure. But there is something more to this lyrical cruelty. Yet another meaning of the Bottom intrudes, which may more fully explain how, in *Sula*, hardship and jeopardy are made to sway toward ecstasy (or, at least, toward tenderness and certain kinds of beauty), so that the Bottom can redirect its pun and be seen as something other than an economic cellar. Not just a neighborhood up in the hills, the bottom is also another locale, a place one can visit, even with others, though it is different in kind from a neighborhood. This is a bodily place, of course: the body's own bottom. The real shock of *Sula* is not so much its lyrical cruelties (though these arrest us); rather, its range of anal allusions and odd bottom scenes (a mother, for example, saving her son by forcing his nutrients up his bottom and "freeing his stools"; a woman sifting her lover's "soil," searching for "loam" with a hand she imagines wielding a chisel and going deep). We can even formulate this shock more succinctly. In Morrison's *Sula*, black women are depicted as the anal penetrators of the Bottom's black men. And these penetrations, I am going to argue, unlock our understanding of the lyrical sorrows and intermittent ecstasies that the Bottom—Morrison's historical exemplum of a certain kind of neighborhood—produces. The bottom helps the Bottom to redirect its metaphor, from economic basement (which the Bottom surely is) to a spread of social and economic holdings (which the Bottom comes to be).

How, exactly, does this redirection work, and why does it collapse by the novel's end? It will take the length of this chapter to explain Morrison's imaginative gloss on black labor and the history of black neighborhoods. Yet consider this: Though it is a place (a place upon the body) this bottom can compete with an economic metaphor (and thus make it sway) because it so dramatically calls up values, but values that run along a track that diverges from a monetary system and an economic basement. That is, for Freud—and strikingly for Morrison in *Sula*, too—the bottom's "productions" (to use Freud's euphemism) are, in certain contexts, more valuable than money, even if they are clearly bound to dirt. They can be the veritable signs of life (for example, successful, relief-filled excretion as the sign of being healthy and fed) or of being alive to certain pleasures (and certain kinds of sex) that only one's stepping aside from conventional values can produce. And yet, bottom values are in constant conversation with the question of money—as Freud's euphemism "production" implies. One could say that bottom values flash the signs of different values that sit beside money. In fact, in *Sula*, anal penetrations surprisingly speak to a neighborhood's values ("tucked up there in the Bottom") in the face of an economic pun.[8]

To explain the Bottom's relation to its values, I will risk two claims: (1) Morrison dares to value debasement; (2) she debases Freud (which means, by the logic that I am going to trace, that she dares to value him). My first claim must be obvious, the second more riddling. As to the first: how does Morrison value debasement? Borrowing on investments in a lowering, Morrison draws on Christian theology's central tenet: what the world puts low, God raises high; what the world deems debased, God elevates. Morrison's peculiar challenge to this view, straining it to the point of rupture, is to run this doctrine around the literal and metaphorical rims of the novel's black bottoms. She particularly tests the extent to which blacks can afford upending values. By doing so, Morrison examines a set of forceful metaphors for downward mobility and what appears to ground them—economic trends. She even exposes herself to the charge of shackling black people to representations that have dogged their determined flight from oppressions: images of a people stalled in the sinkholes of U.S. economies.

Now to the riddle of my second claim: Morrison risks joining hands with a master while she debases him. In hazarding association with Freud (I don't know how intentionally), she cuts in on debates about critical theory's (lack of) value for reading "black" fictions.[9] I am speaking, of course, as if Morrison bears intentions toward Freud. Though critical correctness would suggest that I speak of *Sula*, not Morrison, making moves on Freudian claims, I choose, instead, to name *Sula*'s bundle of interpretive possibilities "Toni Morrison." I wish in this way to emphasize Morrison's parity with Freud as a theorist (and historian) of anal matters, thus according her the pride of place and agency still reserved for theorists but seldom now for novelists (unlike authors, theorists are not dead).[10] Morrison is my name for how I feel asked to sift the loam of *Sula*'s Bottom history; how *Sula* confronts me in the complications of my interpretations. To strike, however, at the trickiest part of my riddling claim—Morrison's actually debasing Freud—let me say only this at the start: to debase Freud is not to ignore but engage his highly influential claims—so as then to bend them against the values of the civilizations he embraced. To debase Freud, in relation to the Bottom, as we will see, is to credit his accounts of feces as coins but to make more sorrowful what he clearly felt some necessity to celebrate: namely, how the bottom is lost, left behind, as one becomes more "civilized."

Here, indeed, with her fondness for the Bottom, Morrison crosses into queer connotations—especially now, with the backdrop of AIDS, which has produced such a public discourse surrounding the dangers of anal penetrations, and which has bound together black and gay communities, largely at the level of public language, by disproportionately striking both.[11] Morrison even directly brings black women into this fold by portraying female orgasm (to take one example) as a species of anal eroticism. In fact, it is precisely the dominant culture's stand against anality that Morrison humiliates by her rich attachment to her novel's Bottom. As she does so, Morrison is tucking a form of rage into corners of her narrative. Like her old woman character Eva, who runs "her fingers around the crevices and sides of the lard can," Morrison is rimming a ring of trouble, lodging us deep in the fat of her concerns.

This is how the novel begins:

> In that place, where they tore the nightshade and blackberry patches from their roots to make room for the Medallion City Golf Course, there was once a neighborhood. It stood in the hills above the valley town of Medallion and spread all the way to the river. It is called the suburbs now, but when black people lived there it was called the Bottom. . . . [J]ust a nigger joke. The kind white folks tell when the mill closes down and they're looking for a little comfort somewhere. The

kind colored folks tell on themselves when the rain doesn't come, or comes for weeks, and they're looking for a little comfort somehow. (3–5)

The black folks in *Sula* live "up" in the Bottom, "above" Medallion—a town whose name bears the trace of "coin."[12] The threat of these reversed relations, bottoms above medallions, comforts town conventions, nonetheless, by remaining "just a nigger joke." A white farmer, as the story goes, had tricked a slave into taking hill land, in payment for some difficult chores. This white trickster had convinced the slave that the hill land was " 'the bottom of heaven—best land there is' "—" 'High up from us,' said the master, 'but when God looks down, it's the bottom. . . .' Which accounted for the fact that white people lived on the rich valley floor in that little river town in Ohio, and the blacks populated the hills above it, taking small consolation in the fact that every day they could literally look down on the white folks. Still, it was lovely up in the Bottom" (5).

Loveliness clings to cruelty in this story—and, literally, to dirt. "Valley land" is, by definition, "bottom land," meaning land that is "rich and fertile." In the "nigger joke," "the Bottom," to begin with, refers to the valley and points to an obvious social "holding": that of land. It is only by getting the slave to think that the Bottom (the rich and fertile land) is actually in the hills that the master gets to keep his land; the Bottom, by consequence, when it begins to refer to the hills, becomes a metaphor for economic struggle. This being said, the Bottom neighborhood's land shifts in value over the course of the neighborhood's history. It starts out as "hilly land, where planting was backbreaking, where the soil slid down and washed away the seeds" (hence the white farmer's "joke"). But the butt of the joke shifted, over time, as the Bottom grew into a neighborhood; for when "the farm land turned into a village and the village into a town and the streets of Medallion were hot and dusty with progress, those heavy trees that sheltered the shacks up in the Bottom were wonderful to see"—though the black folks "had no time to think about it," Morrison tells us, since "they were mightily preoccupied with earthly things— and each other" (5–6). The neighborhood's own difficulty in seeing the beauty of their land, given their struggle to scratch out a living and understand themselves, is part of their dilemma in seeing their own beautiful Bottom. This myopia is another layer of the "nigger joke" that Morrison addresses with her depictions of surprising social "holdings" (in the sense of property and physical actions): bottom stories one could not have foreseen. Yet if, as Freud said, jokes tell aggressive truths, this "nigger joke" besets us at the start with Morrison's own sadistic truth telling.[13]

What is the truth about the Bottom? Coyly, *Sula* claims that the Bottom is up. This is true in a geographical sense, we have already noted, since the Bottom sits perched up in the hills and has its own geographical loveliness. The Bottom also inclines up in terms of the Christian theological paradigm of downward mobility, according to which God descends from Heaven in the form of a servant, proclaiming to His fold that the last shall be first. The Bottom rises up again in terms of the sexual rise (sexual orgasm) that the novel depicts as a form of reaching bottom—a movement, downward, into the soft ecstasy of loam. Confessing caution, even so, Morrison warns that the Bottom is not up: in relation to the national economy, it is literally downwardly mobile, and later, at the end, the Bottom "collapses" when the land becomes valuable and rich white folks from the valley move up.[14] In fact, from the start, one sees that *Sula* positions black folks outside Medallion's capitalist complex, linking the town's whites to the mill but blacks to the Bottom and to the Bottom's unspecified economy. Morrison thus succeeds in displaying, and unbraiding, a knot that many critics fail to see as a tangle: Reaching bottom is theologically encouraged, sexually pleasurable, but economically dangerous for marginalized people.

Black history, of course, has told part of this story (in grounding studies by John Hope Franklin, Philip Foner, and Nicholas Lemann, among many others). Up to and around the point of *Sula*'s publication, blacks' economic progress had made for a sad tale that, if it were a novel, would be noted for its repetitive events and remarkably nonrising plot structure. One repeated narrative riff concerns the promise (made by whites) of blacks' employment and participation in labor unions; migration or mobilization of blacks to grasp the promise; withdrawal of the promise by capitalists and unions; and the consequent unemployment of blacks. In literary terms, this disappointing history has been a "bad read." Fixed to the bottom, black workers' labor history has often amounted to a nonlabor history, a story of the struggle to gain the "privilege" of being exploited.[15]

Sula knows this nonrising plot structure well. Published in 1973, *Sula* bears the stamp of the Nixon default on the federal programs and promises initiated by LBJ. *Sula* is a story also tinged with the unemployment blues for black men who returned from Vietnam. At the novel's close, Morrison's plot bottoms out much the same way that it begins, but with one exception. By the end of the novel (1965), even the richness of Bottom values is being lost by a new generation that has moved beyond its neighborhood without much gain (economic or otherwise). This generation has cut a path to "whiteness" (defined in *Sula* as homes in the valley and the separateness of nuclear families) but has lost its contact with a Bottom that is up. The only bottom they know is the valley; by the time that they have moved down, whites have moved up, and the Bottom "collapses." This peculiar story of how the Bottom was lost requires that Morrison play anal historian and write the sadistic fiction that bruises the reader of *Sula*.

In fact, we should not be perplexed that Morrison, already at the start, concludes that the black Bottom collapsed. Nor should we wonder why she commences with 1919 (all her chapter titles are dates). For 1919 marks a crucial period toward the end of blacks' Great Migration from South to North during World War I, a migration that established a black industrial working class and an efflorescence of black hopes for livelihoods. The motif of promise and letdown figures here (and perhaps forms the structure of another "nigger joke"): lured from the South by "glowing reports of the high wages and better social conditions in the 'Negro Heaven' north of the Mason-Dixon line," blacks found that labor opportunities vanished with the end of the war, confirming their place in this Heaven's bottom. With a raft of soldiers returning from the war, employers replaced working black men with white veterans, while black servicemen found no work.[16]

Morrison's autopsy on the Bottom begins in earnest, as we will see, with a black man returning from World War I, who is "tucked up there in the Bottom" where black men discover the passivity of unemployment. How fitting for his place in this economic bottom, where he is stalled, that he finds his "grave" black face reflected in the toilet bowl's water. And yet, there are other dimensions to this moment.

Theoretical Coins: "The Gold Which the Devil Gives
His Paramours Turns into Excrement"

As we explore this postmortem on the Bottom, it is hard to ignore that other chronicler of anal eroticism, whose theories on anality migrated so successfully into popularized notions of anal-retentive personality types and a child's pleasure in producing its "presents." In *Sula*'s world, black communal life is strangely bound to a Freudian fascination: the obsessions, repressions, and expressions of anal economies in relation to the dominant order. Remarkably, given the dominant culture's stance against it, Morrison comes down on the side of the Bottom and on the side of those whom she depicts as having retained anal eroticism into adult life. Could Morrison be writing *Sula* so as to uproot the kind of negative judgments of debasement that ground even Freud's own views?

Curiously, at this point, a Freudian theorist of gay male sex can help to dramatize why Morrison must value debasement and yet debase theorists such as Freud. In his fraught piece, "Is the Rectum a Grave?," Leo Bersani presses the nerve of debasement's value. I point particularly to Bersani's conclusion that sex can valuably shatter the self (or reveal its shattered state) rather than "phallicize the ego":

> Phallocentrism is exactly that: not primarily the denial of power to women (although it has obviously also led to that, everywhere and at all times), but above all the denial of the *value* of powerlessness in both men and women. I don't mean the value of gentleness, or non-aggressiveness, or even of passivity, but rather of a more radical disintegration and humiliation of the self. For there is finally, beyond the fantasies of bodily power and subordination that I have just discussed, a transgressing of that very polarity which . . . may be the profound sense of both certain mystical experiences and of human sexuality. . . . Freud keeps returning to a line of speculation in which the opposition between pleasure and pain becomes irrelevant, in which the sexual emerges as the *jouissance* of exploded limits, as the ecstatic suffering into which the human organism momentarily plunges when it is "pressed" beyond a certain threshold of endurance. (217)

For the "general public" (Bersani's phrase), this view of sex as that which debases the self is starkly symbolized by the sex act commonly associated with gay men: anal penetration. Even as far back as the Greeks, Bersani notes, "to be penetrated is to abdicate power." "The only 'honorable' sexual behavior," he continues, quoting Foucault, "consists in being active, in dominating, in penetrating, and in thereby exercising one's authority" (212). Domination and the will to exercise authority—presumed masculine pursuits—are demeaned in depictions of men being penetrated anally. This is why these relations are feared and, says Bersani, why they should be embraced. Bersani again:

> But what if we said, for example, not that it is wrong to think of so-called passive sex as "demeaning," but rather that *the value of sexuality*

itself is to demean the seriousness of efforts to redeem it? "AIDS," [Simon] Watney writes, "offers a new sign for the symbolic machinery of repression, making the rectum a grave." . . . But if the rectum is the grave in which the masculine ideal (an ideal shared—differently—by men *and* women) of proud subjectivity is buried, then it should be celebrated for its very potential for death. Tragically, AIDS has literalized that potential as the certainty of biological death, and has therefore reinforced the heterosexual association of anal sex with a self-annihilation. (222)

Clearly, Bersani's celebrations are dangerous. He only hints at the dangers for women involved in the "joys" of powerlessness and does not consider blacks' representational fix as America's bottom class. Demurs not aside, I confess that Bersani holds me in sway because Morrison, actually, runs his risks. She outruns his risks. Bersani, in his essay, indicates that the gay man's embrace of being penetrated is a strike against his full-on identification with the masculinity that would wish him dead.[17] As if they are enabling this very strike, Morrison's women become the anal penetrators of the novel's men, not for love of domination but for reasons of making alive or releasing from suffering black male bodies on the bottom. *Sula's* women actively warn against the loss of Bottom locations and stimulations, since these may be valued for their coinage in partially alternative economies. To this end, by penetrating men, Morrison's women reinforce why, being people of the Bottom, neighborhood blacks (both women and men) must bury in the Bottom their "own perhaps otherwise uncontrollable identification" with the very people—respectable whites—who, in this novel, work against the interests of blacks at every turn.

Can critical theories that are largely European (at least in their origins) address these complications?[18] Barbara Christian was among the first to caution that "critical theories" are not supple enough to speak to an African American literature that seemingly has "the possibilities of rendering the world as large and as complicated as I experienced it, as sensual as I knew it was."[19] For Christian, "people of color have always theorized—but in forms quite different from the Western form of abstract logic"—"in narrative forms, in the stories we create, in riddles and proverbs, in the play with language, since dynamic rather than fixed ideas seem more to our liking" (52). "Theory," to her mind, even that forged by the Black Arts Movement of the 1960s, has been unrightfully "exalted" (Christian's term) over the fictions of black men and women. The words "devalue," "denigrate," and "discredit" pepper Christian's essay as she expresses anger over Western "philosophers'" power "to determine the ideas that we deemed valuable" (52). In this struggle over value, Christian wanted to raise black fictions (by her definition, literature written by African Americans) from a "low" designation ("denigrated" as political or just ignored) to a valued designation as a theorizing force, shattering the grip that a certain version of theory holds.[20]

Taking to heart Christian's complaints, lodged years ago, I propose that rather than avoiding or exalting "critical theories," we should for a time purposefully, thoughtfully, complexly debase them. By this I mean *reveal their limits* by tucking their claims into contexts bound to trouble them.[21] There is a twist, even so, to the critical debasement I propose. If Freud falls down in the face of *Sula*, does his fall, his inadequacy to what Morrison poses, devalue the importance of Freudian theory for reading "black" texts? The value, to the contrary, may reside precisely in the debasement, in what becomes visible if we fold Freudian claims about anality into the Bottom that Morrison champions. What we particularly see at the start, which will illuminate Bottom relations, are the limits of Freudian thought for black gender, since Morrison reverses Freud's gendered expectations.

Let me now schematize Freud on anality so that these reversals of Freud may emerge:

> In [the] early period of [libido-development] a loose sort of organization exists which we shall call *pre-genital*; for during this phase it is not the genital component-instincts, but the *sadistic* and *anal*, which are most prominent. The contrast between *masculine* and *feminine* plays no part as yet; instead of it there is the contrast between *active* and *passive*, which may be described as the forerunner of the sexual polarity with which it also links up later. That which in this period seems masculine to us, regarded from the stand-point of the genital phase, proves to be the expression of an impulse to mastery, which easily passes over into cruelty.[22]

In what he deems the pregenital phase, Freud sees the contrast masculine/feminine as not yet actuated but only foreshadowed through the opposition active/passive. Although Freud states that "the contrast, between masculine and feminine plays no part as yet," he nonetheless "links" masculinity to activity and, specifically, to mastery and cruelty. Morrison reverses precisely these relations as she explores the Gordian relationship of black men and women to capitalist economies. To show us this knot, she joins black women to cruel-seeming mastery while binding black males to forms of passivity.

Also important for Morrison's thinking, the social order, as readers of Freud know so well, is sexual and economic at once, making bodily relations both literal and metaphoric referents for social status.

> The outer world [Freud says] first steps in as . . . a hostile force opposed to the child's desire for pleasure. . . . To induce him to give up these sources of pleasure he is told that everything connected with these functions is "improper," and must be kept concealed. In this way he is first required to exchange pleasure for value in the eyes of others. His own attitude to the excretions is at the outset very different. . . . Even after education has succeeded in alienating him from these tendencies, he continues to feel the same high regard for his "presents" and his "money."[23]

"The outer world"—the dominant economy, one might say—invades the child's pleasure and demands not only that pleasure be exchanged for value but that anal pleasure be repressed as "improper." Even so, one's assimilation into conventional educations does not eliminate bottom pleasures, so that feces as an alternative coin (or medallion) may still count for something. In fact, if bottom values vitalize Morrison's thinking and her fiction, anality would likely receive its due in *Sula*. As for Freud, his ambivalent judgments concerning anality are caught in a comment made when he wrote "Excretory Functions," a preface to John G. Bourke's *Scatologic Rites of All Nations*: "Men have chosen to evade the predicament by so far as possible denying the very existence of this inconvenient 'trace of the Earth.' . . . The wiser course would undoubtedly have been to admit it and to make as much improvement in it as its nature would allow" (220). What would constitute this "improvement" Freud does not say.

A final set of points from Freud further outlines the shape of his ambivalence. There are roughly three paths with regard to anal eroticism, and these are spelled out in his essay "Character and Anal Erotism" and in two of his introductory lectures on psychoanalysis ("Aspects of Development and Regression: Aetiology" and "The Paths of Symptom-Formation"). For the sake of clarity, I will call these paths regression, sublimation, and expression.

REGRESSION · Failure to "migrate" successfully past the anal phase leads to a fixation of the anal impulse that may predispose the libido to *jouissance?*

turn back "when the exercise of its function in a later and more developed form meets with powerful external obstacles, which thus prevent it from attaining the goal of satisfaction" ("Aspects" 350). Regression of the libido to the anal stage, along with repression, frequently forms an obsessional neurosis, in which symptoms substitute for the missing satisfaction but symptoms also convert an earlier satisfaction "into a sensation of suffering" ("Paths" 374).

Folding Freud into black American history, I find his opposition between "success" at "migration," on the one hand, and "arrest" through "fixation," on the other, richly evocative of Morrison's lament. Freud's discussion of "powerful external obstacles" that impede "progress" toward "the goal," and that ordain "suffering" instead of "satisfaction," makes regression to an anal fixation sound like Morrison's Bottom history: migrations that have featured more arrests than success. Freud even offers an analogy to "inhibited development" that veers in the direction of black American history. He makes analogy to the vicissitudes of "migrating people," "small groups or bands" who "halted on the way, and settled down in . . . stopping places, while the main body went further" ("Aspects" 349). When we turn to *Sula*, we must remember this Freudian analogy to psychic stalling—how Freud compares an anal fixation to a people's stalled migration.

Freud also brings regression into close proximity with debasement when he states emphatically: "In reality, wherever archaic modes of thought have predominated or persisted—in the ancient civilizations, in myths, fairy-tales and superstitions, in unconscious thinking, in dreams and in neuroses—money is brought into the most intimate relation with dirt" ("Character" 174). Rounding out the implications of regression as a journey back to more "primitive" stopping places, Freud later invokes "the word 'regression' in its general sense": that is, "reversion from a higher to a lower stage of development" ("Aspects" 351). Freud's association of "excrement" with things "archaic" and "low" shows why Morrison's bottom values risk offense. His penchant for "improvement" shows why Morrison must debase him. In staking her claim with and for the Bottom, Morrison ends up inverting entrenched cultural judgments about regression and, by implication, about debasement.

SUBLIMATION AND EXPRESSION · In contrast to regression, sublimation affirms dominant values—the very values Morrison humiliates. Specifically, according to Freud, sublimation redirects a particular aim:

the aim to make money takes over for anal erotism. As part of the development demanded by civilization, says Freud, shame, disgust, and morality
are formed at the expense of anal excitations. Cleanliness, then, is a
reaction-formation "against an interest in what is unclean and disturbing
and should not be part of the body" ("Character" 172). The character traits
of orderliness, miserliness, and obstinacy result from the sublimation of
anal erotism. Conversely, those individuals who retain anal erotism into
adulthood and therefore express, rather than sublimate, anal interests do
not show signs of anal character. By virtue of anal expressions, "no neurosis results; the libido succeeds in obtaining a real, although not a normal
satisfaction" ("Paths" 368). By "normal" society's standards, Freud continues, one who does not fall ill from expressing anal interests is, nonetheless, "perverse."[24] For Freud, this person is usually a homosexual; in
Sula, it is Sula herself.

I am interested here in the way in which the character traits of sublimation (orderliness, miserliness, obstinacy) sound like a ticket to participation in the reigning economy, whereas regression to and (more so)
expression of anal interests sound like ties to the bottom values Morrison
affirms for her black neighborhood. We will see how these paths relate
to Morrison's development of her characters. But first I will explain why
Morrison, responsive to economic straits, must reverse Freud's expectation that activity foreshadows masculinity, while passivity adumbrates
femininity.

The Bourgeoisie and the Bottom Class: "We're a Typical White Family That Happens to Be Black"

Knowingly, Morrison sees this pair—masculine activity, feminine passivity—as the middle-class coupling of a white world anxious to flee its
bottom. Though she, as much as anyone, grasps "the pain of being black"
(the title of her interview with *Time* magazine in 1989), Morrison refuses
to join the dominant order's plan to "cure" (but also shame) black families.
Specifically, she refuses to join those voices decrying black men's "femi-
nization" and the "devastating" outcome of the "female-headed home."
Morrison, by contrast, mourns the reign of (straight) white gender: how
it seduces blacks away from (what she depicts as) the Bottom's sociality,
leading them into the tight, disappointing configuration of the couple;
how it courts, before it jilts, the expectations of black men and women.

Customarily, feminists have defined masculinity as access to the control of capital and of women. But as numerous commentators have pointed out, problems emerge for extending this definition to black men, for whom masculinity cannot so easily be defined along the axis of economic power. Black masculinity cracks in studies as diverse as the famous *Moynihan Report on the Negro Family* (1965) and Robert Staples's well-known treatise *Black Masculinity: The Black Male's Role in American Society* (1982). Staples's sociological study (published a decade after *Sula*, but with an eye to the period when Morrison would have been writing it) shows his worries over gender reversal: that is, the strain of fitting black men into male supremacy. The dilemma for the "black man," according to Staples, involves his ability to "sire" children through "sexual adventures" (these are Staples's terms) but his inability to provide for them once he has "sired" them (136). This predicament, Staples says, fosters black men's self-destruction. In fact, Staples cites the 1970s as the period in which the "flowering of black manhood turned into a withering away of what little supremacy [black men] had [over women]" (135). Unemployment is the culprit Staples has in mind—but also black men's "refus[al] to compromise their masculinity by indulging in 'feminine work' " (130). Here, for Staples, lies another trouble: he alludes to the "problem" of black women's employment that, to his mind, gives black women a competitive edge over black men and causes black men "to continue to fall behind black women in their education and economic progress" (19). Staples persistently voices his worry over gender reversal, even though at the start of his book he clearly states that, "despite having more education, black women consistently have a higher rate of unemployment and earn less income than black males" (17).

Taking a different line on reversals, black feminists Angela Davis and Hortense Spillers have long argued that black women shatter white gender couplings that color femininity passive. These scholars link black women to work outside their homes, since neither leisure nor their own housework has traditionally formed the focus of black women's lives. Black women, for the most part, have not been privatized in their domestic labors but, rather, have been tied to production circuits in dominant economies—as field laborers, factory laborers, office laborers, domestic laborers, or sexual laborers under white management.[25]

The fix, then, for blacks, in the face of "white" gender, has gone like this: historically, black women have often been blocked from (the bourgeois ideal of) feminine passivity, whereas black men have often been blocked from (the bourgeois ideal of) masculine activity. This "activity" is the "privilege" of participating in the dominant (capitalist) economy as *either* exploiter or exploited (bourgeois or working class). Hence, "activity" in this scheme should not be taken exclusively as "productive labor" in Marxist terms (according to which the proletariat, not the capitalist, performs productive labor). Rather, the bourgeois white man is culturally coded "active," though he does not, technically, "produce." (That is, he himself does not build a bridge, though he actively employs other men to build bridges.) In the same way, the presumed passivity of the bourgeois white woman may involve productive (likely, domestic) labor, or even capitalist professional activity, but she may be culturally defined as more "passive."[26] In other words, as bodies climb the economic ladder of American capitalism, tracing a trajectory from unemployed to working class to white-collar management to capitalist ownership, they move increasingly into a domain that, toward the top, was historically governed (still firmly in the time that *Sula* depicts, though now quite precariously) by a masculine active/feminine passive binary couple.

If, by these remarks, I imply that blacks can be bourgeois only by conforming to a certain color and style of coupling, I am simply tracking *Sula* through labor, sex, and love. That is to say, Morrison makes no bed for a recognizable bourgeoisie among her Bottom characters. After all, *Sula* centers on the forties—a period before blacks could even dream (Martin Luther King–style) of entering an era of corporate positions and suburban lifestyles. And though the novel ends in the civil rights era, the last chapter title, "1965," marks the year of the Moynihan report that spelled out the supposed "tangle of pathology" that makes the Negro family "fail" the "normal" genderings of the white middle class.

Popular national news magazines have told us, pointedly, through the years, that the bottom is defined by a certain configuration of gender: the (black) man unemployed, the (black) woman heading the home. African Americans' sign of success—their bourgeois potential—has often been measured by the extent to which they reverse bottom gender and mime white families. In a *Time* article by Richard Lacayo, from 1989, "Between Two Worlds: The Black Middle Class Has Everything the White Middle Class Has Except a Feeling that It Really Fits In," we learn in a punch line what "fitting in" means:

> For the black middle class, there are new preoccupations. Not just job creation programs, but job promotions. Not just high school diplomas, but college tuition. Not just picket lines, but picket fences.

An agenda, in short, for a full partnership in the American Dream. Superficially, middle-class blacks already seem to be living that dream. Leon and Cora Brooks have spent more than a decade at IBM, where he is a dealer account manager and she is a senior personnel specialist. They have a comfortable home in the affluent and mostly black Los Angeles neighborhood of Baldwin Hills; they have a Mercedes in the garage and a daughter at California State University at Northridge. Leon Brooks jokes, "We're a typical white family that happens to be black." (60)

Just how true is this summary joke? What *Time* and *Newsweek* anxiously index (long after *Sula*'s publication, in fact) is the incomplete entry of African Americans into (white) bourgeois ranks. According to *Newsweek*, bourgeois blacks are dogged by the bottom, for which the operative term is "underclass":

Devastating statistics: The isolation of the underclass was a hazard of the civil-rights movement. As it succeeded, more educated and entre-preneurial blacks moved to integrated neighborhoods, taking their gifts with them. It is an irony that distresses middle-class blacks: a deep class divide among blacks themselves. "We moved up the eco-nomic ladder and away from the old ghettoes," says Roger Wilkins, a senior fellow at the Institute for Policy Studies, a Washington-based think tank.

For those left behind the statistics are devastating. Around 55 per-cent of the families are headed by female parents. . . .

The steady economic growth that benefited many blacks gave way to economic stagnation in the mid-1970s. New plants and industries are taking root in suburban corridors, where poor blacks have little ac-cess to them. "You have to see the poverty of the urban underclass as likely to endure," says Michael Fix of the Urban Institute. "It raises the question of whether we're seeing the emergence of an American caste, a hard bottom class. . . . I do think that the urban underclass remains perhaps the signal issue of the next decade."[27]

What remains specific to American blacks, and recognizable *as* "black," according to these analysts, is their location on the bottom ("hard bot-tom") of a caste system—spelled out for us by a Mr. Fix. We notice that this bottom is truly down (what Morrison also hints at in her final chap-ter, "1965"), depleted of its neighborhoods and social arrangements, says

Fix, by the accomplishments of civil rights, successes that saw blacks part ways on the economic ladder, "buppies" taking with them "gifts," others left as a "hard bottom class."[28]

This much Morrison would not deny, and even foresees, in the early 1970s when she is writing *Sula*. What she would not countenance is how this article warms up and reserves the Moynihan report. The "devastating" specificity of the black bottom family, according to *Newsweek*, is the female-headed home. This specific gender-configuration is how we supposedly know when blacks have failed to make it, when they are (on) the bottom (and, to boot, pathological). Vestiges of Moynihan's matriarchy thesis—strong black women make black men weak; black women are elevated, black men debased—remain in these discussions.[29] By contrast, Morrison, in her public commentary, cuts a kinder path to black gender and pain. In "The Pain of Being Black," appearing in 1989, like Lacayo's article, she speaks to the issues of bottom gender and bottom values that do not copy white family relations:

> *Q:* In one of your books you described young black men who say, "We have found the whole business of being black and men at the same time too difficult." You said that they then turned their interest to flashy clothing and to being hip and abandoned the responsibility of trying to be black and male.
>
> *A:* I said they took their testicles and put them on their chest. I don't know what their responsibility is anymore. They're not given the opportunity to choose what their responsibilities are. There's 60% unemployment for black teenagers in this city. What kind of choice is that?
>
> *Q:* This leads to the problem of the depressingly large number of single-parent households and the crisis in unwed teenage pregnancies. Do you see a way out of that set of worsening circumstances and statistics?
>
> *A:* Well, neither of those things seems to me a debility. I don't think a female running a house is a problem, a broken family. It's perceived as one because of the notion that a head is a man. Two people can't raise a child any more than one. You need a whole community—everybody—to raise a child. The notion that the head is the one who brings in the most money is a patriarchal notion, that a woman—and I have raised two children, alone—is somehow lesser than a male head. Or that I am incomplete without the male. This is not

true. And the little nuclear family is a paradigm that just doesn't work. It doesn't work for white people or for black people. Why we are hanging onto it, I don't know. It isolates people into little units—people need a larger unit. (122)

Morrison refutes the thesis that female headship is a problem. Instead, what she offers is a warning that coupledom constitutes "a paradigm that just doesn't work." As for gender, Morrison specifies black men as those men who wear (in the form of their genitals as their clothes) the failed promise of a dominant sign.

Taking this clue about failed promise, I see Morrison carving out in *Sula* the specific outlines of black masculinity. She does so by recording black men's and women's expectations and letdowns surrounding the promises made by gender. Defining themselves against "feminine work," black men may well expect to participate in the privileges that have so often greeted white men. Black men, however, at least at the time of *Sula*'s composition, are defined by their peculiar relation to capitalist unemployment and their uneven advance if employed. This is a form of masculinity, I would argue, because it promises something not-feminine (not-domestic, not-leisured). But it looks like femininity because of its letdown. Black femininity, in the 1970s, bears a more surprising relation to promise. It is promised nothing by a white culture's sign systems. Yet, against all seeming odds, but, as it happens, for historical reasons (their lower cost to be both capitalized and maintained; their possibilities for sexual and domestic labor in white economies; their active role in black domestic labor; and the lesser threat of their participation in capitalist productions), black women have discovered a promise for activity in capitalist circuits that looks incongruent with a seeming double negative ("black woman").

Importantly, in *Sula*, Morrison circumvents the stereotype of black males as "feminized" by the dominant order or by black women. The way she performs this—a stunning display—is to script the problem (no less harrowing) as black males stalled at an anal economic stage before the division into masculinities and femininities that come with employment. Morrison, by these means, avoids examining black males' binds solely in relation to capitalist "success." Rather, she probes black gender in *Sula* as activity or passivity, mastery or nonmastery, with regard to capitalist *and* Bottom productions. Posing these lessons in anal economics, Morrison concentrates readers on the pain of getting past an impasse, of migrating, of moving on—without, one could say, leaving the pleasures of the Bottom behind.

Morrison Takes Freud Black to the Bottom

I want to begin my examination by taking *Sula*'s first three chapters as a complex: the years 1919–21. Here Morrison not only roots her central issues but also hails her three main characters—Shadrack, Nel, and Sula—in succession. Remarkably, these characters, as if they were playing out some kind of parable of Bottom economics, with its mix of sexual values and monetary struggles, dramatically match the three different paths anal interests may take: regression (Shadrack), sublimation (Nel), and expression (Sula).

Shadrack's year is 1919. In him, we greet a character "blasted and permanently astonished by the events of 1917 . . . [who] returned to Medallion handsome but ravaged" (7). This black man is "arrested" at the start. He is a veteran returning from the war, with no work awaiting him. Morrison even shows this historical type and his economic halt in layered ways: she makes him psychologically shell-shocked as well as physically unemployable. Shadrack cannot control his hands: "Slowly he directed one hand toward the cup and, just as he was about to spread his fingers, they began to grow in higgledy-piggledy fashion like Jack's beanstalk all over the tray and the bed" (9). Next, we are given telling details of the black man's privatized, sequestered position in a nation where he finds no place: Shadrack "wanted desperately to see his own face and connect it with the word 'private'—the word the nurse (and the others who helped bind him) had called him. 'Private' he thought was something secret, and he wondered why they looked at him and called him a secret. Still, if his hands behaved as they had done, what might he expect from his face?"(10). The word "private" binds together the black men in *Sula*—as if to chain-link them through common positionings (the group of colored boys known as the deweys "remained private and completely unhousebroken"; Plum "chuckled as if he had heard some private joke"; even the honorary black Tar Baby wanted a place to die "privately"). But to return to Shadrack's privacy, we catch him in a particularly private moment that joins the questions of hands, face, identity, and "blackness" together at the toilet.

Shadrack is in jail when this moment occurs, released from the hospital, but literally arrested, "booked for vagrancy" (a denigrating name for unemployment):

He lay in this agony for a long while and then realized he was staring at the painted-over letters of a command to fuck himself. . . . Like moonlight stealing under a window shade an idea insinuated itself: his earlier desire to see his own face. He looked for a mirror; there was none. Finally, keeping his hands carefully behind his back he made his way to the toilet bowl and peeped in. The water was unevenly lit by the sun so that he could make nothing out. Returning to his cot he took the blanket and covered his head, rendering the water dark enough to see his reflection. There in the toilet water he saw a grave black face. A black so definite, so unequivocal, it astonished him. He had been harboring a skittish apprehension that he was not real—that he didn't exist at all. But when the blackness greeted him with its indisputable presence, he wanted nothing more. In his joy he took the risk of letting one edge of the blanket drop and glanced at his hands. They were still. Courteously still. (13)

Momentously, in this anal version of the Lacanian imaginary, with the toilet bowl acting as mirror, Shadrack tucks, instead of fucks, himself: tucked up into his blanket ("he took the blanket and covered his head"), he renders the toilet water "dark enough to see his reflection," reversing the more familiar reliance on lightness as a means of revelation. Regression to an anal economy is formative here for existence, and takes this character back to "black" as a greeting—a hailing or arresting of himself. In reference to "blackness," Shadrack's hands can suddenly function—as if, courteously, an anal economy scripts a different scheme of physicality.[30]

Completing his context, Morrison depicts Shadrack, who is "tucked up there in the Bottom," as a kind of obsessional neurotic with a host of peculiar rituals. (Freud, we recall, linked anal regression to obsessional neurosis.) Not surprisingly, it is Shadrack who establishes National Suicide Day: one day each year devoted to the fear of death: a sadistic call, one might say, for neighbors "to kill themselves or each other" (14). Freud, as it happens, pairs obsessive actions and religious practices in an essay by that name, written shortly before "Character and Anal Erotism." He terms the neurotic's obsessive rituals a "private religion" (a nice phrase for Shadrack).

In contrast to Shadrack's regressive embrace of black bottom values, Nel makes a halting movement toward whiteness—really, a kind of valley-girlness. Nel is a character traipsing the path of sublimation. Introduced in the chapter entitled "1920," Nel, we learn, was raised by a proper, repressive mother: "Under Helene's hand the girl became obedient and polite. Any enthusiasms that little Nel showed were calmed by the mother until she drove her daughter's imagination underground" (18). Part of the novel's tension is strung with Nel's equivocal relation to this under-ground—that is, her relation to the Bottom and to Sula, who figures the sadistic pleasures that proper Nel has learned to guard against. Even here, so early on in *Sula*, we are being told that if one is black one cannot flee the bottom, only (incompletely) sublimate it. On a trip south by train, Helene and Nel are visually assaulted by (what they feel are) the denigrat-ing gazes of black American soldiers suited up in their "shit-colored uni-forms." Next, they must bear an affront to their manners by using the so-called "toilets" for "COLORED WOMEN" in the field opening out beyond the stationhouse. Black women, Morrison's novel seems to say, have no ac-cess to white bourgeois manners when they must void themselves in high grass. Nel, however, unlike her mother, and more like Shadrack (whom we saw wrapping himself in his blankets), tucks herself into the bottom darkness that renders identities (or, more precisely, Nel's existence) dark enough to see. (We even find Nel refusing her name as Helene's proper daughter.) " 'I'm me. I'm not their daughter. I'm not Nel.' . . . And then, sinking deeper into the quilts, '. . . I want to be . . . wonderful. Oh, Jesus, make me wonderful' " (28–29).

Morrison moves from Nel to Sula, Nel's good friend who later, sadis-tically, brings Nel back to the Bottom (and the toilet) by laying Nel's hus-band, Jude, on a whim. It is surprising and important that this chapter ("1921"), which should be introducing us to Sula, largely offers a historical retrospective of Sula's grandmother, known as Eva—a woman who mas-ters anal economics on behalf of her son. I refer to the scene in which Eva's baby, Plum, can't defecate and so must be saved by his mother's fortitude in the family outhouse (yet another toilet scene).

On our way to this drama, we are given a sketch of Eva's economic bind. Abandoned by her husband, Boyboy, Eva is left with $1.65, along with five eggs and three beets to her name. She is thus linked to valley productions as a mother forced to contemplate outside employment: "She would have to scrounge around and beg through the winter, until her baby was at least nine months old, then she could plant and maybe hire herself out to valley farms to weed or sow or feed stock until something steadier came along at harvest time" (33). During an event that will change her plans, Eva mobilizes a kind of anal mastery when she learns her baby has stopped having bowel movements:

[S]he resolved to end his misery once and for all. She wrapped him in blankets, ran her finger around the crevices and sides of the lard can and stumbled to the outhouse with him. Deep in its darkness and freezing stench she squatted down, turned the baby over on her knees, exposed his buttocks and shoved the last bit of food she had in the world (besides three beets) up his ass. Softening the insertion with the dab of lard, she probed with her middle finger to loosen his bowels. Her fingernail snagged what felt like a pebble; she pulled it out and others followed. Plum stopped crying as the black hard stools ricocheted onto the frozen ground. And now that it was over, Eva squatted there wondering why she had come all the way out there to free his stools. (34)

We see a wrapping in blankets (again), a tucking linked to an anal feeding, and a literal movement up the bottom—where tucking, by the way, can mean "to gather up in a fold," "to eat or drink heartily," or "to stick, pierce, or poke."[31] Here looms Morrison's clearest figuration of the black male's quandary in relation to the white valley economy: he can't produce—either feces or coins. Eva's mastery of economies is signaled not only by her ability to "free [Plum's] stools" but also by the fact that there, in the outhouse, and later that evening, Eva envisions a strange solution to her family's hardship. What a cruel solution it is: Eva throws herself under a train, in order to lose one of her legs, in order to collect insurance money, in order to raise the children her husband, Boyboy, sired. This strange twist on selling one's body (through the active loss of a part) proves, nonetheless, a masterful move within the white economy.

Eva's loss of her leg also proves a masterful move in castration metaphorics, which have historically (and even literally) dogged depictions of black masculinity. Morrison's novel largely cleaves to an anal stage, so that, in effect, questions of castration are stalled and kept at bay. Even so, *Sula* may be implying that black women, *since* they are promised next to nothing and wear a double negative, are better positioned than black men to work through castration figurations. *Sula*'s black males lack this mastery, stalled as they are at the threshold of production, saddled with the letdown of their phallic sign. That is, a reversal creeps into view, again. In Jacques Lacan's return to Freud, he stresses the penis as that "pound of flesh which is mortgaged in [the male subject's] relationship to the signifier"("Desire and the Interpretation of Desire in *Hamlet*," 28), meaning that the penis-as-organic-reality must be relinquished as the male subject transits into the domain of signification that substitutes language, and cultural privilege, for organic reality. Morrison interrogates the borders of this privilege by scouting black gender. In *Sula*, black males, as one might expect, cannot convert the penis to cultural privilege (hence, the letdown of their phallic sign), whereas women, in ways that surprise us, can manipulate, and even mortgage, penile representatives. For it may be possible to read Eva's leg, along with the later depictions of Nel and Sula's twigs and Sula's hand (described as a pick, by which she offers an anal caress), as a woman's penile proxy. In Eva's case, she parts with her proxy in order to tap white economic power.

There is something even more bizarre we might consider. In his essay "On Transformations of Instinct as Exemplified in Anal Erotism," Freud asserts that the feces are the first piece of the body with which the child has to part; he claims, furthermore, that "in the products of the unconscious . . . the concepts faeces (money, gift), baby, and penis are ill-distinguished from one another and are easily interchangeable" (128). Feces=money= baby=penis. As far-fetched as these equations sound, Morrison is risking some similar equivalence in her astonishing outhouse scene. As if she beguiles these Freudian echoes, Eva solves her baby son's painful inability to part with his feces (a sign, in this case, that the family lacks money) by, productively, planning to part with a proxy of her own, as if she will not only castrate but also excrete her leg, turning this appendage into coins. Later, shockingly, she even parts company with her "baby," Plum himself, as a way to secure him against his own loss.

That is why, at the end of this chapter ("1921"), we are given memories of a scene of cruelty: Eva sets fire to Plum, now grown, while he is sleeping in "snug delight":

> Now there seemed to be some kind of wet light [kerosene] traveling over his legs and stomach with a deeply attractive smell. It wound itself—this wet light—all about him, splashing and running into his skin. He opened his eyes and saw what he imagined was the great wing of an eagle pouring a wet lightness over him. Some kind of baptism, some kind of blessing, he thought. Everything is going to be all right, it said. Knowing that it was so he closed his eyes and sank back into the bright hole of sleep. (47)

As if we've sustained a narrative slap too smooth to sting, we encounter a liquid sadomasochism alive with this novel's aggressive truth telling. The truth being told is that Plum grew up to be a veteran like Shadrack, who, ravaged by war and the unemployment for black men that followed, was exhausting himself in a backward spiral, seeking rebirth. Eva tells it this way: " 'There wasn't space for him in my womb. And he was crawlin' back. Being helpless and thinking baby thoughts and dreaming baby dreams and messing up his pants again and smiling all the time. . . . I birthed him once. I couldn't do it again. He was growed, a big old thing'" (71). In the case of Plum, the bottom truly is a grave, where Eva, helpless to heal, can only demolish the "murderous judgment against him" (Bersani, 222) by tucking him into a final sleep. With a plash of penetration—the splashing kerosene "running into his skin"—Plum is gathered "into the bright hole" of death.

Eva's moment of loving cruelty anticipates a later scene of like kind. Nel and Sula, twelve years old, "wishbone thin and easy-assed," accidentally kill a boy named Chicken Little. The scene occurs after Sula, on her way to the toilet, overhears her mother say that she loves but does not like her daughter. Nel and Sula escape to the woods where curious play with twigs takes place:

> Nel found a thick twig and, with her thumbnail, pulled away its bark until it was stripped to a smooth, creamy innocence. Sula looked about and found one too. When both twigs were undressed Nel moved easily to the next stage and began tearing up rooted grass to make a bare spot of earth. . . . But soon she grew impatient and poked her twig rhythmically and intensely into the earth, making a small neat hole that grew deeper and wider with the least manipulation of her twig. Sula copied her. . . . Together they worked until the two holes were one and the same. (58)

By piercing the ground with their "undressed" twigs ("rhythmically" and "intensely"), the girls make a hole into which they stuff "all of the small defiling things they could find"—"paper, bits of glass, butts of cigarettes." This deep hole, which they have "tucked in," in the senses of both piercing and enfolding, *Sula's* narrator calls "a grave" (59). Moreover, following this scene of construction as if, providentially, they have built a bottom in which to tuck him, Chicken Little slips from Sula's hands, falls into the river, and swiftly drowns.

This young boy is another black male killed by a female who has cruelly or tenderly tucked him into death and taken him forever outside of oppressions. Important for the theological valence to this tucking, the narrator describes the women in church who mourn Chicken Little: "They acknowledged the innocent child hiding in the corner of their hearts, holding a sugar-and-butter sandwich. That one. The one who lodged deep in their fat, thin, old, young skin, and was the one the world had hurt. . . . [They] wondered if that was the way the slim, young Jew felt, he who for them was both son and lover and in whose downy face they could see the sugar-and-butter sandwiches"(65). These are women who tuck the black male into their hearts and into the folds of their various skins, by linking his hurts to the slim young Jew.

Marriage, as it happens, is another kind of tucking—a different attempt to address the economic placement of black men. Nel has one of the few Bottom weddings (weddings being more of a valley affair). If this whitened ceremonial is not enough to put Nel back on the path of sublimation, Nel's husband, Jude, surely does. Jude seeks the (white) masculinity yoked to active work and control over women. More specifically, he seeks to work on the construction of the new Medallion bridge. (Later, the plan for a bridge is dropped in favor of a tunnel.) As readers, we can grasp Jude's impetus to marriage only by unlocking his labor history and his own realization that, ultimately, one cannot escape the bottom.

> More than anything he wanted the camaraderie of the road men: the lunch buckets, the hollering, the body movements that in the end produced something real, something he could point to. . . . It was after he stood in lines for six days running and saw the gang boss pick out thin-armed white boys . . . that he got the message. So it was rage, rage and a determination to take on a man's role anyhow that made him press Nel about settling down. He needed some of his appetites filled, some posture of adulthood recognized. . . . Whatever his fortune, whatever the cut of his garment, there would always be the hem—the tuck and fold that hid his raveling edges; a someone sweet, industrious and loyal to shore him up. And in return he would shelter her, love her, grow old with her. (82–83)

In spite of the valley economy that forcefully stills Jude to forms of passivity, he is determined "to take on a man's role anyhow" by marrying Nel. Yet even his own determinations for sheltering are confused with a representation of tucking, where she is the tucker and he the tuckee. Can we be surprised, then, that this wedding chapter, a chapter that can figure only a partial sublimation of the bottom, ends with a rear view? In the last paragraph, Nel watches Sula leave the wedding, and "even from the rear," the novel informs us, "Nel could tell that it was Sula and that she was smiling" (85).

The novel now skips from 1927 to 1937—a ten-year hiatus in which Sula has left Medallion for a college education while Nel has stayed at home with her husband. These events form yet another view—Eva's was the first—of a black woman's mastery of anal economics. For when Sula returns to the Bottom, during the Bottom's plague of robins and their "pearly shit," she is college-educated *and* conversant with sadistic urges of bottom pleasures—so much so, in fact, that Morrison paints her as someone who is obviously unable to sublimate: "She was completely free of ambition, with no affection for money, property or things, no greed, no desire to command attention or compliments—no ego. For that reason she felt no compulsion to verify herself—be consistent with herself" (119); "Sula never competed; she simply helped others define themselves"(95). Sula's lack of sublimation makes her the bottom of the Bottom and lends her a peculiar theological agency within her community, demonstrated first in relation to Nel. She leads Nel (through the toilet) to God. She tenders Nel's passage to renewal, furthermore, by laying Jude, for no stated reason. The effect is startling: the end of Nel's marriage and the beginning of a long journey back—to Sula, oddly enough.

To mark this shift in Nel, the narrative for the first time leaps to a short first-person narration of Nel's interiority. It is as if Nel's encounter with Sula's alternative economy—which marks property in unaccustomed ways—creates a new space in which different forms of having can appear; a space, no less, in which even the narrator temporarily surrenders full possession. When Morrison returns to omniscient narration, we are at the toilet where Nel is now newly contemplating God. This bathroom, in fact—"small and bright"—shows forth what Plum's "bright hole of sleep" could only shadow: that rebirth needs some form of excretion, the back-end productions of grief over waste:

> The bathroom. It was both small and bright, and she wanted to be in a very small, very bright place. Small enough to contain her grief. Bright enough to throw into relief the dark things that cluttered her. Once inside, she sank to the tile floor next to the toilet. . . . There was stirring, a movement of mud and dead leaves. She thought of the women at Chicken Little's funeral. . . . What she had regarded since as unbecoming behavior seemed fitting to her now; they were screaming at the neck of God, his giant nape, the vast back-of-the-head that he had

turned on them in death. . . . They could not let that heart-smashing event pass unrecorded, unidentified. It was poisonous, unnatural to let the dead go with a mere whimpering, a slight murmur, a rose bouquet of good taste. Good taste was out of place in the company of death, death itself was the essence of bad taste. And there must be much rage and saliva in its presence. (107)[32]

This is bottom theology, one could say—one of rage and saliva, of mud and dead leaves—a communal howl that breaks the (valley) canons of taste.

Morrison's theology, however, is not so simply transgressive. Nor is it simply about transgression. It is about a way of doing sorrow, as we see with Nel above. Morrison's theology also concerns pleasure's backdoor entries—actually, the requirement that pleasure not be taken straight. As Freud admits, if religion "reproduce[s] something of the pleasure which [it is also] designed to prevent," it must also, on the surface of things, still prevent this forbidden pleasure ("Obsessive Actions," 125). Morrison traces this complicated logic and *affirms* the casuistry Freud would regard as religious hypocrisy: Morrison depicts how the Bottom makes Sula represent the devil, the bottom of the Bottom, yet a devil around which the community is able, quite salvifically, to pleasure itself. The narrator reports: "Their conviction of Sula's evil changed them in accountable yet mysterious ways. Once the source of their personal misfortune was identified, they had leave to protect and love one another. They began to cherish their husbands and wives, protect their children, repair their homes and in general band together against the devil in their midst. In their world, aberrations were as much a part of nature as grace. It was not for them to expel or annihilate it" (117–18). Sula stimulates the Bottom's theology, providing a hidden outlet for her community's pleasure. She undermines valley-like sublimation, "the aim to make money that takes over for anal erotism" (as Freud would say), as she works as a devil in the Bottom. Freud, indeed, reminds us that the devil is directly aligned with anality; in fact, in myth and fairy tales, "the gold which the devil gives his paramours turns into excrement" ("Character," 174).

Along this rich associative chain (gold/devil/paramours/excrement), readers can discover, as if uncovering a reward for their pains, Morrison's golden links to orgasm. Female orgasm (of course, it is Sula's) is rendered as a species of anal eroticism, an orgasm seemingly in touch with excrement, or at least with beautiful dirt. Prior to the climactic moment, the narrator has told us that sex is Sula's way of feeling (and doing) deep sorrow. Her lovemaking hollows a space in which she "leap[s] from the edge into soundlessness and [goes] down howling, howling in a stinging awareness of the ending of things" (123). Her dive into endings recalls not only bottom theology (its rage and saliva) but also Bersani's meditations on debasement, especially his celebration of sex "as the *jouissance* of exploded limits, as the ecstatic suffering into which the human organism momentarily plunges when it is 'pressed' beyond a certain threshold of endurance" (217). This is clearly downward mobility in the sexual sense — but a movement down that effects Sula's rise. The narration at this point shifts to Sula in first person, as it earlier did with Nel, suggesting a transformation, even a translation (from one register to another), in the "high silence of orgasm":

> *If I take a chamois and rub real hard on the bone, right on the ledge of your cheek bone, some of the black will disappear. It will flake away into the chamois and underneath there will be gold leaf. . . .*
>
> How high she was over his wand-lean body, how slippery was his sliding sliding smile.
>
> *And if I take a nail file . . . and scrape away at the gold, it will fall away and there will be alabaster. . . .*
>
> The height and the swaying dizzied her, so she bent down and let her breasts graze his chest.
>
> *Then I can take a chisel and small tap hammer and tap away at the alabaster. It will crack then like ice under the pick, and through the breaks I will see the loam, fertile, free of pebbles and twigs. For it is the loam that is giving you that smell. . . . I will put my hand deep into your soil, lift it, sift it with my fingers, feel its warm surface and dewy chill below. . . .*
>
> He swallowed her mouth just as her thighs had swallowed his genitals, and the house was very, very quiet. (130–31)

Even Sula's pleasure cannot be taken straight. Sula (through her direct address) rides the reader, on top of her lover, along a color spectrum — from black to gold leaf to alabaster to loam — beginning at the cheek bone but ending where? "I will put my hand deep into your soil." The passage remains profoundly silent as to the status of lines like these. We know they convey Sula's "thoughts" during sex, but just how imaginative and metaphorical are these descriptions? What is Sula *doing* when she thinks of "sifting" her lover's "fertile" "soil"? And just how far does she drift (in thought, in sex) from his face? Craftily, the novel will not let us know.

These penetrations of a black man's depths (Morrison's riskiest flirtation with anality?) remain under cover. We can only follow Sula's translation of their relations into a register ending with "mud"—the last word Sula is depicted as thinking, as she tries to figure the right kind of mix between her "water" and Ajax's "loam" in the making of a "soil" that is "rich and moist." What we can glean even so from Sula's unusual value-track are the strong echoes of earlier scenes of women's penetrations. Sula's rubbing and scraping and chiseling render her active in sexual intercourse— even, perhaps, as she's being penetrated. Joined to her fond penetration of Ajax's "soil" by her hand, these abrasive invasions (of Ajax's depths) recall Eva's freeing Plum's stools with her finger and Nel and Sula's probings of the ground (their makeshift bottom) with their twigs. This scene's siftings even transform Eva's earlier desperation, lending now suggestions of something languorous, sensual, and sumptuous to (anal) penetration. Since the fertility of Ajax's loam ("free of pebbles and twigs") makes an obvious and stunning contrast with Plum's hard stools, the thrust of Sula's (imaginative) penetrations appears to be to make black men productive of —and also alive to—bottom values. What an odd species of female orgasm that must mentally penetrate soil.[33]

Now we have come full face to a crux: What are the material dangers of black folks' embracing paradigms of downward mobility? Can there be life-sustaining productions without some kind of valley possessions "up" in the Bottom? As *Sula* brings the relations of Nel and Sula to a head, sharpening questions of traditional morality and sexual possession, it draws to a point the novel's economic issues. Sula's parting question, which she puts to Nel—"How do you know who was good?"—extends to competing economies. These kinds of questions are further drawn to a point by a tunnel.

In the chapter "1941," Bottom blacks attack the tunnel that they have been barred from helping to build. The date of the chapter places us during a wartime economy; jobs, once again, have been promised to black men and, once again, the promise reverts to a "nigger joke." By this time, as well, the black community's strongest link to its bottom values, the Bottom's devil, Sula, has died. The narrator laments: "A falling away, a dislocation was taking place. . . . [They] now had nothing to rub up against. The tension was gone and so was the reason for the effort they had made. Without her mockery, affection for others sank into flaccid disrepair" (153). Already one senses the Bottom's collapse, made more dramatic by the suggestion of flaccidity. Another sign of the Bottom's demise: Shadrack is hopeless that National Suicide Day will do, or has ever done, any good for his community. Even so, in a kind of final push, Shadrack leads a parade to the tunnel, where in a strong display of rage, Bottom blacks, who are losing Bottom values, attack the structure that figures their relationship to white employment promises: "Their hooded eyes swept over the place where their hope had lain since 1927. There was the promise: leaf-dead. . . . They didn't mean to go in, to actually go down into the lip of the tunnel, but in their need to kill it all, all of it, to wipe from the face of the earth the work of the thin-armed Virginia boys, the bull-necked Greeks and the knife-faced men who waved the leaf-dead promise, they went too deep, too far . . . A lot of them died there" (161–62; second ellipsis in original). How should we read this angry penetration of a darkened cavity, caused by the failure of a promise made to black men? Does Morrison's affirmation of Bottom values meet its death here? Must Bottom values be put to death, because the Bottom can never economically be truly "up"? Or is the attack itself wrongheaded, the quintessential sign of the neighborhood's loss of what it has valued apart from the valley?

Morrison does not solve this problem for us. Her narrative leaves off in 1965 with the certainty that the Bottom collapsed: black people who made money during the war moved close to the valley, only to find that white people with money had moved up into the hills. The invocation of civil rights through the chapter title, "1965," plays sorrowfully, ironically. The era of civil rights was itself a period of symbolic reversal; civil rights, at least King's brand, was grounded in a bottom theology; and with its struggle over restrooms and buses, civil rights offered a veritable discourse on backseats and toilets. Does Toni Morrison suggest that civil rights, because of its gains, led to blacks' assimilation of values that would then repress the Bottom? Is this why the novel ends with ambivalent Nel calling out in sorrow for Sula—voicing a cry that has "no bottom and . . . no top, just circles and circles of sorrow" (174)?

Morrison, in this novel, seems to worry in this way. What a fix, indeed: if upward mobility proves theologically and sexually depleting, but downward mobility spells economic suicide for economically marginalized people, what economy will not immobilize? Can there be a ceiling that will raise the bottom? Can there be a rising that refuses to leave one's Bottom behind? Can a better Bottom, perhaps, be built?

These, for me, are the questions pressuring Morrison's close. Yet, by *Sula*'s end, it becomes even clearer that this is a novel not so much about racial segregation (though there is that: blacks and whites trading valleys and hills); and not so much about racial separatism (though the Bottom gets signed "black," since the name is a kind of "nigger joke"). Nor is the novel about a blinkered embrace of something "opposite" to the joys of material health. Rather, the bottom's contributions to the Bottom, through a thoughtful chain of anal reference, signal remarkable social holdings that stand apart from money—in fact, amid the sorrows of unequal distributions. The many ways of "tucking" people "up the Bottom" (to use the novel's words) are not an unthinking social debasement. "Tucking," we recall, means at once "to gather up in a fold," "to draw together," "to eat or drink heartily," and, by way of Old French and Middle Dutch, "to stick, pierce, or poke." The verb "tuck" itself seems to trouble distinctions between the poles of activity and passivity, aggressor and receiver, suggesting something of a snug contact that is restless nonetheless. And if "tucking" bears obvious maternal overtones, it avoids the softness that spells a white feminine passivity, being, after all, a folding that is also a piercing, a poking that is also a swallowing.

This is *Sula*'s joke. In the midst of blacks' economic struggles, Morrison has only (but think of all that she folds into "only") traded the pun of being "fucked" for that of being "tucked." Of course, this trade is an imperfect swap. But, for all of that, it is not at all socially insignificant. It is an aggressive, self-reflexive debasement of one's neighbor as oneself, in a neighborly way. For to "tuck" each other in the Bottom is to aggress against each other tenderly. As the novel says, "Just a nigger joke . . . a little comfort somehow."

Chapter Three

WHEN ARE DIRTY DETAILS AND

SCENES COMPELLING? TUCKED IN THE CUTS

OF INTERRACIAL ANAL RAPE

Dirty

Details of beautiful shame are often composite and oxymoronic. Grimy, and sometimes obscene or scatological, but also undeniably compelling, not to mention frequently lyrical: such are the details from which I have already drawn speculations about cloth wounds and the anal history of black bottom neighborhoods. In Genet, a quite depressing thought about faggots spreading like a shawl woven out of shivers; a secret thought of graceful murder, hiding beneath a sailor's pants blacker than any pair known to man; blood running down the inside of a peacoat and over a jersey, coloring while also wounding clothes; Querelle penetrated by a brothel-owner, causing his self-execution to peak in release upon velvet. Then, in Morrison, the stripping of twigs to a smooth, creamy innocence, used to poke rhythmically into the earth for making a hole in which to stuff glass and cigarette butts; the wet light of kerosene poured by a mother killing her son, who, messing up his pants and smiling all the time, was trying to reenter his mother's womb; the sifting of a lover's "soil," during sex, by a hand that is described in terms of a chisel that is penetrating depths. And now these: details from a story of a man's gold watch (details we encounter toward the end of this chapter), a watch that he hides as a treasured heirloom up his rectum while he is in prison (as a POW) before he dies of dysentery, and before he hands the watch to his buddy, a man named Captain Koons, who then hides the timepiece up his bottom (in his Koons cavity); also the tonally various details surrounding the man-to-man rape of a black man (who is called a "nigger," though not a "coon") by hillbilly types in a pawnshop basement.

Now we are ready to ask about the force of these kinds of details, and our fascination with these kinds of scenes, especially as they operate in visual domains.

Beyond the Pale?

We started at the surface of bodily shame in chapter 1: queer clothes, black skin. We then moved on in chapter 2 to the body's tenderly penetrated depths. In that chapter, the sign of queer anality—and dirty bottom pleasures—offered ways to think about strong communal values and disquieting pleasures in (what get tagged as) black bottom neighborhoods. Now, on our way to debasements that sit at the bottom of our minds (chapter 4), or spread themselves along the circuits of the brain (chapter 5), we step back to ask about the modes of depicting and especially reading shame. We even up the ante on the kinds of shame discussed. For on the face of it, it is a challenge to any conception of a beautiful bottom to see, as we see in Quentin Tarantino's film *Pulp Fiction* (1994), an anal rape of a powerful black man (who tells the only witness to his rape: "don't tell nobody about this"). This depiction—deemed debasing by many critics and film spectators—would seem beyond the pale of generative shame that we have been discussing.

I will argue it is not. To be more specific, in the previous chapter we encountered Toni Morrison's edgy depictions of Bottom blacks: her conception of the economic struggles of the "underclass" in African American communities from 1918 to 1965. "Bottom" males, in Morrison's conception, were those black men who were struggling even to get themselves exploited in the capitalist system; who were implicitly raising the question of whether blacks could be bourgeois, pre-1965, in a color caste system; and who, in a set of striking depictions, were being penetrated—in various ways—by black Bottom women seeking to keep their men alive to black Bottom values of neighborhood life. They, black men as well as women, were "tucked in the Bottom" (Morrison's phrase) of this economic strife, which they rendered to themselves (according to Morrison's depiction in *Sula*) as a kind of "nigger joke."

This is aggressive portraiture on Morrison's part. But so is this: an underworld, more than an underclass, black man—a boss, in fact, by every reckoning—making his way in the parallel capitalist system of crime rings, who, even so, ends up raped by redneck whites in a "nigger joke" told by Quentin Tarantino, not Toni Morrison. With this aggressive depiction in mind, and against the backdrop of Morrison's depictions of black male debasements, I want to pose my title's question: when can dirty details and scenes be compelling? Or, at the start, to shift this question so as to begin to explore a part of it: how do the signs attaching to authors (whether Toni Morrison or Quentin Tarantino) control our trust in their experiments with shame? If we were told that black gay filmmakers Marlon Riggs or Isaac Julien, not Tarantino, had written, directed, and produced *Pulp Fiction*, would this film have produced different reads? Or if one believed that a black gay photographer—plausibly, Rotimi Fani-Kayode—had produced the black male nudes attributed to white photographer Robert Mapplethorpe, would there have been a black gay backlash against that work? Out of these questions comes my experiment: to see if we might, indeed how we might, consider *Pulp Fiction* in relation to what José Muñoz has called "black gay male cultural production."[1] What kind of a producer of these signs ("black" and "gay," or "queer") is Tarantino, given that he's not a wearer of them? And how do his productions, in his film *Pulp Fiction*, compel us to encounter the notion of compelling dirty details and scenes?

"Dirty," for the sake of this argument, will trace a set of dictionary definitions of this term: "grimy," "obscene," "scatological," "contemptibly contrary to honor or rules." In this way, different kinds of viewers might agree on a scene's "dirtiness" (at the level of description, or even genre) without agreeing in their judgment on it (without necessarily moralizing against it). Furthermore, my experiment here—to view Tarantino beside the phrase of Muñoz ("black gay male cultural production")—is not meant to save or redeem Tarantino by linking him to this specific phrase. I don't think saving him is interesting or requisite. It would even be ironic, since Tarantino, in *Pulp Fiction*, puts redemption itself into question in ways that confirm its violence most of all, as we are going to see. Rather, by linking Tarantino to "black gay male . . . productions," I aim to show the width of this phrase and broaden our conception of what it might embrace. To do so, even so, I must engage the author's signs. And I must engage certain critics' complaints about the film—about its racist, homophobic acts of violence—that center on the scene of the rape of a black man. I will encounter both of these matters as I advance three interlocking arguments. First, I will show how Tarantino's film fits the definitions of "queer pulp" offered by a recent study of that genre, a point that should remind us that non-normative sexualities were always a staple of pulp fictions generally. Second, I will demonstrate how certain critics' problems with Tarantino's *Pulp* echo, in certain significant ways, debates surrounding Robert Mapplethorpe—specifically, his photographs of black male nudes. I will even argue, in relation to this point, that Tarantino's film puts into motion images reminiscent of Mapplethorpe's photography; and, quite strikingly, puts them into motion right alongside iconic images (pulp fictions) from America's Jim Crow history of lynching and sexually assaulting black Americans. This bold pairing of gay sexuality and Jim Crow history, with which Mapplethorpe himself experimented (see figure 4), intensifies quandaries surrounding what counts as visual pleasure. Which leads me to my third and most difficult argument.

The goal of my first two claims—my assertions about queer pulp and Mapplethorpe echoes—is to confront what we can call our attraction to dirty details and scenes. Eve Kosofsky Sedgwick, working through her thoughts on the work of Silvan Tomkins, has shown how the act of registering shame (and here I am thinking of the film spectator) depends on interest, how, in her words, "without positive affect, there can be no shame: only a scene that offers you enjoyment or engages your interest can make you blush."[2] Or as Sedgwick quotes Tomkins saying: " 'like disgust, [shame] operates only after interest or enjoyment has been activated, and inhibits one or the other or both. The innate activator of shame [he writes] is the incomplete reduction of interest or joy' " (97). I suggest we take these hints, which Sedgwick gleans from Tomkins, and move the question of interest into matters of attraction and full-on visual fascination in the cinematic field. How do scenes of shame stay tethered to matters of attraction? In many respects, this is the question grounding the trauma of Mapplethorpe's nudes. To answer it, I am going to argue against some critics' claims for the viewer's "ambivalence" in the face of Mapplethorpe—and one could say, by extension, Tarantino. Attraction to these images, as I hope to show, does not necessarily involve an ambivalent state of mind, or pious hand-wringing for that matter. The state of mind produced for a viewer may be better described as additive, one

4. *Hooded Man, 1980,* copyright The Robert Mapplethorpe
Foundation, courtesy Art + Commerce Anthology.

allowing for a composite stance in the face of debasement—for fascination, even humor, and sorrow simultaneously, and also allowing for the violence (the uncontrollable force) that can be a part of attraction itself. Like the work of Morrison, Tarantino's film ties flashes of political and historical poignancy—through a forceful bruising of its viewers—to the spectator's visual fascination with pulpy scenes of shame. In fact, visual fascination in *Pulp*, in ways I next explain, may be felt both through and as a cut.

Preliminary Thoughts on Visual Fascination: Attract, Cut, and Hold

I claim throughout this chapter that Tarantino, quite a bit like Morrison, and, I will argue, Mapplethorpe, too, tucks—and, in this way, quasi-hides —black histories of debasements inside cutting details, violent joking, and scenes of force. All three artists treat these histories as fully palpable in American life of the twentieth century—but also, crucially, see them as submerged, as partly occluded from polite view. (Hence, the Bottom that whites rarely visit in Morrison's *Sula*, and "Hooded Man" in Mapplethorpe's corpus.) What links such different cultural producers as Morrison, Mapplethorpe, and Tarantino are their sophisticated ways of showing what lies hidden—or only partly hidden—in cleaned-up versions of American life. Theirs is a brilliance of the commonplace, perhaps—the submerged commonplace of race-sex subtexts. For though the histories in question (violent raced-sexed relations) make their appearance in gay porn movies and hip-hop videos (or, in 2005, in breezy, titillating form in an NFL commercial, with Terrell Owens and Nicolette Sheridan playing with interracial taboos), the work of Tarantino, Morrison, and Mapplethorpe is more aggressive, more thoughtful, more aestheticized, more layered, and dirtier in a compelling sense than these other cultural artifacts. In fact, Tarantino's distinctive contribution to aesthetically engaging these histories of debasement is his complex management of visual fascination.

What exactly constitutes this complicated management—and this fascination—in a film about pulp? At the outset, we can contemplate a possible linkage of these three terms: attract, cut, and hold. We can also contemplate how dirty details highlight what being "compelled"—having our attention "attracted," with or without our consent—might mean. Here is why. A compelling detail (or a set of striking details) is a kind of love—or at least an intensification of our attraction and attention. As this kind of love or attraction, the detail can also be said to cut the text, since it may carry the mind away, and thus in a sense cut the viewer away, from the forward flow of plot or message by drawing attention to itself as a source of fascination. Yet, as odd as this may sound, this cut away from the text is a kind of holding pen. It truly holds our interest, as we commonly say. For tucked in the cut (and, therefore, held in it) is a cache of interest that may take many forms. First and foremost, the detail's cut fundamentally holds the fact of our attraction. That we cut away from the flow of the text, have our attention even momentarily drawn away by the act of fascination, is an obvious sign of our attraction. Second, the detail's cut may also hold any thought the detail launches by association or personal interest. In other words, as the mind is taken away to focus on the detail, various extraneous associations or personal connections may come to mind. One can say that these launched thoughts are held in the cut—the cut away from the text. Third, the cut of the detail can hold an entire history evoked by suggestion and tucked in the cut as a form of hiddenness. We are used to this last dynamic with a film cut—especially an edit. Courtesy of edits, between two frames of a moving film, seconds, days, or years may have passed, or dramatic changes may have taken place in the life of the film's represented protagonist. Entire histories, in the sense of time elapsed, are held inside a cinematic cut. Seen this way, every cut in a film, if we focus on it, points to a hiding: to something more, or just something different, we might have been shown.[3] In a trickier sense than film cuts, I will claim, compelling details—the kind that attract us—themselves make a cut and point to a hiding.

I want to explain this idea of a cut from all these angles: the detail's cut as the sign of our attraction; as the occasion for launching our fantasies; and as the holding of possibly hidden histories. I will also add, quite crucially, a sense of the violent way that the detail cuts the viewer in the act of attraction, sending an arrow to the eye, as it were. In all these ways, we are going to find that *Pulp Fiction* helps us to complicate the highly suggestive theories of Roland Barthes on aesthetic woundings—as we might call the compelling details that Barthes seeks to theorize in *Camera Lucida* (1981). *Pulp Fiction* dramatizes, and thematizes, these aesthetic woundings by using the shock of dirty details surrounding black and queer debasements. Surely Tarantino could count on these details of debasements to compel us, given their political charge. Indeed, his movie relies on the viewer's attractions to its details, even to its pulpiest details, and these attractions open up cuts (of several kinds) that hold hidden histories that the film does not present in the form of a message. These are histories—of the life of pulp in American entertainment and same-sex interracial sexual fantasy in the American imagination at large—that have functioned generally as hidden or partially hidden histories in the mainstream American culture of the mid-to-late twentieth century. Tarantino's film not only opens windows onto these histories: through its dirty details, it opens up cuts that hold these histories. For in Tarantino's exuberant text (with the dark, campy tones we have found, in different ways, in Genet and Morrison) something of the history of black and queer signs, something of the persistent indirections of their sorrows, is humorously, forcefully, launched at the eye.

Preliminary Thoughts on Tarantino's Rape: What Is So Compelling?

In *Pulp Fiction*, as the title suggests, dirty details are the point. In fact, the film begins by defining its term(s): "Pulp (pulp) n. 1. A soft, moist, shapeless mass of matter. 2. A magazine or book containing lurid subject matter and being characteristically printed on rough, unfinished paper." "Pulp," then, refers both to textual matters (paperback fictions) and to their dirty nature (through the "lurid" mess of matter). These dirty details are constantly apparent in Tarantino's film and often quite compelling. The scene of Vincent's shooting heroin is shot with the speed and rhythm of striptease: a case unzipped to reveal a syringe on orange velour; the flick of orange flame repeating the color before a dissolve shows a burning spoon; the puncture of the needle into the skin, giving the look of a magnified mosquito; the backflow of blood into the chamber, kaleidoscopic, a little bit clouded; finally, slowly, the press of the plunger. At certain moments, the reader of *Sula* can find Toni Morrison's dirtiest details echoed here, in another register. There are, for example, a host of penetrations in *Pulp Fiction* by penile proxies (hypodermic needles, bullets from a gun, samurai swords, even a hand). These penetrations are themselves quite bizarrely tied up with the continuous questions of redemption running through the text—can dirty details have redeeming value? Can dirty details themselves be redeemed? In *Pulp Fiction*, redemption proves, as we are going to see, every bit as bent as it did in *Sula*. Here, however, the black bottom male is the gangster-God of some new version of Negro Heaven west of the Mason-Dixon line (in Los Angeles). He's a God, that is, until he suddenly becomes the butt of Tarantino's "nigger joke" (that crucial phrase from *Sula*) and is "tucked" in the bottom, one could say—pierced and poked—though rather less tenderly than we observed in *Sula*'s scenes of cruelty.

Readers familiar with Tarantino's film will remember this scene. (My attractions: the pattern of blood on Butch's shirt, making a mesomorphic pyramid of color; the small puddle of light on the heads of Butch and Marsellus; the squeezable look of red ball gags stuffed in their mouths; The Gimp's leather suit, black from head to toe, zippered at the mouth; and the sound of leather being tapped by fingers.) The black drug lord, Marsellus Wallace, along with his rebellious white employee, Butch Coolidge, is trapped in the cellar of the Mason-Dixon Pawnshop by two white rednecks. Brought up out of hiding (from a space below the basement, a cell beneath the dungeon) is a leather-covered figure in s/m gear, with a comical grin and eerie chuckle, a figure named The Gimp, whose name points the viewer to the question of wounding. Is this leather figure, black from top to bottom, a consenting player in a scene of pleasure or a compelled and imprisoned slave? We never know for sure, for Butch (the straight protagonist with a campy name), waiting to be raped, inadvertently hangs the black-leather figure and escapes unnoticed while Marsellus is brutalized in the next room. Thinking better of it, Butch doesn't run; he decides to rescue Marsellus from their captors. Choosing a samurai sword as his weapon, which he conveniently finds on the wall, Butch creeps back to the pawnshop basement (figure 5) to save Marsellus, who wears a band-aid on the back of his head (figure 6).[4]

At precisely this point, Tarantino's camera shows us what I think we will not be asked to see: the film's black boss being raped from behind. This dirty image hits us right between the eyes. I am attracted—drawn, compelled, caught by what I have rarely if ever seen onscreen outside a gay pornographic film (where this image would not look out of place). "Liking" the image is out of the question. Liking would be a mere pleasant interest, from which I would press on. "Love"—some far more passionate attachment, which does not exclude shades of revulsion—is forced on me here. My response is rapid, but also arresting, which slows down my forward progress. Wed to each other in this moment are flashes of (my own imagination's) historical scenes of interracial rape, lynchings (which I have seen in films and photographs, and which, though they don't exactly pertain to this image, still surround it), and, powerfully, my own undeniable wish to see black men and white men in sexual proximity to each other, as one might see them in gay pornography. (These are some of the palpable strains in my attachment, as I analyze it later.) Then, on

5. Butch with sword, *Pulp Fiction* (1994).
6. Marsellus with band-aid, *Pulp Fiction* (1994).

7. Sword aligned with rape, *Pulp Fiction* (1994).

the sudden heels of this sight, a sword blade cuts across our view. Butch
has raised his weapon to strike. For a flash, the sword aligns with the rape,
and almost obscures it, as if it is cutting our sight of the trauma (figure 7).
But it's too late. We have already seen. Butch frees Marsellus (he cuts a
white Southern rapist with his sword) but does not free the viewer from
what he or she has been made to see: the opening of a black man's wound
in a shot that another film might have edited out.

To the extent that we are surprised to see this rape, if indeed we are,
we are forced to consider what films often cut, what they discreetly hide
in a cut—and what, by contrast, Tarantino puts in view. In this odd way,
we see inside a (would-be) cut. The film, at this point, could even be seen
to be punning on cutting, and, in this way, thematizing form. Marsellus,
with a band-aid on the back of his head (presumably covering some kind
of cut), is anally cut from the back by the rape; Butch is cutting a rapist in
two. In any event, while we see cuttings (in these several ways), the film
is putting a highly compelling visual image (hillbillies raping a powerful
black man) where a film cut might have been made. In place of a film cut
an image arrests us. But this particular image also cuts—at least, it may.
By means of this insistent sight, in a scene begging to be read as dirty
(with its grimy basement, its blood, its Gimp, its view of a rape), the film
may be prompting its own distraction, its own cut away, from the comic
plot of Butch's escape. The film, as it prompts our thoughts through the
Mason-Dixon name and Confederate flag on the pawnshop wall, may poi-
gnantly point us to a history—the American history of racial codes that
affects the fortunes of American blacks—that *Pulp* does not otherwise

track or use. A history of African American pain, as well as a history of hidden attractions (those of a same-sex and interracial nature), resides, it seems, in an anal cut.[5]

But there is something more interesting still, something that tells us to think about these cuttings as a different kind of argument from the kind we commonly associate with a film's so-called message. In a fascinating manner, the opening of Marsellus's (historical) wound leads toward the opening, on a very large scale, of the film's own cuts (its edits) as well. Formally, dramatically, the film is thematizing the opening of film cuts as a kind of opening onto hidden histories—and the hidden life of signs— that can be unleashed at a moment's notice. For when the film proceeds from the rape (and Butch's escape from the rednecks' store), the narrative loops us back to the film's beginning scenes that were previously cut but now are offered to our view. For the rest of the film, as I will unfold, it is as if the viewer is *in* these cuts: from this point on, the viewer is only ever shown scenes—is only ever inside scenes—that are the missing matter, the contents of the cuts, of earlier scenes.[6]

Critics have tended to talk in general terms about Tarantino's postmodern disordering of his plot. Yet my detail-specific analysis yields two claims. After the first out-of-order scenes, the narrative runs in an orderly sequence right to its climax, its narrative end, with the rape-and-escape. For example, if we assign numbers to scenes to indicate where each would come in sequence if the plot were told in a linear fashion, we can see how, and in what order, Tarantino puts the scenes out of order: 6 (coffee shop: beginning of film)-1–7–8–9–10–11–12–13 (rape and escape; END of narrative)-1–2–3–4–5–6 (coffee shop: end of film). When the film proceeds beyond its climax (the rape and escape) by seeming to be starting all over again, it again runs in sequence (scenes 1–6) by now showing what was hidden in its cuts (scenes 2–5) between 1 and 6. That is to say, post-rape-and-escape, as if these events have opened these cuts, we, as viewers, inhabit these cuts; everything we see, from here to the end, is technically, thematically, the inside of a cut. Formally situated in this way, after the climax of the rape and escape we are treated to hit men debating each other about the message (and also the value) of something compelling— and tremendously dirty—that they have seen. We think about the status of dirty details, about the redeeming value of these details, and about the message of redemption itself, while we are inside the film's own cuts.

Given these dynamics, I am struck to find that, writing in the face of this movie's popularity and critical acclaim, negative critics acknowledge

Pulp Fiction's engaging details, noting their nuance, but see the film's message (or its lack of one in the face of dirty scenes) as part of its overall racist picture. "Quentin Tarantino," writes Pat Dowell in the journal *Cineaste*, "the genius of the moment embraced by so many who would never vote Republican, is the hip version of the angry white guy who does." "[H]is thrust is basically conservative," Dowell claims; in fact, the sensibilities of *Forrest Gump* and *Pulp Fiction* "are the two sides of the same coin."[7] Tarantino's film "fancies itself postracist" but "subjects" Marsellus "to the most humiliating of sexual attentions, rape (by a white rapist)." Furthermore, "the structure of *Pulp Fiction* is not so new as it looks"; Tarantino "is first and foremost an ingenious curator of displaying his collection of cultural trivia." Anthony Lane, in *The New Yorker*, concurs. Though "the decoration is a lot of fun" (Lane loves "the details pondered by the camera"), Tarantino is not only playing "an old Godard game," he is also, ultimately, "less an ironist than a chronic fetishist; he has cooked up a world where hamburgers matter, and nothing else."[8] Thomas M. Leitch adds to this view: "Although the characters of *Pulp Fiction* are obsessed with moral problems, the problems they most actively debate . . . are so inconsequential . . . that the tendency is to trivialize all moral discourse."[9]

Beyond these negative assessments, even the three most intelligent essays on this movie are those that severely critique its debasements of blacks and gays. Michael Rogin's passing reference to *Pulp Fiction* in his illuminating treatise "The Two Declarations of American Independence" takes as a sign of the film's racist stance (which "bring[s] *Birth of a Nation* up to date") the fact that "the intimidating black boss [Marsellus] is cut down to size in a graphically depicted anal rape."[10] In a lengthy treatment, Sharon Willis, in *High Contrast*, weaves a wonderfully complicated argument about *Pulp Fiction*'s ahistoricity. Central to her case is her sense that the film is intent, almost above all else, on "catching the big boss with his pants down"—one aspect of the film's "infantile regression to anal sadism." More broadly, Willis claims that *Pulp Fiction* "might resecure racialized representations for a racist imaginary, even as it tries to work them loose from it."[11] Carolyn Dinshaw's complaints are just as strongly stated, in her richly woven essay "Getting Medieval: *Pulp Fiction*, Gawain, Foucault." She calls the film "a very old story" in the grips of a "racist straight white male imaginary" "that ends up supporting . . . a reactionary plot."[12] As part of the film's bold homophobia (wedded to its racism) "sodomy, implicitly suggested and denied . . . as a possibility in male bonding, is then explicitly represented in the pawnshop basement as unconsensual and violent—rape—so that it can't be seen as in any way acceptable" (121). Bottom line: this film goes wrong, say numerous critics, in its debasements of blacks and gays.

I disagree. Something goes positively right in these debasements, which is why I have no interest in redeeming Tarantino from these charges of racist homophobia leveled against him. Something in these scenes with their dirty details, something about my attraction to these details, opens out onto crucial questions of the violent nature of visual fascination and its potential political suggestiveness. For when *Pulp Fiction*'s depictions are most scurrilous, most intensely shameful, but also strangely funny, as they are with Marsellus's rape, they are also most politically resonant—and most firmly anchored in aesthetic experiment. In fact, apropos to my theory of the dirty detail's cut, and to its place in Quentin Tarantino's aesthetic experiments, D. A. Miller and Lee Edelman, in two separate essays, have brilliantly uncovered how Hitchcock, in films such as *Rope* and *Rear Window*, is haunted by an anal cut that these films disavow but suggest. D. A. Miller, in his essay "Anal *Rope*," examines Hitchcock's cinematic fantasy of a film that would have no cuts; though, as Miller proceeds to point out, *Rope* makes cuts that it hides on the backs (the tailcoats) of its homosexual killers, thereby suggesting their castration through this aesthetic experiment. Lee Edelman, in "*Rear Window's* Glasshole," examines a different Hitchcock fantasy: Hitchcock's illusion of pure montage with the seams between cuts all sewn up. This kind of fantasy, Edelman argues, cannot acknowledge (at least, not openly, not affirmatively) its structural reliance on an all-important hole in the camera's vision, which as Edelman smartly unfolds it, seems suggestively, importantly anal.[13]

Writing in the vein of Edelman and Miller, with an eye specifically on formal experiment, I am going to argue that, unlike Hitchcock, Quentin Tarantino, quite a bit like writers as diverse as Morrison and Genet, puts anality—and, moreover, its value—on display. As I have indicated, in *Pulp Fiction*, an openly anal cut is like a film cut: it is a valued place that actually holds important matters that are tucked in its hole. Specifically, the (anal/film) cut is a place that holds our interest, even our attractions; it is a place from which to launch our fantasies; and, in a film entitled *Pulp Fiction*, it opens onto histories that are bound up with the violence of pain and lurid, messy attractions. Among these histories are three in particular: the history of pulp paperback fictions in postwar American mass entertainment; the more hidden histories (for the general public) of gay pornography and s/M, which serve as a source of pulp for paperbacks; and, quite importantly, the history some Americans wish they could forget (and sometimes do): the Jim Crow history—with its historical pulp fictions, we might say—of murderous white violence against black Americans, which includes, through lynchings and rape, a murderous desire to sexually possess them.

These are three historical strands, three quasi-hidden historical strands, of violent attractions and pulp entertainments braided together in Tarantino's film. And with these braided strands in mind, I now want to locate Tarantino's film in relation to issues dotting the landscape of black gay male cultural production. Not because Quentin Tarantino wears these signs as a cultural producer (he certainly does not), but because he seems to circulate them in such violent ways, bringing "black" signs into such a violent collision with "queer" ones.

The Worlds of Queer Pulp and Mapplethorpe's Nudes

Surprisingly few of Tarantino's critics give pulp genres serious play in their discussions; none that I know of mentions queer pulp. Queer pulp, of course, is almost redundant as a term. The paperback books steeped in sex and lurid plots that became so popular mid-twentieth century were paperback perversions for a mass audience. And queer sexualities, whether broadly or narrowly defined, were a tailor-made source of pulp for paperbacks that trafficked in salacious reads. A range of titles conveys the sexualities on tap for pulp fictions and shows that often they were being sold as titillating oddities of one sort or another: *The Last Days of Sodom and Gomorrah* ("Passions and Debauchery Explode in History's Most Wicked City," 1957, by the author of *Secrets of Mary Magdalene*); *Frisco Gal* ("A Rich Man's Darling—A Young Man's Slave—A Strong Man's Passion. All Three Were Hers for the Choosing," 1949); *Muscle Boy* ("They Got Their Kicks from Forbidden Feats of Strength," 1958); *World without Men* ("They Had Forgotten What Men Looked Like," 1958); *Bold Desires* ("Refused by His Wife, Harry Felt His Desires Were Undeniable, However Timid or Bold They Might Be," 1959); *Strange Fulfillment* ("Men and Women in a Jungle of Emotion," 1958); *Taxi Dancers* ("For Need of Money and Desire for Sex, the Taxi Dancers Wandered to All Corners of Life's Gutters," 1958); *Triangle of Sin* ("A Delicate Subject, Boldly Treated," 1952); *The Strange Three* ("One of the Three . . . a Sister . . . Who Strongly Opposed the Basic Convention and Taboos against Incest," 1957); *Hang-*

out for Queers ("It was a Haven for Oddballs . . . Sex Weirdos in Search of Offbeat Thrills," 1965).

The overlap between queer sex and pulp paperbacks becomes apparent in Susan Stryker's *Queer Pulp: Perverted Passions from the Golden Age of the Paperback* (2001), in which she sketches what her book cover deems a "lost chapter in American publishing history." Stryker reminds us in her study that "wayward sexuality is what mid-century paperbacks peddled par excellence." Pulp novels were "the venue of choice for exploring and exploiting certain taboo topics disallowed in movies and radio and the pages of reputable hardcover books." She continues: "Before the sexual revolution of the 1960s, and the explosion of soft- and hard-core pornographic magazines that came in its wake, paperback books were pretty much the only game in town when it came to explicit portrayals of sexuality in the mass media" — "a world of sin and sex and drugs and booze and every ugly thing human beings could conspire to do to one another."[14]

From these descriptions, one sees that Tarantino could use pulp fictions in a visual medium to thematize the question: what can be shown in a nonpornographic American entertainment? It is as if Quentin Tarantino takes his camera through the "peephole" cover of a pulp paperback. For, as Stryker tells us, "the popular 'peephole' style of cover art [on paperback pulps], suggesting stolen glimpses into exotic interior territories at once psychological and geographical, literalized the voyeuristic appeal of early postwar paperback art." Says Stryker: "Through the peephole covers we saw slovenly white trash swamp-dwellers, libidinous inner-city Blacks, suburban wife-swappers, lesbian girl-gangs, and other such denizens of the dominant culture's overheated imagination. Featuring eye-grabbing illustrations of primal scenes blatantly displayed in the public sphere, the covers seduced readers with the imagined pleasures and forbidden knowledge within" (7–8).

What does Tarantino choose to serve his viewers for the flavor of taboo in the 1990s? A primal scene from American history, with a new twist from the age of AIDS: two white men (hillbilly rednecks) forcing anal sex on an unwilling black man. One could say that Tarantino serves his viewers a composite flavor of American taboo, crafted from a crossing of signs. Tarantino crosses miscegenous relations (of a violent sort) with violent same-sex (unprotected?) sex. Anything less, one is tempted to say, would seem mundane; but this combination of signs — especially in a scene played in part for comic effect — seems calculated to carry a charge.

This being said, it may seem surprising to read *Pulp Fiction* in relation to "black gay male . . . productions" from the same period. I do so for these reasons: to show how *Pulp Fiction* fits certain descriptions intelligently attached to this phrase by José Muñoz (in his *Disidentifications: Queers of Color and the Performance of Politics*); to show simultaneously how Tarantino would raise more strongly the problems Mapplethorpe raised for the would-be keepers of this phrase (especially in Tarantino's directly debasing, objectifying, penetrating gaze at a black male body in his film); and, finally, by virtue of this linkage *and* this trouble, to stretch the phrase itself.

To start, I will take some descriptions from Muñoz. In his highly suggestive essay "Photographies of Mourning: Melancholia and Ambivalence in Van Der Zee, Mapplethorpe, and *Looking for Langston*," Muñoz argues for the central importance (to what he deems a "movement" of black gay artists) of Isaac Julien's experimental 1989 film on the black American poet Langston Hughes, who may have been gay, a film "that meditates," as Muñoz puts it, "on queer cadences that can be heard in Hughes when studying Hughes' life and work."[15] Muñoz starts by placing this film — and, presumably, Isaac Julien himself as a black gay filmmaker — in the context of "black gay male productions" that "experienced a boom of sorts in the late 1980s and early 1990s" (57). (*Pulp Fiction* was released in 1994.) What makes Isaac Julien's film, one might ask, a "slippery center" of these productions (of work by Essex Hemphill, Marlon Riggs, Melvin Dixon, Blackberri, Bill T. Jones, and Rotimi Fani-Kayode, among others)?

To answer this question, we should look at what Muñoz wants to embrace about this film. Perhaps out of worry that *Looking for Langston* will be dismissed as overly aestheticizing, to the point of obscuring historicity, Muñoz points to this "exemplary and central text's densely layered, aestheticized, and politicized workings." As its own "mode of history writing," *Looking for Langston* is a "montage of attractions"; it is a "calculus of juxtapositions" using a "strategy of emotional combination that produces what [Sergei Eisenstein] has called 'emotional dynamization.'" Muñoz continues: "It is important to keep in mind that this queer black cultural imaginary is in no way ahistorical. Its filaments are historically specific and the overall project is more nearly *transhistorical*" (his emphasis, 60). Strikingly, given what I have proposed for *Pulp Fiction*, Muñoz draws attention to the fact that Julien's film "attempts to represent . . . a few different histories that have . . . been cloaked." As a result, *Looking for Langston* accomplishes "a dialectical interchange between present and past tenses" and "a complex relation of fragments to a whole" (61), while fulfilling a "task" central to black gay male productions: the job of "(re)telling elided histories that need to be both excavated and (re)imagined" (57).

Tarantino, I will argue, unquestionably offers aesthetic experiments in his film that fit Muñoz's favored descriptions, including a transhistorical homage to a genre in his title, *Pulp Fiction*. Furthermore, an aspect of Julien's film that receives among the most extended discussions by José Muñoz is the film's indication of "the compositional influence of Mapplethorpe's photography" (68): "Perfectly chiseled black male bodies, framed in striking black-and-white monochromes, occupy the central dream sequences of the film . . . [though Julien] is rewriting the Mapplethorpe scene by letting these men relate to each other's bodies and not just the viewer's penetrating gaze" (69). At stake in this particular claim—that Isaac Julien signifies on Mapplethorpe, using his aesthetic but revising his gaze—is a nest of issues hotly debated by respondents to Mapplethorpe, especially by black gay critics Isaac Julien and Kobena Mercer. Julien and Mercer, in "Race, Sexual Politics and Black Masculinity," indict Mapplethorpe for "objectifying" black nude men in his photography, showing himself, as José Muñoz puts this complaint, "as the exploitative author who sees these black bodies only as meat." Issues for reading Tarantino, I suggest, arise from these critiques. For Tarantino's film offers the kind of visual-pleasure quagmires that Robert Mapplethorpe's photography creates. *Pulp*, for its part, like Mapplethorpe's photography, reveals these quagmires most profoundly where it brings "black" and "queer" into congress. To be sure, if Mapplethorpe, who also produced a famous series of s/m photographs (largely of white queer men), is guilty of exploiting black men's *beauty* for the camera, using in some ways the visual codes of gay pornography, is it any wonder Tarantino would be charged with racist homophobia in his depiction of a black man being raped?

In their essay, Mercer and Julien explain how the beauty of black men —in and through the Mapplethorpe images—serves to debase them, how their beauty comes back to them (and to their viewers) in the form of violence and aggression (again, figure 4). If this criticism of beauty sounds familiar from feminist writings, it should be noted how directly Mercer and Julien draw on these materials. After they situate Mapplethorpe as a media star, "the prints of darkness," an artist with a fundamentally "conservative" aesthetic in "pursuit of perfection in photographic technique," "reworking [as he does] the old modernist tactic [of] 'shock the bourgeoisie,'" they accuse Mapplethorpe's black nude photographs of "fetishistic structure" (figure 8).[16] For example, "When Phillip [one of Mapplethorpe's models] is placed on a pedestal," he, like the others, "is 'sacrificed' on the altar of some aesthetic ideal to affirm the sovereign mastery of the white man's gaze"(147; see figure 9). In some of these nudes, moreover, "the camera cuts away like a knife, allowing the viewer's gaze to scrutinize 'the goods' with fetishistic attention to detail" (148) by means of which "each fragment seduces the eye to ever more intense fascination" (149). This fascination even "spreads itself" over the surface of skin, since, say these authors, "the racial fetish of skin colour and skin texture is 'the most visible of fetishes.' " They proceed to add, in a way that further speaks to Tarantino's scene, that "the fascination with black leather . . . suggests [that this leather is] a simulacrum of black skin, an outward extension of an intense curiosity and fascination with black skin among white people" (150).

Given these views, one can see why, when discussing Mapplethorpe, Mercer and Julien end up making so many references to pornography — here "gay porn and the male pin up genre" (144). But by their essay's end, these critics take a turn. Mercer and Julien cannot help but recognize a problem with their argument that leads to their "ambivalence," at the least. Unlike straight women feminists who can plausibly claim, or so it seems, that they do not find the images of women that they criticize attractive or seductive for themselves, Mercer and Julien must confess that Mapplethorpe's beautiful black nude men speak to them and also seduce them. As one of these writers admits at the close: "In revising this essay I'm . . . more aware of how the ambivalence cuts both ways, that I am also equally implicated in the fascination these images arouse and the fantasies and pleasures they offer" (152). This implication in fascination would emerge rather boldly for Julien in his short s/m film "The Attendant," which was released in 1993, one year before *Pulp*. Ten minutes long, this film depicts a black man's sexual fantasies of sadomasochism (in which he alternately plays top and bottom) with a white man, fantasies prompted by a painting on the wall of the museum where he works: F. A. Biard's 1840 abolitionist painting "The Slave Trade (Scene on the Coast of Africa)."

Strikingly, however, more than causing these writers to probe and explain in print the relation of Mapplethorpe's visual violence to their attractions (which, to be fair, they do in some ways), their ambivalence toward Mapplethorpe leads them to find new ways to redeem him from their own charges. Or perhaps historical circumstances change, which then allow for this new embrace. In any event, one can see from the writings and cultural productions of Julien, Mercer, and Muñoz that as they start

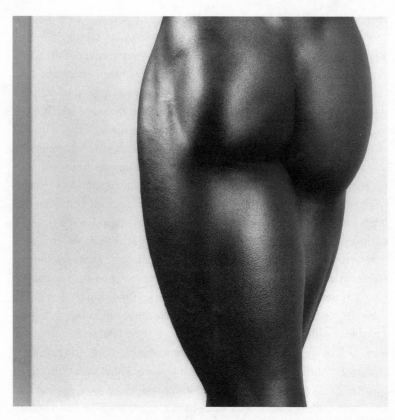

8. *Derrick Cross, 1983*, copyright The Robert Mapplethorpe
Foundation, courtesy Art + Commerce Anthology.

9. *Phillip Prioleau, 1979*, copyright The Robert Mapplethorpe
Foundation, courtesy Art + Commerce Anthology.

to link Robert Mapplethorpe more and more to themselves (through the signs of "gay artist" and "AIDS"), they trust his dangers more and more, or find ways to rescript the debasement they initially seemed to discover in his work. One can see these reassessments in Mercer's later essays: "Skin Head Sex Thing: Racial Difference and the Homoerotic Imaginary" (1991); and "Looking for Trouble" (1991). Mercer begins the former piece by repeating his confession from 1988 in even stronger terms. "We were fascinated," he admits again, "by the beautiful bodies" in Mapplethorpe's photographs—"shocked and disturbed . . . angered . . . [but] unable to make sense of our own implication in the emotions brought into play by Mapplethorpe's imaginary"—the fact that "the objectified black male [is] also an image of the object chosen by my own fantasies and erotic investments."[17] Still, in his reassessment of Mapplethorpe, Mercer argues for a "change of context," owing to Mapplethorpe's death, the Whitney Museum's retrospective of his work, and federal arts policies shaped by the right in response to Mapplethorpe. Mercer admits, "the subversive dimension [of Mapplethorpe's photography] was underplayed in my earlier analysis . . . [I] minimized the homosexual specificity of Mapplethorpe's eroticism"—and, as Mercer later adds, the "specificity of Robert Mapplethorpe's authorial identity as a gay artist" with "a sense of humor that might otherwise escape the sensibilities of nongay or antigay viewers" (197). Mercer, intriguingly, also compares Mapplethorpe's effects to those of Jean Genet (who embraced the Black Panthers, Mercer reminds us, and their black leather), making, he claims, both Jean Genet and Robert Mapplethorpe "niggers with attitude" (210).

Importantly, moreover, for our assessment of Tarantino's film with its gangster-God, Mercer now appreciates the very "pedestalization" of black men that so initially offended him in Mapplethorpe. "Some of the men," Mercer writes, "who in all probability came from this [African American] underclass are elevated onto the pedestal of the transcendental Western aesthetic ideal."[18] Sounding even as if he is gingerly embracing debasement, Mercer states that "the over-valued genre of the fine art nude" is, in this way, usefully "'contaminated' by the connotative yield of racist fears and fantasies secreted into mass media stereotypes" (356). Mercer, that is, seems to imply that Mapplethorpe vengefully, and perhaps politically, pulps up art through black queer signs. Partly for this reason, Mercer takes extreme umbrage at the censorship Jesse Helms and others had begun to forge "on the new cultural grounds of 'offensiveness' to minorities," objecting to art that "'denigrates, debases, or reviles a person,

group, or class of citizens on the basis of race, creed, sex, handicap or national origin,'" though earlier Mercer and Julien themselves had objected
to this art on similar grounds (359).

Overall, however, what marks the turning point for Mercer and Julien,
making these writers newly emphasize the signifier "gay" in Robert Mapplethorpe as a "white (gay) male author" (Mercer's phrasing), is the photographer's death by AIDS. "It was the death of the author," Mercer states,
"and the sense of loss by which the AIDS crisis has affected all our lives,
that made me reread the subversive and deconstructive dimension of
Mapplethorpe's modernist erotica" (355–56). Given that many (all?) of
Mapplethorpe's black gay models died of AIDS (half of them before Mapplethorpe himself), Mercer deems Mapplethorpe's photographs of them
"*memento mori*," with "the intense emotional residue Barthes described
when he wrote about the photographs of his mother."[19] José Muñoz, too,
ends his essay by regarding *Black Book* (Mapplethorpe's book of black
male nudes) as "a mourning text," reminding us that "mourning [Langs-
ton] Hughes, [James] Baldwin, [Robert] Mapplethorpe, or the beautiful
men in *Black Book* is about mourning for oneself, for one's community,
for one's very history."[20]

Nevertheless, something is absent from these texts that invoke Roland
Barthes on photography and mourning. Missing is a summary or a recon-
sideration of Barthes's own remarkable tendency to theorize aesthetic attraction, or aesthetic pleasure, or aesthetic recognition, as a violent force.
This is a tendency in *Camera Lucida* that sometimes displaces beauty for
force as the heart of Barthes's aesthetic or makes beauty (and sorrow, too)
inseparable from the violence of attraction in and of itself. Before we turn
to Tarantino's pulp—and his telling use of cuts—it is helpful to investigate Barthes's implied theory of aesthetic woundings, a theory *Pulp Fiction* could be said to extend and, in some ways, revise.

The Force of Attraction: Roland Barthes's Aesthetic Woundings

Roland Barthes's passion for photography—in some respects, his Passion—uses a rhetoric of violence at its major junctures, especially as he
ties his love for certain photographs to his own suffering: "Each time I
would read something about Photography, I would think of some photograph I loved. . . . what you are seeing here [Barthes would say to him-
self] . . . makes you suffer. . . ."[21] On his way to presenting this connection between aesthetic attraction and suffering, Barthes, in a now familiar

postmodern gesture, claims that objectification, loss of self, and alienation are built into the act of being photographed. In this sense, the dilemma of Mapplethorpe's beautiful black nude men (or even Tarantino's framing of Marsellus) is not a special, politicized instance of violent intent, but is emblematic—really, allegorical—of a general aesthetic effect.

But what effect? Barthes in front of the camera, as he tells us, is a "passive victim, its *plastron*, as Sade would say"; "they [photographs and readers of photographs] turn me, ferociously, into an object, they put me at their mercy, at their disposal, classified in a file, ready for the subtlest deceptions" (14). (Barthes recalls that "in order to take the first portraits . . . the subject had to assume long poses under a glass roof in bright sunlight; to become an object made one suffer as much as a surgical operation," 13). This kind of language is echoed in Barthes's reference to the thing or person being photographed as a "target" (9); "the Photograph," he says, "creates my body or mortifies it, according to its caprice." Barthes is "captured" (11). "Invariably," he writes, "I suffer from a sensation of inauthenticity, sometimes of imposture (comparable to certain nightmares)." "The disturbance," he says, "is ultimately one of ownership. . . . to whom does the photograph belong?" (13). As a figure being photographed, Barthes is even pulled through the peephole of the camera, "the keyhole of the *camera obscura*," as he puts it: " 'the little hole' (*stenope*) through which [the photographer] looks, limits, frames, and perspectivizes when he wants to 'take' (to surprise)" (9–10). This particular rendering of a "taking"—by surprise, no less—makes the photograph resemble the "peephole" style of cover art on pulp paperbacks that draws the reader through its "keyhole."

Ultimately, more than the suffering posture of the one being photographed, Barthes is anxious to explore the passion of the readerly position. He wants to convey the forceful attractions that come to the eye that looks at a photograph, which is the view, the result of a view, through a camera's peephole. And so he takes his treatise down the path of attraction, trying to understand why he's compelled by certain photographs, especially by their details. "I decided . . . to take as a guide for my analysis the attraction I felt for certain photographs" (18); "I realized," writes Barthes, "that some [photographs] provoked tiny jubilations, as if they referred to a stilled center, an erotic or lacerating value buried in myself (however harmless the subject may have appeared)" (16). "I wanted to explore it [photography] not as a question (a theme) but as a wound," "keeping with me, like a treasure, my desire or my grief" (21).

These are somewhat odd and striking terms. Just as he joined his love of certain photographs to a sense of suffering (his passion for them), here Barthes brings erotic and lacerating values together in the photographs' peculiar provocations, making for a wound he might explore. If we did not know otherwise, we might think this was Mercer on the complex effects of a black male nude: something, he might say, that "referred to . . . an erotic or lacerating value buried in myself." Barthes, however, is talking in general about the effects of compelling, attractive photographic details; for this intriguing reason, he might regard Mercer's discussion of a Mapplethorpe photograph from *Black Book*, or my analysis of Tarantino's *Pulp*, as a powerful dramatization—almost a thematization—of his own general claims about aesthetic woundings.

Indeed, Barthes's seeming turn from the political to the formal and affective dimensions of photography deepens as he further explains his "attractions." Here is Barthes himself on his liking and his loving: one he calls *studium* (later glossed as "liking"), the other he calls *punctum* (his violence-tinged term for "love" of a photographic detail). Political pictures of the war in Nicaragua are the context for his comments:

> The first [order of interest: "liking"] . . . refers to a . . . body of information: rebellion, Nicaragua, and all the signs of both: wretched un-uniformed soldiers, ruined streets, corpses, grief, the sun, and the heavy-lidded Indian eyes. Thousands of photographs consist of this field, and in these photographs I can, of course, take a kind of general interest, one that is even stirred sometimes, but in regard to them my emotion requires the rational intermediary of an ethical and political culture. What I feel about these photographs derives from an *average* affect ["liking"]. . . . [In Latin] it is *studium* . . . a kind of general, enthusiastic commitment, of course, but without special acuity. It is by *studium* that I am interested in so many photographs, whether I receive them as political testimony or enjoy them as good historical scenes. . . .
>
> The second [order of interest: "loving"] will break (or punctuate) the *studium*. . . . [T]his element . . . rises from the scene, shoots out of it like an arrow, and pierces me. A Latin word exists to designate this wound, this prick, this mark made by a pointed instrument: the word suits me all the better in that it also refers to the notion of punctuation. . . . This second element which will disturb the *studium* I shall therefore call *punctum*; for *punctum* is also: sting, speck, cut, little hole—and also a cast of the dice. A photograph's *punctum* is that accident which pricks

me (but also bruises me, is poignant to me).... [O]ccasionally ... a "detail" attracts me. I feel that its mere presence changes my reading, that I am looking at a new photograph, marked in my eyes with a higher value. This "detail" is the *punctum*. (25–27, 42)

At least two things are surprising here. First of all, we find the language of force (even violence) once again. Words like "break," "shoots out like an arrow," "pierces," "wound," "prick," "disturb," and "bruise" lead up to the word "attracts"—all of which elucidate "loving" a "detail." Second, political Barthes sounds bored. Never have wretched, ruined streets, corpses, and grief seemed so banal, rising to the level of an only "general" interest, an "average" affect, requiring (kiss of death) "the rational intermediary" of the political. By contrast, *punctum* excites by marking (punctuating) information. Somewhere between a decorative brooch and the pin-pricks decorative brooches make, the *punctum* is a detail whose allure is its "sting," or even its "cut," pricking and bruising its viewer as much as "disturbing" its relay of "information." In other words, for Barthes, at a visual level, "political testimony" or "good historical scenes" are not moving in and of themselves. (They are not "traversed, lashed, striped" by something which "attracts or distresses me.")

To be sure, a *punctum* breaks into a *studium* but does not replace it, just as a fascinating jewel punctures cloth (and can even overwhelm it) but does not replace clothes. The *punctum*, importantly, is "an addition" (55). It is even a "subtle beyond," "a blind field"—"as if the image launched desire beyond what it permits us to see" (59). Rather than leaving history or politics behind, however, the *punctum* opens a cut through which we may all the more passionately return to them. In a photograph of Queen Victoria, for example, Barthes discovers that "the *punctum* fantastically 'brings out' the Victorian nature (what else can one call it?) of the photograph, it endows this photograph with a blind field" (57). It makes one desire to follow the picture beyond the frame, into that history. In fact, when it is present, *punctum* so connotes "high value" to its viewer that it redirects the whole—"overwhelms the entirety of my reading," as Barthes puts it (42, 49). Figures 10 and 11, and Barthes's captions to them, illustrate how *puncta* (crossed arms and a child's finger bandage, for example) are details that overwhelm one's reading of a photograph. They also indicate the personal nature of a *punctum*-like effect ("the *punctum*, for me, is the second boy's crossed arms . . ."). That is, Barthes imagines that different spectators will receive different *puncta*, since in his view (one I find

10. *Savorgnan De Brazza, 1882*, Nadar. "The *punctum*, for me, is the second boy's crossed arms . . ."

11. *Idiot Children in an Institution, New Jersey, 1924*, Lewis H. Hine. "I dismiss all knowledge, all culture . . . I see only the boy's huge Danton collar, the girl's finger bandage . . ."

only partially persuasive), the photographer cannot will a *punctum* into being. (Tarantino, I will claim, to a certain degree intends to and succeeds in directing key visual arrows to the eye.)[22]

But if we are struck by the detail of a bandage, what do we lose? What is sacrificed because of a *punctum*? When something rises arrow-like out of a photograph to strike Barthes's eyes, his is not the only wound. The *studium*—the domain of cultural information, historical scenes, and political testimony—is also, in some way, according to Barthes, "broken" and "disturbed," to some extent sacrificed to the *punctum*'s stinging allure. Or put another way: if Barthes sacrifices something of himself when he receives the *punctum* (more on this in just a moment), the photograph, strangely, falls on its own sword, wounding its own *studium* (its relay of messages and cultural information) by the very arrow it sends out as *punctum* ("I dismiss all knowledge, all culture," Barthes informs us, "I see only the boy's huge Danton collar, the girl's finger bandage"). In reference to this photograph, "Idiot Children in an Institution," Barthes would have us think that the details of the bandage or the large shirt collar wound the photograph's information about the children or institutions.

But how does a detail come to wound? How much damage can a detail do? The *punctum* does two significant things, according to Barthes: (1) it draws inordinate attention to itself, diverting attention away from the *studium*; the detail is diverting ("I dismiss all knowledge, all culture . . ."); (2) the *punctum* wounds the act of naming its effect; the detail is dumbfounding: "What I can name cannot really prick me. The incapacity to name is a good symptom of disturbance. . . . The effect [of *punctum*] is certain but unlocatable, it does not find its sign, its name; it is sharp and yet lands in a vague zone of myself . . . it cries out in silence. Odd contradiction: a floating flash" (51, 53). A floating flash, a poignant haze, signals something valuable tied to a loss. It's as if you're made to say: "I cannot name what I so value here." And the more one values a particular photograph (because it launches *punctum*), the more one feels what it means to lose a naming of it.

Barthes feels this loss. For in part 2 of *Camera Lucida*, Barthes goes searching for a photograph of his deceased mother. In part 1 of his book, Barthes's "getting pricked" by something in a photograph was the sign of Barthes's "loving" something in that photograph. Now Barthes starts with loving his mother and, therefore, he tries to get pricked by her photograph. He wants to be wounded—by her photograph with a *punctum*, one by which he might not "recognize" his mother (at least not simply so) but actually "find" her. (Barthes finds his mother in a picture of a child: his mother at the age of five.)[23]

Here again, but differently, something political comes back into play, showing us how politics ("political testimony" and/or "good historical scenes") can be tied, in highly sophisticated ways, to the art of the detail— are themselves an art of the detail, in many circumstances. We see this political dynamic in Barthes, whatever he may claim, whatever may seem like Roland Barthes's discarding dull political testimony in favor of the sexy, exciting, and sometimes ill-bred *punctum*. In other words, we cannot forget the composite dynamics Barthes has specified for photographs that move him and also wound him. Indeed, as Barthes goes looking for a *punctum* in his photographs, for a mother-*punctum*, his search reveals a complicated politics of motherhood. This is how he puts it:

> [N]o more than I would reduce my family to the Family, would I reduce my mother to the Mother. Reading certain general studies, I saw that they might apply quite convincingly to my situation. . . . Thus I could understand my generality; but having understood it, invincibly

I escaped from it. In the Mother, there was a radiant, irreducible core: my mother. (75)

One begins strongly to suspect that Barthes is using some established political myth of the Mother, and also his politically keen critique of it, *in order to draw out* the photographic *punctum* that pierces this (general) political myth. For though he himself never puts it this way, Barthes uses *studium* ("a body of information" about the figure of the Mother) to draw out *punctum* that wounds *studium*. Or to say it slightly differently: Barthes's acute sense of the politics of Motherhood is absolutely crucial to drawing out the arrow that will wound it, producing "attraction," "adventure," "animation," and "excitement." For Barthes will register a photographic *punctum*, will himself be capable of perceiving *punctum*, only if it seems to wound the *studium* of Mother (which the picture of his mother-as-a-child would likely do). But here, it seems to me, is where we can see that wounding a *studium* can mean something more like layering it with stripes, lashing it with stripes, of different insights and ranging tonalities (since *punctum* is additive) and therefore can mean extending the *studium* in heretofore unforeseen ways (since *punctum*, says Barthes, "launches desire beyond what it permits us to see"). In relation to a photograph of Queen Victoria, Barthes had said: "the *punctum* fantastically 'brings out' the Victorian nature . . . of the photograph." Now, with this photograph of his mother, one senses how the *punctum*, at least as Barthes presents it, creates a blind field. It creates the urge—or, in Barthes's case, matches his desire—to launch beyond the frame of even this photograph into the history of his mother, which is the history of her irreducibility. In this way, this *punctual* launch into her history does not destroy the *studium* of his mother's picture. Rather, it points toward a more extensive and richer possibility for a politics of motherhood—made of particular mothers (such as his) who surprise the very myth. In other words, the *punctum* opens up a wound that can speak to the hidden histories of the *studium*.

Furthermore, in spite of what Barthes may seem to say, quite a bit of naming, or at least analytical talking, does get done around a *punctum*. Barthes's own riveting discussions—even of the silencing effect of a *punctum*—speak to his need to discuss the highly textured, and in some cases layered, politics of disturbance. Barthes on expression:

Or again (for I am trying to express this truth) this [one photograph of my mother] was for me like the last music Schumann wrote before collapsing . . . I could not express this accord except by an infinite series of adjectives, *which I omit,* convinced however that this photograph collected all the possible predicates from which my mother's being was constituted. (70; emphasis mine)

Barthes, at the last, makes the photograph-with-*punctum* that so attracts him (and therefore supposedly wounds the act of political naming) sound as though it holds, in the form of a hiding, the history of his mother's particular being. (Attract, cut, hold.) Indeed, the cut of the *punctum* contains all the adjectives and predicates that make fascinations (in which I include political poignancies) hard to convey. Never has the luxury of a detail looked so necessary.

Pulp Punctum: Tucked in the Cuts of Tarantino's Dirty Scenes

Quentin Tarantino has his own peculiar ways of making his viewer confront aesthetic woundings, and the subtle politics emerging from them. In fact, these ways recall those of Barthes, Morrison, and Mapplethorpe all at once. With a scene of rape that compels our attention, a scene itself of compelled relations, Tarantino can thematize the force of compelling dirty details on a cinema screen. Being visually struck by a rape, along with other sights, viewers find themselves assaulted in the eyes, whether humorously or seriously so (or both at once), whether they would like to be ravished or not. This is the violence of visual—and other—attractions that Tarantino explores.[24]

And this is the benefit of thematizing cutting, as Tarantino's film also seems to do. Making the opening of a black man's body (through the cutting act of rape) underscore the formal and narrative opening of the camera's cuts in Tarantino's film, as I earlier explained, Tarantino's movie can powerfully thematize histories, or relations, or even information hidden in the cuts of bodies and films. The history (in the sense of a historical phenomenon) most directly thematized in *Pulp Fiction* (a film about a genre) is the role of pulp, the importance of pulp, in American entertainment (whether one considers paperbacks or movies). As *Pulp Fiction* itself proceeds to demonstrate, when you open up the somewhat elided history of pulp, you pull up out of hiding (out of the basement, in the case of this film) queer sexualities (such as s/m) that are a source of pulp; and, perhaps, surprisingly, drag out into view iconic scenes from American history (white on black same-sex rape) that remind us that American racial relations are themselves a source for pulp—and queer pulp at that. In fact, it appears that Tarantino intensely layers this scene by giving what could be a gay porn scenario a strangely evocative historical context (with the Confederate flag on the wall, the Mason-Dixon Pawnshop name, and the hillbillies using "nigger" for Marsellus). No wonder Tarantino's film can feel like work by Morrison, in this specific sense: both these artists tuck (and almost hide) intense political histories and sorrows inside aggressive joking and dirty scenes of force. Both take the risk of crafting "nigger jokes" that require of their readers a composite stance in the face of their tonalities. "Can't you take a joke?," their texts seem to say, knowing full well that to "take" the comic effects of their narratives is to be open to emotional combinations of unusual sorts.

For all of this family resemblance, however, Tarantino risks being read by critics as someone shaming blacks (and gays). As I have said, I think there is something quite right about this reading, and something quite right about Tarantino's scenes of shaming that operate in ways similar to the strong embrace of debasement in works by Morrison and Mapplethorpe. Obviously, the point of comparing Tarantino to Morrison is not to sanitize his particular aesthetic but to underscore the breadth and dare of hers. And, as I have urged, we might also widen our sense of what the phrase "black gay male . . . productions" could include. This is precisely why José Muñoz aids our understanding. His appreciative reading of *Looking for Langston* gives definitions of this phrase that put Tarantino into novel light—a light that reflects back onto the phrase and the room inside the phrase for unexpected twists. For Quentin Tarantino can be seen as "(re)telling elided histories" of pulp fictions surrounding the signs of black and queer, through his "densely layered, aestheticized and politicized workings" of form and story in his film. He, too, has his own "mode of history writing" in *Pulp Fiction*, using not only a "montage of attractions" and "emotional combination" but also, quite directly, "historical filaments that refer to different times" and that "uncloak" "different histories." I would even emphasize, leaning toward Barthes, that Tarantino layers historical *studium* in the rape scene with stripes of different insights and ranging tonalities, as I am going to show.

Before we return to the rape, however, I want to make a few more detailed observations that link *Pulp Fiction* to the conceptual interests of Morrison, Barthes, and Mapplethorpe. First of all, one can easily see that Tarantino's film, in ways Barthes might appreciate, is formally thematizing the movie-camera's violence. The camera at times acts like a gun, giving some shots the feel of a stick-up—sometimes of a character, sometimes of the viewer—making one feel one's been shot in the eye or taken hostage at camera-point. The moment when Vince by mistake shoots Marvin, in the face no less, making the spectator feel the splatter, is perhaps *Pulp*'s most dramatic example of this dynamic. Thus we are made aware, as Barthes was aware in still photography, of the camera's ability both to objectify and wound what it shoots, on the one hand, and, on the other, to arrest and wound the one who looks. In *Pulp Fiction*, both these propensities are worked out in interesting ways on Marsellus. In the scene where we meet him, Marsellus, described in a previous scene as "black and bald," is shot from behind, the camera squarely focused on the back of his head (black and bald) as he is ordering Butch to throw a fight. We do not see his face. Instead, befitting his role as controller of other men's fates, we are given Old Testament–like revelations of his "back parts" (Exodus 33: 20–23): namely, his head.[25] Marsellus is clearly positioned in this scene as a gangster and a god. The camera even "pedestalizes" Marsellus, as Kobena Mercer might note, in a way reminiscent of a Mapplethorpe photograph—especially since the camera holds steady on Marsellus for the length of several minutes. In fact, the view produced of Marsellus in this scene—the evocation of his mightiness—in some ways resembles a back-of-the-head shot Mapplethorpe made famous for evoking power (see figure 12). And yet, at the same time, a flesh-colored band-aid worn on the back of Marsellus's head, which underscores his blackness, gives the strange impression that the hovering camera has somehow wounded the back of his skull with its penetrating gaze—or at least over-zealously caressed him with its violent look. Later, in the scene of the rape itself, the camera pulls in tight on Marsellus just as he is chosen to be the one assaulted, making it look, in this striking shot, as if the camera itself has selected him. As one would expect, Marsellus's eyes open wide, with shock and protest, miming the viewer's reaction to numerous nonconsensual sights in the film. Still more intriguing, the camera literally turns Marsellus upside down right before he is raped, visually announcing the violence about to befall both his person and his position. As viewers will recall, in the scene that leads to the rape in the basement, Marsellus is finally seen as something other than a powerful backside, especially as he crosses the street with his coffee and donuts in hand. After Butch rams Marsellus with his vehicle, Marsellus is shown, upside down, on the hood of the car, by means of a full camera shot to the face, as if the camera's catching him is prelude to his rape.

12. *Ken Moody, 1984*, copyright The Robert Mapplethorpe
Foundation, courtesy Art + Commerce Anthology.

The camera's capture of Marsellus in these scenes, making him first an all-powerful force, then a victim of rape, creates a link to a novel like *Sula*—and not just because he is a penetrated man. Like Toni Morrison, Tarantino situates black men partly inside and partly outside of capitalism. Specifically, Tarantino represents the drug world (a staple of pulp fictions)—which in part results from the black unemployment Morrison depicts—allowing him to represent a black male lumpenproletariat boss in the parallel capitalist world of the crime ring. Such an alternative world could be seen as an upside-down world (in 1994) in which a black man sits atop a financial empire (an idea which his Roman name reinforces). What this positioning of Marsellus can demonstrate (underscored formally by the camera's violence) is his vulnerability, at any moment, to historical pulp fictions circulating inside our culture: the established violence of cultural codes that surrounds American racial relations, making a man not a boss but a "nigger" in a matter of moments. These available historical codes—pulp fictions in their own right—haunt any black man on a pedestal, whether he is filmed stilled by Robert Mapplethorpe (figure 9) or put into motion by Quentin Tarantino.

Tarantino's camera causes further violence in ways whose effect on tone recall *Sula*. In Morrison's fiction, one is struck by how she undercuts the sentimental feelings she herself builds up (dramatically and lyrically) by striking acts of violence: mothers dousing sons, who are messing up their pants, with flammable fuel and striking a match with maternal love; a daughter watching her mother burn, fascinated by the flames. These scenes of violence, some effected through dirty details and cutting forms of humor, allow a certain sentimental thread to snake through Morrison, buying her the right to speak of love or sorrow without losing edge. Tarantino has his version of this strategy. Undermining standard visual pleasure in his film—even turning beautiful Uma Thurman into a green, vomiting corpse in her near-death scene—Tarantino's aggressive camera clears a space for a kind of remarkably tender (and hilariously campy) domesticity to take firm hold among its couples ("Honey Bun" and "Pumpkin"; Lance and his overly pierced wife, whom he refers to as "Honey"; Butch and his girlfriend, whom he calls "sugar pop" and sometimes "lemon pie"). Men who are determined to please their women—who are fearful of letting them down—drive major stretches of Tarantino's *Pulp*. This mix of tones—the sentimental, even the beautiful, with the violent—forged through a camera launching arrows at the eye is critical to the film's embrace of pulp.

13. The Gimp, *Pulp Fiction* (1994).

Keeping in mind Tarantino's taste for disturbing kinds of visual pleasure, we now return to the scene of the rape and all that follows from it in Tarantino's narrative. This scene has an enigmatic detail, at least for most of Tarantino's viewers: a walking dirty detail that attracts our surprise: a figure that its captors call The Gimp, referring, presumably, to some form of woundedness hidden from our eyes (The Gimp, intriguingly, walks just fine). What has wounded him? Where is he hurt? What is his relation to his hillbilly captors, one of whom is dressed as a security guard (which makes this latter figure seem a member of the law—corrupt Southern law)? The blackened Gimp looks as if he had escaped from a Mapplethorpe photograph (see figure 13). Not the photographs of Robert Mapplethorpe's black nude men; rather, another kind of Mapplethorpe photograph, featuring, prominently, black leather figures (see figure 14). In Tarantino's film, this Mapplethorpe-reminiscent animated icon is clothed in a kind of black leather skin—skin-tight and all-encompassing—with gloves, boots, and full-on hood. This is the perfect wedding, maybe even mixed marriage, between queer cloth and jet-black skin. (Mercer, we recall, regards black leather as, in the eyes of whites, simulating black skin.) Whether this outfit is put on or forced on (that is to say, compelled or not), we are never told. The Gimp just giggles in ways that seem calculated to unnerve, after he's been led on a leash to the room where Butch and Marsellus are bound to their chairs and indecorously trussed with red-ball gags. Butch and Marsellus express as much puzzlement, at least as much as one can convey with a fierce tilt of one's head and eyes, as

14. *Brian Ridley and Lyle Heeter, 1979*, copyright The Robert Mapplethorpe Foundation, courtesy Art + Commerce Anthology.

viewers likely feel to encounter such a figure on the screen in this moment. What is this riddling Mapplethorpe composite—a figure blackened by the cloak of queerness, shrouded but announcing some violent submerged attraction—doing here? It is as if the film were rehearsing as a joke a more serious arrow it will offer to the eye. That is, courtesy of this striking image, the camera, already, before it shows the rape, points to a hidden history of wounds (The Gimp's own history in the hillbillies' basement) and to a stock figure who peoples the worlds of queer paperbacks and, later, gay porn (not to mention Mapplethorpe's stylized photography). Therefore, slyly, the camera is pointing to unspoken attractions, those circulating in some way between the rednecks and The Gimp, suggesting that a history of attractions may be hiding in a (zippered) cut. The Gimp's zippered mouth, shutting off his speech, keeps him from speaking about his situation, if he were inclined to. Strikingly, the audience, for its own part, invariably laughs at the sight of The Gimp. There is a tense comic excitement to seeing how this set of incongruous characters—hillbillies, queer-looking s/m slave, white rebellious boxer, and moneyed black drug god—will end up consorting with each other. The answer is that they (con)sort historically.

For many viewers, the visual power of Marsellus's rape comes from, even as it points to, a history of racial codes that lie in wait like traps to be sprung. By "racial codes" I mean stereotypes and semiotic signs (whether positive or negative) by which we are made or asked to see "race" in American life. These racial codes have intricate histories, being no less crude (in the sense of pulp fictions) for having often long and complicated developments. The brilliant effect of Tarantino's film is to spring such a trap, a racial trap, so that we may see it as a form of hiddenness—see it as a history of racialized pulp fictions that is intimate with American entertainments, yet, at times, occluded from view until it springs forth.[26] In essence, by the way both Tarantino's *puncta* and his cuts are structured in and around this central scene, we glimpse the hidden history of a crude racial code, which at any moment can leap into view and cause a total turnaround of personal fate. (The black boss, Marsellus, ruler of his world, falls through the Mason-Dixon trap of the pawnshop to its basement.) With the anal rape, Tarantino hits us in the eyes with a reduction (a crude racial code), which has a full (if, here, hidden) history. *Punctum* is drawing its arrow from a massive and traumatic body of cultural information— a *studium* field, which is powerfully summoned as we are pricked. The camera's pricking of the spectator's eye is announcing something hidden on a very large scale: America's history of sexed race relations, especially white men's violent passion for black male bodies.[27]

Indeed, the tilting of queer codes toward racial ones in the pulpy composite of The Gimp keeps the unsettling note of attraction (even entertainment and humor) alive in the scene's pastiche of brutal clips. All the more so when The Gimp is "lynched." Viewers will recall that as Butch is escaping unnoticed from the rapists, who are in the next room, he punches The Gimp, who is chained to a pipe. The mysterious strung-up figure in black is immediately hanged, left by Butch to dangle as a reminiscent image from American history—a hung black body— though surely queerly so. Reminiscent for this scene (and the scene of the hillbillies raping Marsellus) are the criss-crossing dramas of attractions imagined, falsified, denied, yet enacted in the historical lynchings that were often photographed as communal entertainments, as David Marriott informs us in his essay " 'I'm gonna borrer me a Kodak': Photography and Lynching." What is hard to "see" in these photographs of lynchings, though its presence seems duly captured by these acts of violence, is the passion, murderous in intensity, that the crowds feel for the bodies that they sexualize. The crowds repay the attractions they imagine have spurred the rapes (they have also imagined) with an attraction of their own. They want black flesh, want to inspect and possess its sex. Marriott writes of a lynching that was photographed:

> A hot August night in Marion, Indiana. 1930. Accused of rape and murder, a young black man stands—a bloody mass—on the courthouse lawn. There's a noose around his neck. The mob surrounds him: thousands of people baying. Above him, the bodies of Thomas Shipp and Abram Smith hang from the trees. . . . "To think they wanted me that bad!" [writes the man who escaped this lynching].
>
> [W]hite men, and women, demand a keepsake, a memento mori: toes, fingers, or—most highly prized—a black penis, a black scrotum.[28]

In Pulp Fiction, the hillbillies want to get inside a black man. They choose Marsellus to penetrate first, not white Butch. And we are struck, pricked in the eye, by the action of their violent possession.

Still, this explanation may not account for all the shades of attraction to this rape. One may be struck by the sight of interracial same-sex penetration given its relative rarity in either Hollywood or independent cinema—or, conversely, given its prevalence in gay pornography, which Tarantino is clearly drawing on. In either case, one may be struck precisely by its visual allure, its power to launch the sexual fantasies of its spectator in many, and many different kinds of, directions—as Isaac Julien and Kobena Mercer experienced with the Mapplethorpe photographs that disturbed, angered, and appealed to them. (Gay) spectators in another era often found an erotic charge—and a launch for fantasies of outright sexiness—in the often violent images surrounding homosexual characters on the screen.[29] (Sometimes these homosexuals were violent; and often they were the objects of violence—to the extreme.) Spectators now, in films and photographs, may find themselves attracted—against their will or not, but also to their pleasure—to the varied images of black/white interracial same-sex sex that jump to strike the eye. Black queer writers Robert Reid-Pharr and the late Gary Fisher (see my introduction) would also remind us of the enormously complicated circuits of desire and attraction in interracial same-sex fantasies. Black men seeking to be tenderly or not so tenderly fucked by white men may, with a range of emotions, contemplate "sleeping with the enemy" (Reid-Pharr's phrase).[30] Or, as Gary Fisher writes of himself: "I haven't read Hegel yet. Why haven't I read Hegel when I'm somewhat in love with this? I'm afraid to know. . . . So I want to be a slave, a sex slave and a slave beneath another man's (a white man or a big man, preferably a big white man) power. Someone more aware of the game (and the reality of it) than myself. I want to relinquish responsibility and at the same time give up all power. . . . This made Roy (Southerner, white, 40+ man) attractive to me—not wholly this."[31] These thoughts should remind us of the myriad ways the rape could attract a viewer's attention.

One should even wonder if Quentin Tarantino, through Marsellus's rape, is teasing viewers with a history of hidden interracial attractions that emerge precisely as submerged in a culture that pretends these attractions are not taboo. (This is a tease Tarantino returns to in *Jackie Brown*, 1997.) For in *Pulp Fiction*, he withholds any congress at all between the members of the only two interracial couples in his film: Mia and Marsellus, Bonnie and Jimmie. For all the other couples on the screen, their domestic tenderness is borne out by their fervent interactions, their intensely shared space, their reciprocal traumas worked out with each other, or their lovemaking. "Honey Bun" and "Pumpkin" are joined at the hip, from their cosy, criminal, coffee-klatch chats at the film's beginning to their stick-up and Mexican standoff at the end; drug-dealer Lance and his wife scramble frantically in their pajamas to find the needle for Mia's antidote; Butch, still sweat-stained from his boxing match, gives his girlfriend "oral pleasure." In stark contrast, Mia/Marsellus and Jimmie/Bonnie are barely seen together in a single frame of film, leaving us to picture their relations as tucked in the cuts between scenes that we are never shown. Mia, who is white, shares with Vincent (also white) detailed conversations about expensive milkshakes and a Samoan man's access to her feet; next, she shares with Vincent her retro dancing moves in those same bare feet; only then to share with him her near-death experience from using his drugs (through which he gets up close to her breastbone). Mia, however, is only glimpsed with her husband, Marsellus, whom she barely touches or looks at in passing. Jimmie and Bonnie (white and black respectively) are pictured for a mere split-second in an imaginary scene that never happens. These submerged relations of the interracial couples make the rape the film's only moment of interracial sexual touching—when white skin touches black skin—never mind the film's sole moment of any kind of interracial sex. The rape, in this respect, is the wound that releases the kind of contact the film is coyly hiding precisely in its cuttings. And so the issue of attraction to violence keeps getting turned by this film in the direction of the violence (the bodily invasion) that may be embedded in being attracted—even to an image on a cinema screen. This is what I read as the film's sophisticated way of exploring the value of its dirty details.

Two significant points emerge from what I have so far examined and said. First, we should notice how certain *puncta* in *Pulp* are planned. Contrary to Barthes's pronouncements, Tarantino's *puncta* are in no way accidental. They are planned and they are crude. They are planned to be crude (in the sense of "raw"). In fact, they're pulp, offering us the spectacle of a pulp *punctum*: a pulpy image that is striking to the eye. Barthes himself understands this allure, for he informs us: "the *punctum* shows no preference for morality or good taste: the *punctum* can be ill-bred" (43). Second, one pulp *punctum* in particular (the rape of Marsellus) plays a central role in opening the camera's cuts to reveal the film's own debate about whether pulp can have redeeming value. Tethered to this question is another query: can the viewer's sight of rape, and, more importantly, the history of racial codes that surrounds it, be redeemed? And why does this seemingly uncompromising film even mess with redemption? Does *Pulp* bend the very concept of redemption as dramatically as Morrison does in *Sula* or as Genet bends grace in *Querelle*?

In a sense, the dual debates about pulp's redeeming value and about redeeming pulp take place all along in the film's tug and pull between its offering of its *puncta* (its often dirty details) and its flirtation with the message of redemption. I say flirtation, because until the film cuts are opened to reveal two hit men debating the question of redemption, the issue of redemption is only hinted at. Really, it is pointed at, through visual arrows and pulpy details. This kind of pointing appears in one of the first planned *puncta* that Tarantino launches. I am referring to the optical shock (the pulpy *punctum*) of Mia's "resurrection" through the hypodermic needle thrust into her chest. Nearly dead from an overdose of heroin, Mia is saved when her escort for the evening, Vincent Vega, in a riotously comical scene, undertakes the frightful stab required to revive her. This is an ill-bred arrow to our eyes, and, for many viewers, it is probably unforgettable. "Showing no preference for morality or good taste," it is the *punctum*, as Barthes would predict, that draws our interest solely to itself (as do the details of the hastily drawn red magic-markered spot on Mia's chest; the berserk manner of her coming to life; and the way she holds her long-fingered hands to the side of her face as she mutters "something"). Yet, though this image, this optical stab, is surely not reducible to a set message, it vaguely points at some issue of redemption. What are we to make of Mia's coming back from death?

To give this question of redemption its due, we need to notice how even certain narrative scenes, with dirty details encircling the anus, touch on redemption: specifically, on redeeming time, in the sense of taking time, or even history, back. Butch's taking back his watch, for instance—and the story spun around it. This treasured heirloom—passed down over successive generations, marked by key historical events in the form of famous wars—is given back to Butch by Captain Koons. Koons says to Butch: "It was your great-granddaddy's war watch. . . . [W]hen he had done his duty, he . . . took the watch off his wrist and put it in an ol' coffee can. And in that can it stayed 'til your grandfather Dane Coolidge was called upon by his country to go overseas and fight the Germans once again." And so on, until Koons comes to Butch's father: "This watch was on your Daddy's wrist when he was shot down over Hanoi. . . . So he hid it in the one place he knew he could hide somethin'.' His ass. Five long years, he wore this watch up his ass. Then when he died of dysentery . . . I hid this uncomfortable hunk of metal up my ass for two years. . . . And now, little man, I give the watch to you." Critics (and many viewers, I suspect) treat the details of this scene as a characteristic Tarantino diversion. They seem to go nowhere. (Anthony Lane in *The New Yorker* complains: "It's a joke, but hardly a good joke; and, having written it, Tarantino has to shoehorn the damn thing into his picture whether it fits or not.")[32] However, the detail of Captain Koons's name, with its racial slur, seems suggestive, as do the details of the hiding itself: hiding time in an anal space, hiding time and historical wounds in a Koons's cavity. What can they mean?[33]

Outlandishly, they point. These dirty details, which so bizarrely imagine hiding and then presenting historical time, as if time can be taken back, point toward the racialized scene in the Mason-Dixon Pawnshop. Pawnshops suggest redemption quite directly; they are the scene of a potential buying back. What, if anything, then, is redeemed in the pawnshop basement? Can Marsellus, like Mia, be saved? Can Butch restore himself to Marsellus? Can (one's) history be redeemed?

One could say that Marsellus has been wearing this question on his head, throughout the film, in the form of a detail both distracting and dumbfounding: the band-aid he wears on the back of his skull (figure 6).[34] The detail of the band-aid troubles his omnipotence, even before we see Marsellus brought down to earth in the scene of the rape. The black man's band-aid announces, while hiding—as band-aids always do—some kind of a wound. Can this wound be (ad)dressed? To be sure, some kind of *question* of redemption seems to form here. The film seems to shift from Old Testament vengeance (Marsellus pursuing Butch for revenge) to a focus on grace. The transitional point occurs when Marsellus, after Butch has rescued him, forgives Butch his sins (another central meaning, of course, of "redemption"). Butch inquires in the sparest of theological lingoes: "So we're cool?" "We're cool," says Marsellus. As proof of the pact, Butch rides off from the pawnshop on "Grace," a motorcycle chopper he steals from the rapists.

But can the dirty scene of a black man's rape, and the history of racial codes that surrounds it, be redeemed? Or does this dirtiness itself have a value? *Pulp*'s post-rape scenes probe these questions. In many respects, the film starts again, after the narrative end of the film (not the film's end) culminates with Butch's riding off on Grace. Now, lost details from earlier scenes come back into view, as the movie opens its cuts for our inspection. Two important images earlier withheld from us circle around the issue of redemption. One concerns a near-miss by bullets. The other is the *punctum* of a gunshot to the head.

The first restored scene takes us back to the chronological start of the narrative. Two hit men, Vince and Jules, have gone to collect a debt for their boss, Marsellus Wallace. In doing so, they kill two young white men and recover, as ordered, Marsellus's treasure. When Tarantino returns to this scene (after the rape), we are given missing details. Now we are shown how, after the hit men kill the second of two young men, a third young man, who was hiding in the bathroom, springs from hiding and shoots at Jules (a fitting allegory of hiding in a cut). He misses Jules completely, in spite of the barrage of shots he fires. Jules immediately pronounces a message:

Jules: "We should be fuckin' dead!"

Vince: "Yeah, we were lucky."

Jules: "That shit wasn't luck. That shit was something else. . . . That was . . . divine intervention. . . . God came down from heaven and stopped the bullets."

Vince: "I think we should be going now."

Jules: ". . . . Don't blow this shit off! What just happened was a fuckin' miracle!"

Vince: ". . . . Do you wanna continue this theological discussion in the car, or at the jailhouse with the cops?"

Taking the one remaining young man with them in the car (a young black man, shaken up from the killings), they do, of course, continue discussing. Vincent sees an accident where Jules sees a message—a sign from God that he should retire ("and walk the earth . . . like Caine in 'Kung Fu'"). But just as Vincent turns to include the young black man in the question of this message—"C'mon Marvin. You gotta have an opinion. Do you think God came down from Heaven and stopped the bullets?"—the car hits a bump and Vincent's .45 goes off. An ill-bred *punctum* (to put it mildly), a very dirty detail, violently hits us in the eyes. "I just accidentally shot Marvin in the face." This is a detail earlier withheld from us. Now that it is offered, we cannot forget it. It is a *punctum* that disrupts a message and attracts the spectator's interest to itself—the message of the miracle, for now, is put on hold.

The narrative is literally diverted from here into further channels of further hidden details, many rather pulpy, as we watch Jules and Vincent rush, with the help of Mr. Wolf, to hide dead Marvin from the eyes of the law, though not from the eyes of Tarantino's viewer. Again, by means of a dirty detail (a gunshot to the head), we are being made to see inside a cut—in different senses (formally, thematically) that underscore each other. While we are located inside a film cut, we are now seeing what flows from a cut (a massive wound to a black man's head): the blood and bits of skull that Vince and Jules must clean (from the car, their clothes, and also their hair). And though we might resist it, we are likely seeing one possible face of our fascination, the boldly nonconsensual side of our interest in a dirty sight that bodily invades us. Dead preppy Marvin, rather clean-cut and suburban when we meet him, even becomes a dirty detail for the ear: Jimmie (played by Quentin Tarantino) keeps referring to shot-up Marvin (in a way that is likely calculated to jolt, or even wound us) as a "dead nigger" and to Jimmie's home as "dead nigger storage," forming a second aggressive "nigger joke," in Morrison's phraseology (the rape was the first). Redemption for the matter of Marvin's shot-off face seems patently impossible. Vincent and Jules can't really clean the mess ("just get the big stuff," says Mr. Wolf); they surely can't undo it; they can only hide it—with the help of Jimmie's and Bonnie's (that is to say, the hidden interracial couple's) bed linens. Yet the spectator sees this hiding. The spectator sees, inside these cuts opened up to our eyes, a black man's corpse that is hidden from view—all with the tone of jokey accomplishment. In fact, it is precisely our nonconsensual forced fascination with Marvin's splatter that has pulled us deeper into a problem: what kind of wounds can be undone or even addressed? Here there is no going back, on two counts: Vince cannot undo his action (his infliction of a wound)—only address it by means of other actions (he decides to hide it); we cannot go back to when we had not seen his action, his accidental shooting (given its forceful launch to our eyes), no matter how he decides to address it. Therefore, on both counts, thematically and formally, we are going forward into Tarantino's cuts from woundings there is simply no way to reverse.

Clearly, then, the shooting of Marvin in the face (and thus Tarantino's placement of this *punctum*) is not a simple puncture of the message of redemption, however dramatically it disrupts it. His arrow to our eyes (his arrows throughout) may actually be layering the question of redemption with new complications. For as we saw in Barthes, with the *studium* of Motherhood striped and lashed by the *punctum* of a photo, the art of the detail (as it was in Barthes) can be an unpredictable exploration of, a critical and luxurious extension of, some kind of cutting addition to the *studium*, one that stripes the *studium* with criss-crossing meanings and unexpected tones, and even wounding registers. This, I believe, is the kind of complication one may encounter in a Mapplethorpe photograph, especially in a photograph such as "Hooded Man" (see figure 4)—as viewers like Julien, Mercer, and Muñoz came to give voice to in their writings. They came to accept (though not comfortably) that beauty, mourning, debasement, violence, pornography, despair, objectification, and fascination could all inhere in an image that attracted, or even compelled and wounded, them. Tarantino lends this kind of complication to historical *studium* in his scene of rape, as I have said. Now I want to end by claiming that he makes the concept of redemption just as complex—and as bound to wounds that cannot in themselves ever be undone.

This might sound like a peculiarly dark view of redemption—"wounds that cannot ever be undone"—if it even sounds like redemption at all. But in a sly fashion, Tarantino's film actually elicits and makes newly visible a rather orthodox understanding of redemption as a composite, aggressive, indeed often violent nonequivalence between two different actions at two different times. According to this view, one kind of action (at one point in time) pays the cost for another very different kind of action (at another point in time). (The death of Christ on the cross for the past and future sins of humankind is Christian theology's quintessential example of such redemption.) In some circumstances, redemption actually multiplies violence and multiplies wounds, because redemption is so crucially additive: it adds an action to the one(s) before it: and this new action "addresses" or "pays the cost for" prior actions but cannot undo them or turn back time. History, even in the Christian schema, cannot be taken back or reversed. Redemptive actions must layer themselves on top of prior actions. *Pulp Fiction* follows and plays with this logic. Tarantino shows Butch redeeming his rebellion against Marsellus by violently stopping Marsellus's rape at the narrative's climax, by means of which Marsellus can forgive Butch his sins. But the beauty of this gesture is dramatically striped by a number of different dirty images—many of them violent—none of which is similar to any other in meaning or tone. Sticking to grace are images such as the chuckling Gimp, the hillbilly rapists (one shot up, one sliced in front), the rape itself, and bloody Butch taking off on the chopper, among many others. Redemption here truly proves to be a composite, aggressive nonequivalence between different actions.

This is why the ending of the film in the coffee shop is so intriguing—and so misleading on further reflection. The climax to the scene—and therefore to the movie—is a funny, nonviolent scene of redemption. We are in the coffee shop (where the film began) in the midst of a hard-driving, tense but also funny Mexican standoff between the hit men, Vincent and Jules, and the addled bandits, Pumpkin and Honey Bun, who are attempting to rob the shop. In a surprise move, just when he has them where he wants them, Jules gives money to Pumpkin and Honey Bun— pays them off—so he won't have to kill them. (Or, as he puts it: "Wanna know what I'm buyin,' Ringo? . . . Your life. I'm giving you that money so I don't hafta kill your ass.") If this scene were the end of the film's over-arching narrative, we might feel a simpler, sunnier sense of redemption taking hold than the darker one I have been describing. But given that we know, by this point in the film, that the rape-and-escape is still to come (in narrative terms), as is the violent death of Vince (he dies in a scene just before the rape), we may cleave to a different sense.

We may simply feel that Pumpkin is lucky. For wounds in the world of Tarantino's *Pulp* cannot, once suffered, be undone. Not the (histori-cal) rape of a black man. Not our sight of this (historical) rape. Not the blowing off of a black man's face. Not even our fascination with it. None of these wounds can be undone. They, like Tarantino's treasure-trove of film cuts, can only be opened and given further layers. In fact, Tarantino, throughout *Pulp Fiction*, shows no interest in undoing wounds. Even re-demption cannot undo them, as he proceeds to show. Rather, his interest lies in exploring our attraction to feeling the force of these wounds—and to feeling the force of their nonequivalence to each other or to anything (ad)dressing them. This attraction, to dirty details and scenes of shame, as we know from works by Morrison and Mapplethorpe, can be our way of doing sorrow, political meditation, visual fascination, sexual stimula-tion, or black humor—or all of these in emotional combination, since they need not be antithetical or lead to ambivalence. All of which speaks to the compound potential of compelling debasements: the "layered, aestheti-cized, politicized workings," and the different "mode of history writing" that "(re)tells . . . elided histories," such as we find in black gay productions of the early 1990s, and in Tarantino, too.

Chapter Four

EROTIC CORPSE HOMOSEXUAL MISCEGENATION

AND THE DECOMPOSITION OF ATTRACTION

The Beautiful Bottom of Shameful Attractions

Attraction to people or things marked by shame is a visible thread being pulled through this book. It surfaced first on surface itself in chapter 1. Wrapped in their own kind of stigmatized skins, queers revealed the de-basement aesthetic of beautiful garments on women and men. A wide black cape, from the pen of Genet, was the climax of the chapter—a vest-ment worn coquettishly by a queer lieutenant who gloried in his shame and in the blackened face of a glamorous killer. Shame, we found, to the point of surprise, can attach to the beautiful surface of cloth—in fact, as insistently and sometimes as violently as it adheres to the surface of blackness. Attraction to fabric moves quickly to shame. Yet, quite often, lovingly so.

Shame, less surprisingly, clings to such matters as queer sex acts and the hardships of economic life for black Americans. These are iconic shames for (what we think of) as queers and blacks, and black queers, too. To be sure, attraction to—a definite captivation by, a full-on pull toward—shameful matters seems to be embedded in queer sexualities, even for the proudest of sexual participants. One is left to wonder how a person creatively, consciously, obliquely, consistently, or sometimes automatically negotiates the kind of shame so powerfully attached by laws, religion, and culture to this person's most intimate acts—moreover, to intimate acts of pleasure. Can such a person so easily distinguish between the shame she learns to deny, or work around, and the shame that perhaps generates her attractions? Uncomfortable, pleasing, thrilling, saddening, remarkably changing in color attraction to shame itself—not just attraction to what shame sticks to—is what Genet explores for us. But what about attraction to shame for straight blacks? Especially in reference to economic binds, markers of attraction would seem hard to fathom. But they do appear. In fact, we can grasp these startling attachments, or so I have claimed, only by grasping the crucial metaphorical force of such concepts as bottoms and dirt, shading into fertile soil and bottom land, which Toni Morrison asks us to consider. Her beautiful Bottom up in the hills, where Sula penetrates the "loam" her lover offers, is an index to Morrison's materializing metaphors. By grasping their force, we see how queer bodily pleasures (such as Sula's) and black neighborhoods from a certain historical time (as depicted by Morrison's Bottom) together suggest comprehensible attractions—which are also violent attractions—for people who question the highly compromising values of the "civilized." Refusing to flee one's bottom (even in a doubled sense for Morrison) suggests an attraction to the seat of one's shame.

Of course, we have also shown that some attractions to shame are uncontrollable. We do not elect them, or always consent to them. Uncontrollable mental fascinations often violently strike our eyes. (Brutal interracial same-sex sex; a blown-off face.) Sometimes to our incomprehension. Sometimes to the effect of a pleasure we embrace or deny. Sometimes to the dictates of a history we cannot redeem or decompose. Entire histories of hidden attractions can leap forth immediately from a single image, as Tarantino showed us with a black man's anal rape. In ways that are both confusing and complex, some of these histories of forceful attractions (the Jim Crow history *Pulp Fiction* invokes) are histories of tremendous suffering and threat. Our sorrow can stick to visual fascination, and even at times to sexual fantasy, of an importantly undeniable sort.

This chapter turns up the flame of this dilemma. Can one dispose of shameful attractions seemingly put in the mind by time, or by that force that we tend to call history? Here we find a switchpoint between black and queer more directly shaped by authors who think about the "problem" of miscegenation. This is a highly embodied switchpoint. It is embodied by black and white men who engage in homosexual miscegenation, even if it only occurs in their thoughts. Intimately sharing their signs with each other, if not always their actual bodies, they engage in (what they consider) shameful attractions and struggle with their attraction to shame. Frequently, they are rewarded with violence, against their bodies or their minds. This sort of shame, we are going to be told, can fester in the mind like a rotting corpse. Pointedly, the image of a decomposing corpse—something beyond Marvin's shot-up face, which Tarantino plays with—becomes a dirty detail for two quite different writers. This corpse image connects the shameful attractions considered by James Baldwin to those imagined by Eldridge Cleaver, even as it separates their two different efforts to decompose attraction.

Here, at first glance, then, with these authors, we find less interest than we found in Morrison, Genet, and Tarantino to acknowledge shame's generative powers, its propensity to lure its devotees into violent, illuminating states of mind. Baldwin, however, emerges in his own way as the great reader of Genet that he was. Alongside Genet in the 1950s, and ahead of Morrison, Baldwin ridicules white men's virginal fussiness about being tucked in a bottom, sexually, geographically. *Giovanni's Room*, as the title implies, makes the place of penetration an actual physical, urban space— a dirty spot in Paris—that becomes a mental state. "Beautiful bottom," in this chapter, refers not just to the surface or the depths of a body, or to a place; it refers as well to the bottom of a mind, where the thought of a lover lies decomposing. In the course of my book, debasement has crawled ever inward on the body, until it has reached the depths of the mind, where debasement's actions often take place. There are social holdings, we dramatically discover, even in this loneliest place.

Why Decompose a Mental Obsession?

What happens to a dream deferred? Does it stink like rotten meat?
—Langston Hughes

Giovanni will be rotting soon in unhallowed ground.
—James Baldwin

What if you cannot have a man when you want him? What if you cannot get him out of your mind? Does he live there, die there, or change his form, decompose, over time? Having him perpetually on your mind, what are you? A slave to attraction? A fool for love? A glutton for punishment—yours or his?

Cleaver and Baldwin have men on their minds. They think of white men thinking of them. White men are men whose heads they inhabit (or so they believe), men who cannot get them out of their brains. Though they have neither made nor asked for this state of affairs, they—American Negroes, black men—are forced, they imply, to lie down in this bed, to be the mental obsession of white men. And so they become, Cleaver and Baldwin, bedfellows of a curious sort.

Making Cleaver lie down with Baldwin, for any reason, will seem strange: counter, even opposite, to our usual understanding of these black authors largely taken as antagonists.[1] (Eldridge Cleaver, the '60s Panther, was famously homophobic; James Baldwin, the '50s Negro, was famously homosexual.)[2] Less strange, certainly the more one thinks about it, will be the suggestion, which I offer here, that, in the turbulent racial times of the 1950s and '60s, white men and dark men may be driven toward each other when they obey the common dictum, the grand heterosexual cliché, that says "opposites attract"—even when they search for sexual excitement with (what would feel like) "the opposite sex." Which is why, for Cleaver and Baldwin, being driven toward one's sexual "opposite" often amounts to what is rarely named: homosexual miscegenation.

Racist worries over miscegenation, it has long been said, were greatly inflamed by the judicial decision in *Brown v. Board of Education* (1954) to desegregate the public schools.[3] Desegregation, beyond the schools, would supposedly allow the races to mix in dangerous ways. Miscegenation was the most feared result. Whites and blacks might now, with greater frequency and ease, interbreed. Yet, in public commentaries on racial mixing from this period, even in their ugliest forms, no one named another kind of miscegenation: dark men with light men.[4] Presumably, men could not interbreed. After all, what would get "mixed" in such relations? The sexual exchange of bodily fluids that could have any lasting result—that could change what "the races" are—was imagined to be a straight affair. As for men who were sexually seeking men (sometimes only in their minds), what could ever be bred from this mix?

What could be bred was not a baby, but a corpse. This is the sorrowful, forceful answer given in *Giovanni's Room*, Baldwin's novel from 1956. Even in *Soul on Ice*, Cleaver's essays from the 1960s, miscegenation (if only his desire for it) finds itself tied to decomposition, as I will explain. Something about interracial attraction, Cleaver avers, can lead a lover so moved to decay. But here our writers do part ways, in spite of a shared and serious sense of miscegenation's lasting effects. Cleaver seeks to be freed from racial mixing and "healed" from his participation in it (even from desires that are only in his thoughts), though he continues surreptitiously to savor how white men have black men on their minds. Baldwin takes another tack. He attempts to occupy white men's minds in order to think attraction through their thoughts.[5] In fact, in *Giovanni's Room*, Baldwin turns this particular perplex into a genre rather unusual for a black author. We could call this genre the white man's slave narrative, in which the labor-against-one's-will (one's slave labor) is mental labor and one is captive to something (or someone) in the prison of one's mind. Menaced by a "bulldog in [his] own back yard," mastered by desires imposed from within (or so they seem), locked inside the room of his head, the blond narrator of *Giovanni's Room*, whose only action is to think about attraction, obsessively thinks about a dark man's corpse. *Giovanni's Room* is a white man's meditation, through the use of flashbacks, on his lover who, at the time of the novel's narration, is on his way to death by guillotine: "Giovanni will be rotting soon in unhallowed ground."[6]

Decomposition, I am going to argue, is not just a physical act of decay, though it is surely that. Decomposition also names a mental process we can see in Baldwin—at least, in his narration—and in Cleaver, too. It is a way of thinking—a sad epistemological force. To decompose attraction is to break it down in thought. To decompose attraction, especially by thinking of a lover as a corpse, is to think, with sorrow, about the relation of time to attraction. When did your attraction to a lover go bad? Was the timing wrong? Did historical relations war against it, even as they prompted it? Are we in a world not ready to receive it? Is your historical context your excuse for relational breakdowns that come from many causes? Given your historical context, can you know?

Decomposition names the thick and formal way, for both of these writers, of thinking through these problems. Thick because they both see dilemmas of attraction from so many angles—many more than they can handle. Formal because they at times use an image—of a decomposing corpse—that can *figure* what's at stake. The corpse suggests not only the lingering death of some attractions (or their present dangers) but the thickened sight, the mental apprehension, of what overwhelms the mind. Picasso conveyed this mental overpowerment in the form of his own decompositions, especially in his cubist experiments, where something or some relation is seen, is mentally broken down, from so many angles that the image is asked to hold a rarely seen analysis. The decomposed form represents a thick sight.[7] Decomposition, this chapter will argue, is Cleaver's and Baldwin's way of knowing the sad configuration of sexual relations in the wake of a desegregation that had not, by the time of their writings, and still never has, by the time of this study, actually come.[8]

Not that one could tell this sad configuration to Norman Mailer.

Mailer's Happy Mix

Norman Mailer's "white Negro"—Mailer's term for "hipster" white men drawn to black men—does not go about his knowing in this way. In fact, the "white Negro" does not know this sorrow. There is no sad delay of sexual relations in Mailer's energetic essay, published one year after Baldwin's novel; only a giddy homosocial affair between white and black men. Mailer states his eager "attract[ion] to what the Negro had to offer," in tones ranging from exuberance, to wonderment, to thoughtfulness, to warning, though never sadness.[9] Cleaver, ironically, was drawn to Mailer's happy attraction; Baldwin not at all. Deeming himself "a student" of the essay, Cleaver pronounced it "prophetic and penetrating in its understanding of the psychology involved in the accelerating confrontation of black and white in America," adding, "I was therefore personally insulted by Baldwin's flippant, schoolmarmish dismissal of 'The White Negro'": "[The essay] may contain an excess of esoteric verbal husk, but one can forgive Mailer for that because of the solid kernel of truth he gave us."[10] The "truth," according to Cleaver, is "the depth of ferment, on a personal level, in the white world." Cleaver puts it this way: "People are feverishly, and at great psychic and social expense, seeking *fundamental and irrevocable liberation*—and, what is more important, *are succeeding in escaping*—from the big white lies that compose the monolithic myth of White Supremacy/Black Inferiority" (98, his emphases). Whites, as much as anyone, according to Cleaver, must seek "liberation" from enslavement to a "lie."

How does Mailer express this matter? What, exactly, do white men need? They need a mental jailbreak. In fact, they require a peculiar American existentialism, which will address "a collective failure of nerve" (338), a sense of being "jailed in the prison air of other people's habits, other people's defeats, boredom, quiet desperation, and muted icy self-destroying rage" (339). This is something of an abstract prison, not entirely of one's own making, something (whether fear or boredom or a general inaction) that can jail you by being "in" the "air." Therefore, one needs, in Mailer's estimation, if one is white, an entire mental shake-up: the will "to divorce oneself from society, to exist without roots, to set out on that uncharted journey into the rebellious imperatives of the self" (339). One may sense "the Negro" lurking here, since black men exemplify — as strange as that may sound, given their *forced* relation to rootlessness — Mailer's idea of a mental shake-up. Negroes point the way out of "prison air." Even so, by the terms of Mailer's essay, intellectual influences on this imperative (for a mental jailbreak) turn out to be white: D. H. Lawrence, Henry Miller, Wilhelm Reich, and, most of all, Ernest Hemingway. The latter, above all, emphasizes "courage," of course through adventure, and something that links the problem of (white) men to sexual solutions: "Hemingway's categorical imperative that what made him feel good became therefore The Good."[11]

Never mind that both Cleaver and Baldwin will find this last point enormously troubling, separately confirming that what feels good may lead to attractions one cannot control—which themselves may lead to a less than meaningful death. The point for Mailer (and this is remarkable) appears to be that feeling good may need to come from American Negroes, and thus from some kind of nuptial with them. Hence, Mailer's memorable sexual metaphorics: "In such places as Greenwich Village, a ménage-à-trois was completed—the bohemian and the juvenile delinquent came face-to-face with the Negro, and the hipster was a fact in American life"; "in this wedding of the white and the black it was the Negro who brought the cultural dowry" (340). Alluringly, this grand metaphorical angle on cultural inheritance later runs into a striking parenthetical that Mailer never sees any need to explain: "(many hipsters are bisexual)" (351).

What do Negroes bring to Mailer's metaphorical marriage? What can whites not feel on their own? Threatened, it seems. What will spring white men from the "prison air of other people's habits" is other people's danger—and, really, deprivation. Danger is the heart of another people's orgasm, which, apparently, is part of their "dowry." Here are the lines that follow from this word:

. . . . dowry. Any Negro who wishes to live must live with danger from his first day . . . no Negro can saunter down a street with any real certainty that violence will not visit him on his walk. The cameos of security for the average white: mother and the home, job and the family, are not even a mockery to millions of Negroes; they are impossible. The Negro has the simplest of alternatives: live a life of constant humility or ever-threatening danger. . . . [For this reason, the Negro] lived in the enormous present . . . relinquishing the pleasures of the mind for the more obligatory pleasures of his body, and in his music he gave voice to the character and quality of his existence, to his rage and the infinite variations of joy, lust, languor, growl, cramp, pinch, scream and despair of his orgasm. For jazz is orgasm. . . . [I]t said, "I feel this, and now you do too." (340–41)

For the urban white male, Mailer implies, no (formerly elaborate) journey away from his "cameos of security" is now required. It is enough to know that these particular cameos are impossible for Negroes. One's own danger through (a Hemingway-like) adventure is replaced by knowing that the Negro is threatened on the streets. The complications of whites' "collective failure of nerve" can be simplified by Negroes' "simplest of alternatives" (constant humility or danger); which then, as if they are restoring complication, blossom into "the infinite variations" of jazz. Mailer is not just copping a feel. He is theorizing how racial bodies interpenetrate, how they mix, even if they never formally touch. He is conceiving a wholesale energy transfer from black men to the minds and bodies of "hip" white men. Thinking and hearing about deprivations, and about how many black people feel about the violence and danger that surround them—or simply catching the physical pulse of the Negro music born of these feelings—whites can be energized. The goal for "white" Negroes, in fact, is nothing short of their imagination and creation of "a new nervous system" (345)—hard-wired circuits that skip to the beat of someone else's energy. "Therefore [Mailer says] one finds words like go, and make it, and with it, and swing: 'Go' with its sense that after hours or days or months or years of monotony, boredom, and depression. . . . [one] can make a little better nervous system, make it a little more possible to go again, to go faster next time" (350) and maybe even tap into "the paradise of limitless energy and perception just beyond the next wave of the next orgasm" (351). In this sense, "the hipster," in an odd racial mixing, "absorb[s] the existentialist synapses of the Negro" (341).

Tellingly, such claims slip into warnings: not just that "incompatibles have come to bed," so to speak, but, literally, that "animosities, antipathies and new conflicts of interest" (356) will result. The example Mailer gives is miscegenation:

To take the desegregation of the schools in the South as an example, it is quite likely that the reactionary sees the reality more closely than the liberal when he argues that the deeper issue is not desegregation but miscegenation. . . . [For] the average liberal whose mind has been dulled by the committee-ish cant of the professional liberal, miscegenation is not an issue because he has been told that the Negro does not desire it. So, when it comes, miscegenation will be a terror. (356)

One wants to know how this miscegenation relates to the same-sex energy transfers Mailer extols. Is the absorbing of a Negro synapse (which reproduces Negro energy) a miscegenation? Are white men at risk for psychic or bodily harm when they succeed at taking (something of) black men in? Mailer doesn't say. He only ends his essay by reaffirming what Cleaver likely took as a compliment: "The Negro holds more of the tail of the expanding elephant of truth than the radical, and if this is so, the radical humanist could do worse than to brood upon this phenomenon" (359).

Baldwin broods. In *Giovanni's Room*, his narrator broods. Mailer's sunny mix, however, makes no appearance in this novel. The dark man's dangers and deprivations do not inspire or energize. Things slow down. Energy sags. The white man's brain is remade to receive the dark man's dilemmas. The expanding elephant of truth is a corpse too sad to comprehend. But if *Giovanni's Room* can be read as a kind of prescient response to Mailer's essay before he wrote it, a later Baldwin essay makes a more direct reply. In a piece that Baldwin termed "a love letter" to Norman Mailer—"The Black Boy Looks at the White Boy," published in *Esquire* magazine in 1961—Baldwin speaks of Mailer in a set of shifting tones. There is fondness and admiration here, but there is critique that cuts through both.[12]

In general points at his essay's start, Baldwin particularly contests Norman Mailer's claims for courage. Far from the fine sense of risk that Mailer portrays in his existentialist stance (one he "absorbs" from the Negro, we recall), Baldwin accuses him of seeking security:

There is a difference . . . between Norman and myself in that I think he still imagines that he has something to save, whereas I have never had anything to lose. . . . [T]he things that most white people imagine that they can salvage from the storm of life is really, in sum, their innocence. . . . I am afraid that most of the white people I have ever known impressed me as being in the grip of a weird nostalgia, dreaming of a vanished state of security and order.[13]

Baldwin, rightly or wrongly, interprets Mailer's search for rootless rebellion as, at heart, a wish for safety, and almost virginity (a saving, an "innocence," a "vanished state of security"), in a new and dangerous world, the threat of which, both men agree, is registered by Negroes. Mailer's dream of danger, then, leading to the jazz orgasm Negroes lend to white men, is "but a way," says Baldwin, "of avoiding all of the terrors of life and love" ("Black Boy," 229). Such a dodge, Baldwin implies, makes Mailer's "The White Negro" an "impenetrable" piece, causing Baldwin to ask "*why* should it be necessary to borrow the Depression language of deprived Negroes . . . in order to justify such a grim system of delusions? . . . Why malign the sorely menaced sexuality of Negroes in order to justify the white man's own sexual panic?" ("Black Boy," 229–30).

So much for the sense that Mailer is complimenting blacks in his essay. "One pays," Baldwin warns, "in one's own personality, for the sexual insecurity of others"; "the relationship, therefore, of a black boy to a white boy is a very complex thing".("Black Boy," 217). Mailer, according to the black boy looking at him, is insecure, innocent, impenetrable, and panicked. Moreover, "the Negro jazz musicians, among whom we sometimes found ourselves, who really liked Norman, did not for an instant consider him as being even remotely 'hip' and Norman did not know this and I could not tell him" (221). So much for a love letter.

Cleaver's Convalescence

Cleaver, however, takes revenge for Norman Mailer through his own love and admiration for Baldwin, and in a way that elucidates relations between homosexuality and miscegenation. That is, Cleaver excoriates Baldwin in *Soul on Ice*, even though he starts by avowing "lust" for Baldwin's compositions:

> After reading a couple of James Baldwin's books, I began experiencing that continuous delight one feels upon discovering a fascinating, brilliant talent on the scene, a talent capable of penetrating so profoundly into one's own little world. . . . I, as I imagine many others did and still do, lusted for anything Baldwin had written. It would have been a gas for me to sit on a pillow beneath the womb of Baldwin's typewriter and catch each newborn page as it entered this world of ours. (97)

The tease of Cleaver's metaphorics must have been carefully chosen, since the heart of Cleaver's complaint against Baldwin—against the black intelligentsia, in general—is Baldwin's presumed wish to create ("each newborn page") that swiftly becomes a wish to miscegenate, bodily and intellectually, it seems.[14] Something about how Baldwin writes, what he writes about, what he doesn't write about, and how he reads Norman Mailer and novelist Richard Wright marks him as a lover of whites. Cleaver is not subtle:

> There is in James Baldwin's work the most grueling, agonizing, total hatred of the blacks, particularly of himself, and the most shameful, fanatical, fawning, sycophantic love of the whites that one can find in the writings of any black American writer of note in our time. This is an appalling contradiction and the implications of it are vast. (*si*, 99)

In a fascinating move, Cleaver states that the black intellectual, "who becomes the white man's most valuable tool in oppressing other blacks" (*si*, 103), finds his "extreme embodiment" in "the black homosexual." Having the white man in or on your mind is apparently analogous, by Cleaver's reckoning, to having him inside you. And having him inside you deranges the mind. Thus Cleaver:

> The case of James Baldwin aside for a moment, it seems that many Negro homosexuals, acquiescing in this racial death-wish, are outraged and frustrated because in their sickness they are unable to have a baby by a white man. The cross they have to bear is that, already bending over and touching their toes for the white man, the fruit of their miscegenation is not the little half-white offspring of their dreams but an increase in the unwinding of their nerves. (*si*, 102)

We can imagine that "the case of James Baldwin" and his uterine typewriter are not laid aside. The essay is about them. Baldwin must bear the cross of his fruit: the birth, it seems, of a half-white page. At bottom, Cleaver claims, what explains Baldwin's "attack on Mailer," his "violent repudiation" of Mailer's "The White Negro," his "revulsion" from blacks like Richard Wright who "glory in their blackness, seeking and showing their pride in Negritude and the African Personality," is Baldwin's "despicable underground guerilla war, waged on paper, against black masculinity" (*si*, 109).[15] The (predictable) sign of this war is his character Rufus Scott (in *Another Country*) who, in double-duty miscegenation, "let a white bisexual homosexual fuck him in his ass, and who took a Southern Jezebel for his woman, with all that these tortured relationships imply" (*si*, 107).[16] In a tender let-up, Cleaver admits (almost comically, if one reads for puns) that "Baldwin has a superb touch when he speaks of human beings, when he is inside of them—especially his homosexuals—but he flounders when he looks beyond the skin" (109). In fact, Cleaver claims, Baldwin's work is "void of a political, economic, or even a social reference."[17]

Something is striking in Cleaver's invective throughout this essay—something quite aside from the question of its truth. Cleaver's charge against the homosexual's "sickness" and "miscegenation" echoes his indictment of *himself* at the start of *Soul on Ice*, insofar as Cleaver begins by confessing his attraction to white women. In fact, the volume of his essays could almost be read as a novel of patchwork forms—confession, essay, letter, allegory, incantation—all in the service of an overarching plot: escaping, being cured of, miscegenation. The volume ends, after all, with the essay "Convalescence" and Cleaver's final incantatory call "To All Black Women from All Black Men."[18]

At the other end of this telos—at the start of *Soul on Ice*—is Cleaver's "sickness." The volume begins with Cleaver's going to prison when *Brown v. Board of Education* "was only one month old" (3). In a jolt I imagine most readers don't foresee, the effect of this decision to outlaw segregation was Cleaver's "awakening" to his own indignity. As if this decision made the past come alive in a hideous form, and made the present desegregation seem depressingly, impossibly future, the law that lifted legal strictures made Cleaver feel his disturbing position: "inwardly I turned away from America with horror, disgust and outrage. . . . I became an extreme iconoclast" (4, 6). However, this act of breaking "idols"—"God, patriotism, the Constitution, the founding fathers"—reveals an idol he cannot "smash."

Unlike other idols, this one breeds attraction. "Out of the center of *Esquire*," he writes, "I married a voluptuous bride"—a white pin-up. Cleaver narrates: "And then, one evening . . . I was shocked and enraged to find that the guard had entered my cell, ripped my sugar from the wall, torn her into little pieces, and left the pieces floating in the commode: it was like seeing a dead body floating in a lake" (*si*, 7). Cleaver has his bride decomposed for him (really, dismembered) but left to float, so Cleaver can see, as the guard would clearly like him to see, the form of the pin-up reconfigured. Crucial to the guard and his pointed message, decomposition still takes a form. Cleaver seems to obey the prompt by "seeing a dead body floating in a lake." This aesthetic translation (via simile)—torn paper pieces become a dead body, a toilet a lake—supplies an image and form for the dangers of racial mixing. Moreover, the anecdote is telling to Cleaver not so much for its revelation of the power of guards but for its shocking unveiling of a "sickness" that makes him choose (and all the other black inmates choose, Cleaver claims) white women over black women. (Only the cells of the homosexuals had no pin-ups.)

Extending our view of decomposition (Cleaver's analysis of his attractions) as being bound, at times, to the image of a literal corpse, Cleaver next narrates the revelation that broke his nerves:

> [A]nd then, in 1955, an event took place in Mississippi which turned me inside out: Emmett Till, a young Negro down from Chicago on a visit, was murdered, allegedly for flirting with a white woman. He had been shot, his head crushed from repeated blows . . . [H]is badly decomposed body was recovered from the river. . . . I was, of course, angry over the whole bit, but one day I saw in a magazine a picture of the white woman with whom Emmett Till was said to have flirted. While looking at the picture, I felt that little tension in my chest I experience when a woman appeals to me. . . . I flew into a rage at myself, at America, at white women, at the history that had placed those tensions of lust and desire in my chest. Two days later, I had a "nervous breakdown." . . . When I came to myself I was locked in a padded cell. (10–11)

We may wish to note that when the Till case was in court, Baldwin was about to begin final edits on *Giovanni's Room*. In a truly strange convergence, while Eldridge Cleaver was in prison in the grips of a nervous collapse—over his attraction to Till's white accuser—Baldwin may have been turning the tables on these dynamics, writing a novel in which a white man, jailed in his mind, suffers an uncontrollable attraction for a dark man who is becoming a corpse.[19] In any event, as readers will remember, the case of the fourteen-year-old Till was famous for a literal decomposition, caused by what got taken as attraction. (After parading a picture of a white girl he said was his girl, outside a white Southerner's store, Till allegedly said "Bye Baby" to the white woman working behind the counter.) As we learn from *Eyes on the Prize*, "the tortured, distended body pulled from the river became the focus of attention."[20] It was identified only from a ring—initialed, as it happens—worn on the hand. The sheriff sought to bury the body immediately. Emmett Till's mother, however, demanded the body come home to rest in Chicago; then demanded, against all orders, the casket be opened; then demanded an open-casket funeral, so the world could see him "so horribly battered and water-logged that someone needs to tell [me] this sickening sight is [my] son" (44) (see figures 15 and 16). Ten thousand people (mostly black people) saw Till's corpse. And *Jet* magazine, in a famous editorial decision, ran the photo of the decomposed face, surely knowing that readers' visual fascination with this sight would be inseparable from their sorrow—and their remembrance. Till, *Jet* determined, will long decompose in the minds that beheld him. His unrecognizable water-logged form would give a face to race relations post–*Brown v. Board of Education*.[21]

The fame of this photograph makes Cleaver's comments all the more striking, since he displaces the photo of Till with the white woman's picture. Yet, in all fairness, how could he not? To fight against what Till's face means is, for Cleaver, to face an attraction he is still decomposing. In several different senses, the passage dramatizes the incomplete process of decomposition in the mind's cell. Just as Till's mutilation makes an image able to offer unending decay, so the flushing of a pin-up, or Eldridge Cleaver's rage against a woman, does not spell death to a white woman's image. She can live in the mind (and the chest) for a very long while. In this strong sense, Emmett Till's corpse, its stunning deformation, helps Cleaver know something key about attraction. Attraction is often a function of time. History (specific relations over time) can produce attractions and, simultaneously, deem them unnatural—as (un)recognizable as a corpse. "History," says Cleaver, has put the insistent "tensions" of a particular attraction in his chest, which he cannot extract. In fact, white racist cultures have insisted on miscegenous desire, since they have launched white women as idols. They stimulate (and, therefore, make familiar) the attractions they insist are unnatural. Most interesting of all, this historically conjured heterosexuality (black men and white women) makes Eldridge Cleaver resemble his depiction of a black homosexual, on two bold counts. He feels a publicly tabooed attraction that holds an enormous power over him; and he bears the fruit of miscegenous desire, the remarkable, frightening "unwinding of his nerves" (which he assigns to Baldwin).[22]

Cleaver in no way misses this resemblance. He theorizes it, at least on some level. Even Cleaver confesses that sexual attractions across the racial divide (of black and white) amount to "a most weird and complex dialectic of inversion" (181). "Inversion," of course, is a well-known term from the "science" of sexology for homosexuality—but did Cleaver know it? What Cleaver does know (or, I should say, believes) is that "normal," heterosexual relations between black men and black women are plagued

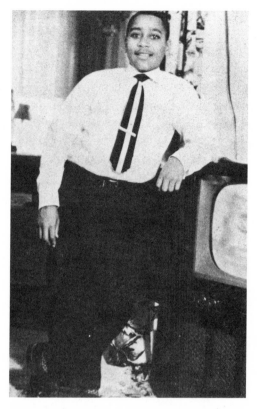

15. Last photo of Till (Christmas 1954) before lynching, courtesy of Mamie Till Mobley.

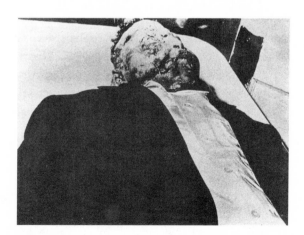

16. Till in casket after lynching, 1955, courtesy of the *Chicago Defender*.

by their *loss* of sexual opposition. Black men and women are too much the same. They are classed to be the same; and their class positions, Cleaver argues, are read by white culture as "founded in biology" (189). By their class positions—race keeping them "down" in class—black men and black women, according to Cleaver, are strong-bodied, full of fight, lacking in sovereignty, virile in labor, split from their minds and drenched in their sex. This shared positioning makes them victims of sexual sameness and, so, they pursue, as if they must, white men and white women as their opposite sex. Cleaver's theory of cultural types names the four players in these relations: the white male Omnipotent Administrator, the Ultra-feminine white woman, the black male Supermasculine Menial, and the black female Subfeminine Amazon. These types "handcuff" black men and women, at least at the level of sexual desire, to white women and men.

Two things seem astonishing here. Cleaver believes, as if it were some biological law, that only so-called opposites attract. Speaking allegorically, and seeming to borrow from the Aristophanic myth in Plato's *Symposium*, Cleaver writes:

> The roots of heterosexuality are buried in that evolutionary choice made long ago in some misty past. . . . Struggling up from some murky swamp, some stagnant mudhole . . . that unknown ancestor of Man/Woman . . . divided its Unitary Self in half—into the male and female hemispheres of the Primeval Sphere. . . . When the Primeval Sphere divided itself, it established a basic tension of attraction, a dynamic magnetism of opposites—the Primeval Urge—which exerts an irresistable attraction between the male and female hemispheres. (177)

Anything other than magnetic attraction between established opposites is homosexuality. Black on black, for instance. That is to say, and this is the second astonishing point, Cleaver reckons that, by virtue of class, blacks are largely masculine (Supermasculine and Subfeminine) and whites are all effeminate. Within "the races," differences are only matters of degree:

> Thus the upper classes, or Omnipotent Administrators, are perenially associated with physical weakness, decay, underdeveloped bodies, effeminacy, sexual impotence, and frigidity. . . . [This] is decisive for the image of the woman of the elite classes. Even though her man is effeminate, she is required to possess and project an image that is in sharp contrast to his, more sharply feminine than his. . . . Therefore, she becomes "Ultrafeminine." . . . Because he despises weakness of the

body in himself, the Omnipotent Administrator will have a secret or subconscious aversion to the woman of his own class. (180–81)

Taken together, these factors make for an odd result. Fleeing sexual sameness leads to racial mixing that may resemble—or, really, just be—"homosexuality" (as Cleaver calls it):

> The Omnipotent Administrator is launched on a perpetual search for his alienated body, for affirmation of his unstable masculinity. . . . [He] cannot help but covertly, and perhaps in an extremely sublimated guise, envy the bodies and strength of the most alienated men beneath him—those furthest from the apex of administration . . . the men most alienated from the mind. . . . (This is precisely the root, the fountainhead of the homosexuality that is perennially associated with the Omnipotent Administrator.) (182)

No wonder Cleaver admired Mailer's essay. He and Mailer seem to come to the same pass. Sort of.

Really, not at all. What Mailer celebrates—a largely mental homosocial brotherhood—is highly antagonistic in Cleaver and smacks of faggotry. ("There is a Pandora's box of sexual aberrations here," Cleaver warns [183].) Moreover, Mailer's celebration can only be produced by (what Cleaver would likely describe as) a failure of straight black relations that puts black folks in danger of miscegenation. Mailer does not approach these concerns, since he mostly absents women (black and white) from his equations. Cleaver cannot absent them. He needs them for his politics ("To All Black Women from All Black Men"). He needs, in fact, to sort them (black from white women)—and, then, remake attraction.

The problem is the mind. Blacks, as ridiculous as this will sound, do not appear to have one. Of course, what Cleaver means is that blacks are not granted mental "sovereignty" (his term) in the public domain. By the dictates of a class divide, the philosophical Mind/Body problem is a solid (and simplified) racial split: black body, white mind. Here, however, Cleaver hits the wall of his own schematics. In order to make his allegory work, Cleaver himself, quite a bit like Norman Mailer, must absent women from his considerations, since white women (unlike Cleaver's white men) have no mental sovereignty and black women (unlike Cleaver's black men) lack the defining mark of Body, the (black man's) penis. Cleaver's foursome also, in this way, whittles down to two; two who seem to supply each other's needs (black male body, white male mind).

What results is a penile parable, nine years prior to the English translation of Lacan's famous essay "The Meaning of the Phallus" (published
in 1977).

Whatever one thinks of Lacanian thought, after reading Cleaver one
must confess that a penis/phallus logic is spelled out independently by
a Black Panther. Cleaver has his own way of showing that the penis is
not the phallus, as Lacan would put it.[23] To wit, Cleaver claims that white
men, via a miscalculation, relinquish "penis" for "omnipotence" in their
accession to social and symbolic power:

> The black man's penis was the monkey wrench in the white man's per-
> fect Machine. The penis, virility, is of the Body. . . . [I]n the deal which
> the white man forced upon the black man, the black man was given
> the Body as his domain while the white man preempted the Brain for
> himself. By and by, the Omnipotent Administrator discovered that in
> the fury of his scheming he had blundered and clipped himself of his
> penis. (164)

Cleaver even has his way—in his own allegorical scheme—of explaining
what feminists have been anxious to explore. Cleaver implies that social
power (particularly the power to make bourgeois myths) enables white
men to cover what they lack in their very embrace of the omnipotence-
that-relinquishes-penis:

> So he [the white man] reneged on the bargain. He called the Super-
> masculine Menial back and said: "Look, Boy, we have a final little ad-
> justment to make. . . . I will bind your rod with my omnipotent will,
> and place a limit on its aspiration. . . . I forbid you access to the white
> woman. . . . By subjecting your manhood to the control of my will, I
> shall control you. The stem of the Body, the penis, must submit to the
> will of the Brain." (165)

It is not surprising, at this turn in his argument, to find the white
woman sneaking her way back into view. Cleaver, we discover, also has
a version of "having" the phallus versus "being" the phallus. Consider
Judith Butler's gloss on Lacan, on his notion that women must be the
phallus that men presume to have.[24] Butler does not directly mention
race, although she cites Hegel on the master/slave relation:

> "Being" the Phallus and "having" the Phallus denote divergent sexual
> positions. . . . For women to "be" the Phallus means, then, to reflect

the power of the Phallus . . . to "embody" the Phallus, *to supply the site to which it penetrates.* . . . The interdependency of these positions recalls the Hegelian structure of . . . the unexpected dependency of the master on the slave in order to establish his own identity through reflection.[25]

Cleaver sees that black men of the 1960s, chafing at the bit of (their metaphorical) slavery, (mis)recognize white women as their wished-for phallus. "She" is their freedom because she "embodies" the white man's omnipotence (literally by supplying the site to which he penetrates). Cleaver puts it this way:

[W]hen I put my arms around a white woman, well, I'm hugging freedom. . . . Men die for freedom, but black men die for white women, who are the symbol of freedom. . . . I will not be free until the day I can have a white woman in my bed and a white man minds his own business. Until that day comes, my entire existence is tainted, poisoned, and I will still be a slave. (160–61)[26]

An unexpected blurring of Cleaver's racial logic comes, with a last twist of the knife, in Cleaver's mysterious attraction to his lawyer in *Soul on Ice*. Making us believe that his lawyer might be a marvelously progressive Omnipotent Administrator—"if you read the papers, you are no doubt aware of my lawyer's incessant involvement in agitation against all manifestations of the monstrous evil of our system, such as our intervention in the internal affairs of the Vietnamese people" (21)—Cleaver soon lifts this momentary tease of homosexuality: "I suppose that I should be honest and, before going any further, admit that my lawyer is a woman— or maybe I should have held back with that piece of the puzzle—a very excellent, unusual, beautiful woman" (21).

Cleaver fails to tell us that she is not black. In point of fact, she's Jewish. Where does this attraction (to a female Jewish lawyer) fit in Cleaver's system of racial relations? Is she the fly in the ointment of his cure? A sign that his break from white women doesn't take? Or is a Jewish woman, with a smart legal mind, neither, exactly, an Ominipotent Administrator nor an Ultrafeminine? Can she even be said to be a lover, since their only intercourse (at least, that Cleaver mentions) comes through their letters and verbal exchange?

Cleaver said that *Brown v. Board of Education*, "striking at the very root of the practice of segregation," "was meant to graft the nation's Mind back onto its Body" (192). But what if it only put a body in (a) mind? What if it only made whites and blacks, men and women, see their separation from what they bed in thought?

Baldwin's Branded Brain

In a book that should have fascinated Cleaver—*Giovanni's Room*—Baldwin shows a white man thinking obsessively about a dark man, from whom he is now strikingly severed.[27] Baldwin even fashions a scaffolding of characters that remarkably resembles Eldridge Cleaver's semiotic skeleton, beating Cleaver, in 1956, to a worry over "sameness" (and the loss of sexy sexual opposition).

Here the white American narrator, by the name of David—a kind of Omnipotent Administrator living abroad in France—finds that his affair with a white American woman threatens to numb him with a sameness.[28] And indeed, as Americans in Paris, they share unmistakable similarities, which emerge in the novel's American Express office scene. Here the narrator is "forced to admit" that, though he could have distinguished each from the other on American soil, "this . . . disquietingly cheerful horde struck the eye, at once, as a unit . . . as though they had just arrived from Nebraska."[29] His girlfriend Hella Lincoln (she of the Nebraskan name from Minnesota) seems to understand and, therefore, worry that she makes gender trouble for the narrator, too.[30] "Very intelligent, very complex," and even "very bitterly handsome" (with short hair and a "wide-legged boyish stance," to boot), Hella, who goes off to Spain "to think," struggles to be more feminine than David. "I'm not really the emancipated girl I try to be at all," she says in desperation. But can she, a Lincoln, emancipate her lover and free him from his mind? As Cleaver's semiotic plan would predict, the white male narrator's relations with men are coded, by contrast, as ones of sexy class and ethnic opposition (first with the "brown" American, Joey, and later with the "dark" Italian, Giovanni, a poor waiter). Ultimately, Baldwin makes his narrator attracted, then strongly repelled, by this mixing.

Importantly, however, this is a mixing of dark with light, only sometimes rendered as mixing black with white.[31] This seeming substitution of class for race, through which it appears that Baldwin writes a novel with no black characters, may explain why Cleaver never mentions *Giovanni's Room* in *Soul on Ice*. Otherwise, Cleaver might have seen in the novel something the novel's critics have missed: the logic of a flight from sexual sameness produces homosexual miscegenation, just as Cleaver later spelled it out. In fact, Baldwin offers something Cleaver would have liked: a slave narrative, written from the cell of a white man's mind, showing what Cleaver praised in Mailer, "the depth of ferment, on a personal level, in the white world." Indeed, we have a narrator—tall, blond—who is "locked" in his "reflection" at the novel's beginning. He thinks about himself, only to find, as he says, that the "germ of [my] dilemma which resolved itself . . . into flight" is "trapped in the room with me" (16). This will not be a pretty reflection. *Pace* Cleaver, it could vindicate Baldwin from any charge of a sycophantic love of whites. Baldwin, rather than complimenting whites, awakens white men to their own indignities. He uses (what Cleaver said was) his "superb touch when he is inside of . . . homosexuals," to wage a "guerilla war" (Cleaver's phrase) against white, not dark, men's masculinity. To do so, he must first reflect on attraction through a white man's thoughts.

In their rush to unfold a theme, critics often fail to focus squarely on the novel's narration, which would remind us that the action of the novel is simply reflection.[32] Over one night, the narrator reflects on his sexual attraction to the dark Italian waiter who, by morning, will be "rotting soon in unhallowed ground." Taking us deeper into decomposition—the novel's analysis of these attractions—I want to explain how carefully the novel is composed around corpses. By doing so, I hope to show how (what I would call) "the Cleaver plot" of *Giovanni's Room* (white men seeking dark men) is strongly overlaid with narrative thickenings surrounding each of the novel's corpses.

Only two corpses are ever described and both appear at the start of the novel. This is where the narrative inexplicably billows out around a first attraction. Trying to understand why he fled from his attraction to a boy named Joey, the narrator remembers (in a sad epistemological reach) the troubled time before their attraction—when his mother's corpse was strongly on his mind. He then leaps forward to a point past Joey, using the corpse of their mutual relation as a marker of his right-angled swerve from his family. The result is a hunt, surrounded on both sides by corpses, for what is "the germ" of the narrator's "dilemma."

As the narrator, locked in his deathwatch, anticipates the next day's sameness—"the train will be the same, the people . . . will be the same, and I will be the same. . . . it will all be the same, only I will be stiller" (*GR*, 8)—he unearths the meaning of his buried attraction and sexual relation to the teenage Joey, "very quick and dark and always laughing," with whom he walked "the dark, tropical" streets of Brooklyn (11–12). There is so much happening around the bones of this attraction, white boy to dark boy. It's as if the clean theoretical lines of a Cleaver plot are being both shown and smudged. Not the least of this smudging is Baldwin's rendering of how sensations rise up out of many possibilities and, then, mysteriously, shape what comes to look like attraction. Thus the narrator: "I think it began in the shower. I know that I felt something . . . which I had not felt before, which mysteriously, and yet aimlessly, included him" (12).

Here there is no discourse like Cleaver's about a history's putting tensions in the chest (though that exact phrase "I felt a tension in my chest" occurs several times throughout the novel). Rather, at the very moment that Baldwin is founding his paradigm—light drawn to dark—he shapes a discourse on attraction's mysterious and aimless inclusions, at a specific moment in time. To underscore this aimlessness, and even the quirky role of time, Baldwin offers a thematics of "accident." Joey and the narrator kiss by accident; later, they meet again by accident; and the chapter ends with the narrator's accident—almost fatal—that he suffers in his car. Packed around the darkness of Joey are details that don't make an obvious semiotic pattern: his rarity, exhaustion, innocence, and smallness. Perhaps they are forgotten by the narrator, who, in any case, eventually recalls how his shame coalesced around a semiotic shock: "I was suddenly afraid. It was borne in on me: *But Joey is a boy*" (15; his emphasis). Strikingly, from here, this reading of the body to a category changes the odd assortment of Joey images into a body of concentrated force:

> I saw suddenly the power in his thighs, in his arms, and in his loosely curled fists. The power and the promise and the mystery of that body made me suddenly afraid. That body suddenly seemed the black opening of a cavern in which I would be tortured till madness came, in which I would lose my manhood. Precisely, I wanted to know that mystery and feel that power and have that promise fulfilled through me. (15)

This is, surely, a bizarre progression. The positive/negative valence of the narrator's attraction to Joey shifts three times—from the seemingly positive discovery of power in a boy's body, to sudden fear (of torture, madness, and even emasculation), to a final wish for "precisely" what he fears. This is that descent to the body below that Cleaver imagines white men will make, losing one kind of manhood in a kind of trade for another. Here, in this passage, though the body is "the black opening" of this "cavern," the language boomerangs to the narrator's mind: "A cavern opened in my mind, black, full of rumor, suggestion, of half-heard, half-forgotten, half-understood stories, full of dirty words. I thought I saw my future in that cavern" (15). Notice how the black opening of a body, through sexual attraction, registers as a strange kind of filling in the white man's mind. Beyond this, consider how the sought-for "mystery" and "promise" and "power" of Joey's body so immediately decays or bloats into rumor, suggestion and strange linguistic halflings. Is the future of things only half themselves ("half-heard, half-forgotten, half-understood") the fruit of this homosexual miscegenation?

The dismissal of Joey based on these fears is soon followed, in narrative terms, by two dead bodies—both in the brain—both of which generate seemingly extraneous narrative material. The first dead body is the narrator's mother's, the description of which heads the ensuing narration of the narrator's family relations—a "long battle," which "had everything to do with my dead mother":

> I scarcely remember her at all, yet she figured in my nightmares, blind with worms, her hair as dry as metal and brittle as a twig, straining to press me against her body; that body so putrescent, so sickening soft, that it opened, as I clawed and cried, into a breach so enormous as to swallow me alive. . . . [P]erhaps [my father and aunt] thought that I was grieving for her. And I may have been, but if that is so, then I am grieving still.[33]

Now begin a series of passages that are unrecognizable for their use in the novel's later chapters. Why do they extend so? We are being shown how the narrator analyzes. He is scouting something important: how alliances form or curve around the holes where bodies or their attractions used to be. Relations, he suggests, take very complicated cues from missing bodies—from the degeneration of their influence and the influence of their degeneration within the mind. ("No matter what was happening in that room, my mother was watching it. . . . Her spirit dominated that air and controlled us all," 20; 18.) No wonder the Joey attraction lives beyond the point of its dismissal. No wonder the narrator's link to him carries the status of a long-decaying corpse.

> I could not discuss [the "Joey incident"] . . . with anyone, I could not even admit it to myself; and, while I never thought about it, it remained, nevertheless, at the bottom of my mind, as still and as awful

as a decomposing corpse. And it changed, it thickened, it soured the atmosphere of my mind. (24)

From here the narrative is off and running with the narrator's dense, deceptively close relations with his father that represent—if one remembers the descriptions—a changing, a thickening, a souring of what the father blithely thinks is his resemblance to his son. The narrator's brush with death, however, lets David know, "at the bottom of [his] heart," that "we had never talked, that now we never would" (29). This is the start of the narrator's flight, from his own white father, that sends him eventually into Giovanni's room. It is also the first of several junctures at which David knows something crucial "at the bottom" of his heart or mind, where the Joey connection decomposes.

Clearly, the narrator knows, at the start, the futility of his intended escape. Contra Mailer and his vision of energy, the narrator's "constant motion" (Baldwin's phrase) in the service of escape will only loop back to what he knows "at bottom":

> I think now that if I had had any intimation that the self I was going to find would turn out to be only the same self from which I had spent so much time in flight, I would have stayed at home. But, again, I think I knew, at the very bottom of my heart, exactly what I was doing when I took the boat for France. (31)

What leads him into Giovanni's room, as I have already suggested, is the narrator's full-on flight from sameness: from resemblance to his father, from resemblance to Americans, and even from a subtly feared resemblance to what he implies is the screaming effeminacy of gay men.[34] Giovanni offers a departure and a draw ("it was like moving into the field of a magnet or like approaching a small circle of heat"). "He stood, insolent and dark and leonine" (39). Giovanni's darkness, often cited by David (as was Joey's darkness), is not a mere break from American sameness. Nor is it solely an unnamed lure, though it is both a departure and a draw, as I have claimed. Giovanni's darkness (as was Joey's darkness) is also a metaphorical blackness. David describes Giovanni, via metaphor, as a potential gay man's slave. David imagines the poor Italian barman, in the face of rich gay "bidders," as "in effect, for sale . . . on an auction block" (40). Perhaps more telling, the dividing line between blond David and dark Giovanni is made apparent by their different orientations to time. "The Americans are funny," says Giovanni, as if he were addressing Mailer's white Negro. "You have a funny sense of time . . . as though with enough time and all that fearful energy and virtue you people have, everything will be settled, solved, put in its place" (48).

What David cannot solve is Giovanni's room. Befitting the problem of their beleaguered mixing, it is an architectural womb, from which nothing issues. A highly fraught space, an overwrought symbol, the room serves to question what form a man's attraction to a man might take at this historical moment. Complicating matters, Giovanni's room may even be the space of what Cleaver later called "the accelerating confrontation of black and white in America"—only partially, and thinly, disguised by Baldwin's substituting dark Italians for American blacks. This room, at any rate, defies any sense of happy mixing. Literally, a "maid's room," "out by the zoo," Giovanni's room is not the great escape that Mailer imagines Negroes offer white men. Ominously, the narrator reports: "[Giovanni] knew . . . at the very bottom of his heart, that I, helplessly, at the very bottom of mine, resisted him with all my strength" (109). Of course, what the narrator resists is a bottom. He knows the pull is down, not up. Absorbing the existential synapse of the man below you on the class pole is not, alas, automatically energizing. Nor does it give life. Within the space of ten short lines, the narrator's description of "life in that room" turns "newborn" "joy" toward his sense of Giovanni's becoming some kind of skeleton or corpse:

> In the beginning, our life together held a joy and amazement which was newborn every day. . . . [But soon] anguish and fear had become the surface on which we slipped and slid, losing balance, dignity, and pride. Giovanni's face, which I had memorized so many mornings, noons, and nights, hardened before my eyes, began to give in secret places, began to crack. The light in the eyes became a glitter; the wide and beautiful brow began to suggest the skull beneath. (99)

Within two pages of this depiction, the narrator starts the narration of his "escape" from this room, working against a magnetic attraction. David's drawn-out intention to flee the very room to which he's fled takes several months and half the book. Moreover, his escape proves incomplete.

Earlier, Giovanni had said, "if I had to beat you, chain you, starve you — *if* I could make you stay, I would" (189). He cannot make David stay. However, by virtue of what Giovanni signifies—a complex matter the novel never summarizes—he can enslave the narrator's mind. As if he himself has become a slave to what he flees, David is branded in his brain:

His body, which I had come to know so well, glowed in the light and charged and thickened the air between us. Then something opened in my brain, a secret, noiseless door swung open, frightening me: it had not occurred to me until that instant that, in fleeing from his body, I confirmed and perpetuated his body's power over me. Now, as though I had been branded, his body was burned into my mind, into my dreams. (191)

So many points in this passage echo the Joey relation and its demise. The "charging" and "thickening" of the air between Giovanni and David may recall the "changing" and "thickening" of "the atmosphere of [David's] mind" in the wake of Joey. The "something open[ing] in [his] brain" ("a secret, noiseless door swung open, frightening me") may echo the narrator's earlier confession that, with Joey, "a cavern opened in my mind, black, full of rumor . . . full of dirty words" (15). Even the confirmation of a body's power over him, "burned into [his] mind," is pre-drawn in the image of Joey (or, at least, of their attraction) as "remain[ing] . . . at the bottom of my mind, as still and as awful as a decomposing corpse" (24). This is not exactly the Emmett Till corpse. Still, this sense of a corpse in the brain can only be strengthened by the reader's realization that the book is a deathwatch for a dark man, who is going to lose his head. Sadly, the way a body stays in the brain, even (or especially) past the point of its life, is figured by Giovanni's memories of his baby, who, as it happens, became an early corpse. Giovanni relates this story when David tries to break off their relations:

"Yes, I had made a baby but it was born dead. It was all grey and twisted when I saw it and it made no sound. . . . It was a little boy, it would have been a wonderful, strong man, perhaps even the kind of man you . . . and all your disgusting band of fairies spend all your days and nights . . . dreaming of—but it was dead." (185)

Then, as if to warn against the kind of virginal, looking-for-safety manhood that Baldwin associates with Mailer, dark Giovanni accuses blond David of "immaculate manhood" (to quote another character). Giovanni states:

"You love your purity . . . you are just like a little virgin, you walk around with your hands in front of you as though you had . . . maybe *diamonds* down there between your legs! You will never give it to anybody, you will never let anybody *touch* it—man *or* woman. You want to be *clean*.

You think you came here covered with soap and you think you will go out covered with soap. . . . You want to leave Giovanni because he makes you stink." (187)

Baldwin is contesting any sense (Mailer's sense) that white American males could ever easily, without mental struggle, follow dark men not just into their rooms but, further, into their lives. White men are rarely man enough, in Baldwin's estimation, to lose a certain manhood. They are virgin men. Yet, like many virgins, they bed down in thought. David is mentally screwed, and enslaved, by his thoughts of Giovanni as a lover and a corpse. In perhaps the novel's strangest echo, David reflects on his draw to Giovanni, who goes to meet his death for killing an Omnipotent Administrator type who bore toward Giovanni a fatal attraction. These dense reflections are contained, I suggest, like a box within a box, by the overall structure of the narrative's deathwatch. It is because of his mental branding, which enslaves him to a body in his brain, that the narrator, in the novel's final pages, can imagine Giovanni's death. For the death is in his mind. He does not literally, actually see it. It is still, by the time of his telling, out ahead of him. Giovanni's death, and subsequent decay, is only the inevitable future result of their relations.

As he did once before, the narrator now puffs out his story—this time by multiplying possible details for what he's seeing with his mind's inner eye:

Perhaps he begins to moan, perhaps he makes no sound. . . . Or, perhaps, when he cries out, he does not stop crying; perhaps his voice is crying now. . . . They drag him, or he walks. (222)

Are these narrative speculations buying time? In a sense, yes. They extend the telling that is leading up to death. But these extensions are no more able to stall the production of a corpse than they have been able all along to comprehend one. Pulling apart Giovanni's death is not a breaking down of its linguistic construction, so as to understand it. It hasn't happened yet; it is not yet composed. Pulling apart Giovanni's death is a *layering on* of linguistic phrases, so as, aesthetically, to compose—and, therefore, picture—a future decay. Or a future in decay. The future is stalled at the point of its richly pictured demise, though this demise is oddly seen from too many angles to seem precise.

In much the same way, Baldwin may already know in 1954–55, when he is in the midst of writing *Giovanni's Room*, barely after the decision in

Brown v. Board of Education, that the promise of desegregation is dying. Its very potential is stillborn and corpse-like. And Baldwin seems to know this corpse-like nature from too many angles to be what Cleaver (and Baldwin's readers) may recognize as obviously "political." Baldwin is a more surprising, if hidden, political writer. He knows the death of desegregation through the obliquities of male-to-male attractions and aggressions and repulsions, which bespeak attractions. He knows it also through decomposed forms, the sign of time's complex workings on what has been promised to American black men and women.

And yet, we notice: Baldwin's narrator (pale, blond) has discovered his manhood, just as Cleaver himself would predict, in the bodies of dark men. This is a manhood against expectations. It knows the sorrow of holding a man, beholding a man, who decomposes in other men's minds.

Chapter Five

PROPHYLACTICS AND BRAINS

SLAVERY IN THE CYBERNETIC AGE OF AIDS

Most of the blacks [I photograph] don't have health insurance and therefore can't afford [the AIDS drug] AZT. They all died quickly. . . . If I go through my *Black Book*, half of them are dead.
—Robert Mapplethorpe, "The Long Goodbye," 1989

To date, sixty-five million people around the world have become infected with HIV, most of them in Africa. Twenty-five million have died. In the next twenty years . . . the number could more than double. . . . The disease represents the worst disaster that we can reasonably expect to befall humanity in our lifetime.
—"The Vaccine," *The New Yorker*, 2003

Sixty Million and more.
—Toni Morrison, dedication to *Beloved*, 1987

Giving a different spin to his so-called objectification of nude black men, photographer Robert Mapplethorpe matter-of-factly refers to their status as going-to-be-dead men. (This was a status he shared with his models.) As a matter of fact, through their endeavors, so different on the surface, Mapplethorpe and Morrison meet at the crossroads of dying black people. He through his *Black Book* (1986) and, evidently, she through hers. As we learn from an interview with Toni Morrison in 1987, "the idea for the plot of *Beloved* came from an actual event—gleaned from a 19th-century newspaper story she'd discovered while editing *The Black Book* (an overview of black American history) at Random House."[1]

The actual event, as transformed by Toni Morrison, may be more disturbing than Quentin Tarantino's controversial depiction of a black man being anally raped, an image prepared for, in Tarantino's film, by the hanging of a black-leather captive reminiscent of a Mapplethorpe photograph (see chapter 3). Morrison's event is also more unusual, and likely more haunting, than the accidental shooting (again, in *Pulp Fiction*) of a black man in the face. The event—a slave mother's killing her daughter— becomes in *Beloved* something on the order of what clearly haunted both James Baldwin and Eldridge Cleaver: Emmett Till's death (see chapter 4). A body decomposing in groups of human minds. A future in decay. Or, for Toni Morrison, millions of futures in decline.

As it happens, Emmett Till was on Morrison's mind, at least at some point, during the process of writing *Beloved*. Either because she was frightened by her novel and thus had reached an impasse (so some say) or because she needed a break from this project, Morrison took time out to write a play while finishing *Beloved*.[2] She called it *Dreaming Emmett* (1985). Describing it in terms that could work for *Beloved*, Morrison explains: "I wanted to see a collision of three or four levels of time through the eyes of one person who could come back to life and seek vengeance. Emmett Till became that person."[3] Till's important function as a sign of early death—and a sign seeking vengeance down through the years— seems implied by the *New York Times* when it deems Till's death, in its interview with Morrison, "a shared collective nightmare of the American soul" "intended [by Morrison] to symbolize the plight of contemporary black urban youth—their disproportionately high rate of death by violence." "Like many Americans," the *Times* proceeds to say, "Miss Morrison is deeply perturbed by this tragedy of anonymous and wasted Emmett Tills."[4] And to be sure, Morrison's play, in its initial staging, underscored this contemporary edge to her sorrow over Emmett Till by using 1950s props, from the time of Till, with the spoken idioms and black argot of 1985.[5]

Dreaming Emmett, I suggest, was the perfect intermission in Morrison's five-year writing of *Beloved*. It allowed the author to rehearse a historical fiction that was also avowedly contemporary. It made attraction— uncontrollable attraction (allegedly that of a young black man for a white

Southern woman; later, in *Beloved*, a mother's for her daughter)—tangle with shame and violent revenge. But it did something more, something that opened the door to *Beloved*'s peculiar depictions of shared collective memories as a shameful virus. Morrison's play made one of the black community's most beloved dead, the dead Emmett Till, more troubling and dangerous than the rotting dead. No longer just the image of a de- composing face from *Jet* magazine (again, see chapter 4), this Till ghost, in Morrison's play, looks and breathes, walks and talks. In *Beloved*, the ghost (of the slave-ship dead: "Sixty Million and more") penetrates bodies and minds—and spreads.

AIDS, one could say, provides the most dramatic switchpoint between "black" and "queer" we might consider. In current public discourse, AIDS is the most intense and sorrowful place where the signs "black" and "queer" (or "gay" or "homosexual") consistently meet. Rates of infection among black Americans or black Africans are routinely compared to those of that original icon of AIDS in America: gay men. (Rarely are black gays mentioned as such.)[6] Access to drugs that may sustain life, we are now told, breaks along divisions between gay men (of economic means) and people of color, who often cannot afford these drugs. So the absolute dead- liness of AIDS is frequently depicted now as breaking between "black" and "queer," with Africa—the once iconic victim of American slavery—the new AIDS icon of certain, and gruesome, untimely death.[7]

With these dramatic developments in mind, this chapter is the culmi- nation to a book that has looked at debasements attached to the various actions of clothing, penetrating bottoms, anal rape, (mental) decomposi- tion, and, now, viral hauntings (by untimely deaths). A final switchpoint: the dangerous transmissions linked to AIDS (in 1987, when *Beloved* is pub- lished) as a way to understand a black slave mother's dangerous exchanges with her dead daughter. The focus here on surface (a mother's skin as a faulty prophylactic) and her body's penetration by material, viral, invasive signs, which lodge in her brain, bring surface, bodily depths, and the brain together as places where shame can manifest. This self-debasement of re- membering Beloved—of having her sign, "Sixty Million and more," inside one's head—is the climactic demonstration of a social self-debasement: the action of holding a veritable congress of the much beloved dead.

We know the dead live, for they reside, with strange intermittence, behind our eyes, in the room of our brain. We wonder how they breathe inside us, at the length of such an intimate remove. Really, the dead are a cybernetic problem. Alive in the virtual world of ideas—we think of them often—they pose a problem of storage and transfer. And they do spread.

I want to read *Beloved* as it is never read—as a novel born in 1987, in the cybernetic age of AIDS. Its melancholy pairing of untimely deaths with dangerous transmissions (between the living and the living dead) is the major issue I wish to consider. This is not to read *Beloved* as an AIDS book—not exactly so—but to claim its kinship to 1987 in its conception of a viral gothic. That is, *Beloved*, perhaps not accidentally, forges a model of viral memory.

As any reader is likely to remember, Beloved is the poster child of untimely death. She is a baby who was murdered by her mother, in order to be saved from a future of enslavement. Beloved first appears as the ghost of a baby who is haunting her mother. Then, in a more unusual form, Beloved returns as a teenage baby (at the age she would have been had she lived) to invade, flood-like—literally, in a fluids exchange—her mother's present life, and to open her mother to dangerous memories. Upon her mother's severe decline from a wasting illness, the neighborhood women drive off Beloved (by now she is a pregnant teen), leaving her memory to haunt the novel with what amounts to a dormancy. Why a black mother should have an auto-immune reaction to (the idea of) her dead daughter is the question I pose.

Mothers and their memories of their dead daughters, who could have been mothers, are one indication of Morrison's clever complication of time. As she conjures slavery's past, setting the novel in the 1870s, Morrison can look like a prophet of the future ills of 1987. AIDS, of course, would appear on the list of 1987's black American worries. But so would other versions of early demise: infant mortality (often caused by AIDS) and teen homicide (murders of and by teens).[8] Media reports on early death for black Americans even now routinely list AIDS, teen homicide, and infant mortality—even as they slide, unhelpfully, carelessly, into a dirge on pregnant teens, as if reproduction is being seen more as a kind of transmission, the replication of early death. Policy experts have long joined the media in this act, sliding the sorrow of early death under their larger concern over rates of black reproduction.

Morrison may make a canny reply. She makes the early death of Beloved, a teenage infant when she appears, her book's most layered sorrow. (The reader is even asked, in this way, to mourn the loss of a pregnant teen.) At the same time, Morrison turns the stereotype of the black-pregnant-teen-as-a-reproductive-threat toward a different kind of sadness that permeates *Beloved*. Through an image of threatening reproduction, Toni Morrison examines how *the dead* reproduce, how they spread in human memory, and, as the ultimate act of embrace, how we face and store the dead as they travel, aggressively alive, in our minds.

There is even prescience to Morrison's depictions of mental copies. Remarkably, the model of memory she forges in the middle eighties shares key concepts with 1990s developments in cloning and the world of cyberspace. There are narrative reasons for this prescience. That is to say, in writing *Beloved*, and offering its particular sorrows, Morrison needed to shape for herself two critical notions. First, her novel required the notion of a virtual future for those who have died, a future "in effect though not in fact" (according to the dictionary definition of "virtual"), a future lived only as someone's idea (for example, a parent's idea of a future for an embryonic child), such as we find in human cloning. Second, *Beloved* needed the notion of how ideas occupy a physical space and, therefore, travel and physically enter human brains, which is a concept that grounds the world of cyberspace.

With the now foreseeable procedure of cloning human embryos, we can imagine new lives for the dead. We can conceive of replacing a dead child with its exact genetic equivalent, starting it over by raising its copy from an embryo, which becomes a child—again. For less urgent reasons, according to *Time*, couples who set aside clone embryos of a particular child "could give birth to the same child every few years" at different intervals. In that sense, *Time* magazine says, "an exact template for what a child could become in 10 or 20 years could be before them in the form of an older sibling."[9] And yet, we should notice the virtual nature of even these futures, which disproves the logic of *Time*. One can likely clone an embryo; however, one cannot clone a child at different intervals precisely because, with the passing of time, one cannot clone a future. Even with the eerie resurrection of the dead, a dead child's future is lost irretrievably. A future dies once and can never live again, except as a thought kept alive in someone's mind. That is to say, a copy-child, as it viewed its "template," would see a future the copy-child could never possess (as anything other than an idea), since its interval from its clone-sibling would always assure that it would live in a different world than that its clone inhabited at the same age. Contrary to the logic of *Time* magazine, the copy would grow up watching the death of its original possibilities, just as a woman who gave birth to her own twin, by incubating her own clone embryo, could never truly relive her past. Her ungraspable personal past would be an impossible future for her twin. In any case, the future of such futures is on ice: "there are . . . floating embryos [*Time* magazine says] floating around in liquid nitrogen baths . . . in a kind of icy limbo."[10]

Beloved depicts the sorrow surrounding virtual futures, held for the dead in human brains. As it happens, it is hard to keep someone "in mind." The novel also knows the invasive force (and the viral force) of such ideas, which truly have a life of their own. They move, they spread, they insist themselves against the will of those who hold them. This is why *Beloved*, with such strange prescience, seems to belong to the cybernetic fold. The novel depicts the potential fright of how we take information to ourselves.

Of course, on the face of it, since it is mere confabulation (not flesh), the world of cyberspace seems a fairly benign domain of transmissions and copies. Companies, at the outset, were scrambling to simplify the task of "cruising the information highway," making intellectual promiscuity more efficient and, intriguingly, more anonymous. The goal, in fact, said AT&T, was to enable users to find "where information is buried" without having to learn "where it comes from [or] how it got there."[11] The breakthrough began in 1993 with the creation of the World Wide Web, famous for its "hyperlinking." Hyperlinks, as is now familiar, are simply key words—"Beloved" could be one—that appear in bold type. When clicked on, they transmit Web users to further discussion of that keyword on other Web pages, which may be stored in other computers thousands of miles away. Sounds safe for such rampant transmissions. In fact, *Business Week*, which explained hyperlinking techniques to its readers in 1995, did not appear to notice its ironic choice of a keyword example: namely, "antigen" (a substance that, when introduced into the body, stimulates the production of an antibody).

Indeed, fears of invasion have grown. Cyberprophylactics are being developed, meant to protect against viral floodings of information and the pranks of cyberpunks roaming the Net.[12] "The technology is in the hands of the children," *60 Minutes* complained in a story, citing kids and teens as the masterminds of cyberinvasions and giving us, as their sole example, a black, streetwise, gold-toothed hacker with an impish grin. The upshot?

"No one is immune," says one article; "the potential for invasion of privacy [is] severe"; "[they] can get in and [they] can be you."[13]

Hackers, for their part, lend a viral edge to these fears. They celebrate their viral powers, their ability to invade the control of information. In this way (and let me lean on this point, since it matches key divisions between Beloved and her mother), hackers heighten generational divides between themselves and their cyberphobic elders who fear their invasions. Some hackers even claim for their actions a radical purpose and civic good, seeing their stealth and viral tactics as corrective to government discourse on AIDS, the environment, psychedelics, sexuality, and spiritual life on this planet. Take the example of Generation X writers R. U. Sirius of *Mondo 2000* and Douglas Rushkoff of *Media Virus!* Both urge activist youth to inject their own "agendas into the datastream in the form of *ideological code*."[14] They deem Generation X the first American generation "fully engaged in a symbiotic relationship with media" (31), owing to this generation's unprecedented ability to "feed back" and "change what's on the screen" (30). In his characteristic rush of optimism, arguing for the "power of virology to effect social change," Rushkoff cheerfully argues that a virus acts as a kind of reality-tracker, since a virus "will always make the system it is attacking appear as confusing and unresolvable as it really is" (36).[15] Santa Cruz hacker Bill Me Tuesday goes so far as to fashion "a healing medical model" when he suggests that "viruses can act like a logic analyzer. . . . [and] serve as a means of creating a self-repairing system" (248). A similar point is made by *Newsweek* in a story on the unacknowledged benefits of computer viruses: "a few scientists [for example, Fred Cohen in his book *It's Alive*] have begun to argue that [computer] viruses are actually living organisms, capable someday of evolving into autonomous Net-runners that will retrieve information for their owners."[16]

With much sadder tones, *Beloved* itself forges a model of data retrieval, one derived from older forms. We could tag it "viral gothic." The novel's ghost, ambiguously alive, retrieves information not just on the slave experience that her mother never had (Beloved's ghostly connections to slaves on their middle passage), but on the virtual, viral life of dead bodies in one's brain. "Beloved" is a version of autonomous retrieval: a keyword with a life of its own. The word first appears as a name on a tombstone and thus as a site of buried information. And yet, soon enough, "Beloved" becomes an idea on a romp, hounding the living to get inside them. More than that, Sethe's single beloved seems to stand for the nameless dead, perhaps for the "Sixty Million and more" dead slaves invoked in Morrison's dedication. To encounter "Beloved" in Morrison's book is to find oneself carried to (the idea of) hyperlinked files (Sixty Million and more) existing as a series of virtual futures. This is slavery in a way we have often failed to grasp it: bondage to a set of virtual remains.

To be sure, Beloved, when she is dead, is a virtual child, kept alive in a watery limbo. (Beloved refers to "the water in the place where we crouched," to the sea, to a bridge over water where she waited; she speaks of coming out of blue water.)[17] When she returns as a teenage infant (no small trick), she seems to come back as a clone of herself: the idea of herself embodied at a different interval from herself. In fact, she is an interval. She now embodies in ghostly fashion the interval between her death and her mother's current life, as if she's been marking time while dead. Killed by her mother before the age of two, she returns eighteen years past her murder, as a nineteen-year-old baby-woman.[18] (Denver, her once baby-sister, still alive, is age eighteen.) I am going to argue that Beloved makes her mother ill with interval when she enters her as an idea. Moreover, according to the book's depictions, Sethe becomes memory-infected, surely at Beloved's death, but recognizably (as if she's testing positive for infection) at Beloved's return. By the end of the book, Sethe has clearly gone into symptoms (of some strange sort), which is why the women want to unload Beloved from the house.

Interlaced with interval is a sense of latency, the feeling that something suspended pursues.[19] Recall that when *Beloved* was written and published, "latency" or "interval" formed a distinguishing medical feature of the medical category HIV-positive. HIV was not only the infection of a body with the virus that causes AIDS (as it still is). It was also medically conceived as the interval between infection and the onset of symptoms (as it may be). For this reason, HIV, in the absence of symptoms, was (and can be) a strange state of latency in which you are ill with an idea, the frightening idea of your possible death, making you dramatically nostalgic for yourself before you decline. You find you fall ill with nostalgia for a future, a time in which you clearly saw a future before you.

This is the sickness Sethe enters when her daughter makes her ill with interval: Sethe increasingly starts going back, into her past, by a series of hyperlinks on her web, activating keywords that open files on shame, beauty, fascination, and a future of virtual remains.[20]

No wonder *Beloved* scouts the need for a mental prophylactic, a kind of mental condom, protecting against invasive, viral memory. In mid-eighties fashion, Morrison reaches for surface protections. She offers figuration of a surface sheath. In fact, the narrative imagines Sethe's focus-on-her-surface *as* a form of brain protection, one that defends against some logic alive and loose in Sethe's mind. And so, at the start, just three pages in, following a pointed count of the children Sethe and her mother-in-law have lost (Baby Suggs, eight; Sethe, three), we find this first long passage on memory:

> [Sethe] worked hard to remember as close to nothing as was safe. Unfortunately her brain was devious. She might be hurrying across a field, running practically, to get to the pump quickly and rinse the chamomile sap from her legs. Nothing else would be in her mind. The picture of the men coming to nurse her was as lifeless as the nerves in her back where the skin buckled like a washboard. Nor was there the faintest scent of ink or the cherry gum and oak bark from which it was made. Nothing. Just the breeze cooling her face as she rushed toward water. And then sopping the chamomile away with pump water and rags, her mind fixed on getting every last bit of sap off. . . . Then something. The plash of water, the sight of her shoes and stockings awry on the path where she had flung them; or Here Boy lapping in the puddle near her feet, and suddenly there was Sweet Home rolling, rolling, rolling out before her eyes, and although there was not a leaf on that farm that did not make her want to scream, it rolled itself out before her in shameless beauty. . . . Boys hanging from the most beautiful sycamores in the world. It shamed her—remembering the wonderful soughing trees rather than the boys. Try as she might to make it otherwise, the sycamores beat out the children every time and she could not forgive her memory for that. (6)

This beginning captures the workings of the mind, making them a topic for the narrative's own discussion of the brain. But it does more. It offers a structural clue to how other scenes in the novel may take place: how keywords ("remember," in this scene's first sentence, or, later, "a plash of water") open doors in the novel's plot, suspending (or slowing) narrative time as the novel's readers are moved, through these keywords, into scenes in characters' brains, which we are unprepared to receive.[21] There, we are captive to their mental cameras, riding the blind curve of images they would keep from rolling out.

In this scene, *Beloved*'s obsession with safety is suddenly made precarious by a brain Morrison typifies as "devious." Sethe's brain is a house divided, the "devious" part working against some other form of benign intent—that (more sensible) part of her "mind fixed on getting every last bit of sap off" her skin. Indeed, the image of chamomile sap on Sethe's skin draws attention to her surface, her body's surface sheath. The sap even seems to stick in opposition to the contents of her mind that, blessedly, are absent. But if we look again, we see that this image, or intent, or sensation of sap-on-skin is itself in Sethe's mind. It's just that "nothing else" is. Her brain, for the moment, is focused on her surface. It sees only skin. Lurking but "lifeless," however, is a picture—a threatening scene of "men coming to nurse her." This picture's ambiguous status—"lifeless" but not forever dead?—is conveyed by comparison: "as lifeless as" nerve-dead skin. Another specific sensation—a scent—is positively not there, implying that on other occasions it must be a frequent visitor, since her brain, or maybe just the narrative, has caught it not at home. Nothing is there, we are told, "just the breeze cooling her face as she rushed toward water." Again, a sensation is *in* the brain, though rendered as if it is worn on the skin. Remarkably, then, as narratively ordered, the danger images (nursing and ink) are narratively sheathed, wrapped round before and aft, by skinflickerings (sap on legs, breeze on face) imagined as a form of brain protection. These brain contents—skinflicks, I'll call them—keep the brain's internal camera focused out, tracking skin, as a way to protect against the (here) obscure but possibly pornographic contents of the nursing picture and the scent of ink.

"Then something." Not the willed flipping of a switch. Rather, links accidentally tripped—a plash of water, the sight of shoes, a dog drinking—that when they enter Sethe's brain, through ear or eye, mysteriously open an inside file. In fact, she is its hapless prey in a brain competition she is always poised to lose. For with an evident agency of its own— "it rolled itself out before her"—its insistence linguistically captured by word copies ("rolling, rolling, rolling")—"it" selects beautiful trees, not the boys who are lynched, as the point of her remembrance. Shame, it appears, is a brain fascination one cannot control or perhaps understand. For "try as she might to make it otherwise, the sycamores beat out the children every time and she could not forgive her memory for that."

Sethe's skinflicks and their breach recall the side of Freud now taboo.

Hardwire Freud: the speculative Freud of *Beyond the Pleasure Principle*. Even though Freud, in this treatise and others, was fixed on invasions of the mind from within, his detailed address to the brain's "protective shields" in *Beyond the Pleasure Principle* concerns "floodings" from the outside world, how the mind does or does not get "flooded with large amounts of stimulus."[22] In part, Freud's focus is available storage space in the brain, especially space for consciousness; for if every excitation were retained as something conscious, the mind would quickly reach its limit for "receiving fresh excitations" (27). Drawing on Helmholz's and Fechner's physical energy theories, Freud declares: *"protection against* stimuli is an almost more important function for the living organism than *reception of* stimuli" (30; his emphasis).

So much so, it seems, that Freud writes his own prophylactic story. He spins a rather speculative tale about how the human brain develops from the skin and, along the way, explains how the skin protects the brain. Embryology, Freud explains, "actually shows" that "the central nervous system originates from the ectoderm . . . and may have inherited some of its essential properties" (29). Along these lines, Freud suggests that the brain's gray matter was originally a highly receptive skin that "in highly developed organisms . . . has long been withdrawn into the depths of the interior of the body, though portions of it [in the form of sense organs] have been left behind on the surface immediately beneath the general shield against stimuli" (31). This "general shield" (in human beings, skin) allows the energy of the external world to pass into the organism's next layers "with only a fragment of their original intensity" (30). In his example of primitive living vesicles, Freud imagines this layer as dead: "[This] outermost surface ceases to have the structure proper to living matter . . . and thenceforward functions as a special envelope . . . resistant to stimuli." "By its death," Freud concludes, "the outer layer has saved all the deeper ones from a similar fate" (30).

Intriguingly, Morrison, writing her own prophylactic fiction, conjures relations resembling Freud's (from his hardwire tale). For starters, she gives her protagonist, Sethe, a back full of nerve-dead skin, the result of a whipping that opened Sethe's back and closed it with a scar in the shape of a tree. Time and again, Morrison, in *Beloved*, plays with depictions of surface protections, often at the level of bodily envelope, only to dramatize the dangerously permeable borders between the brain and its visitors. Freud himself believed that the mind had no shield toward the inside. The organism's solution? Projection (Freud's own theory of skinflicks).

"[T]here is a tendency to treat [excitations] as though they were acting, not from the inside, but from the outside, so that it may be possible to bring the shield against stimuli into operation as a means of defense against them." "This is the origin of *projection*," says Freud (33; his emphasis).

Beloved is full of projective display: brain excitations projected out to the body's perimeters so as to shield one's interior against them. Largely, however, these shieldings fail. Consider the milk on Sethe's mind and the tree that appears on the surface of her back. The tree, composed of nerve-dead skin, is (the sign of) a possible surface-protection. Milk, by contrast, as strange as it sounds, signals bodily borders breached; milk is a dangerous bodily fluid in *Beloved*, since its ingestion often signals external invasion. "Milk," in fact, keeps swamping "tree" with its suggestions of danger and loss. Paul D asks, "what tree on your back?" (15), only to retreat from Sethe's advancing meditation on milk ("I had milk for my baby girl. . . . Nobody was going to nurse her like me," 16). When Paul D at last interjects, the narrative makes its careful weave between the signs of "milk" and "tree":

> "We was talking 'bout a tree, Sethe."
> "After I left you, those boys came in there and took my milk. . . . Held me down and took it. I told Mrs. Garner on em. . . . Them boys found out I told on em. School-teacher made one open up my back, and when it closed it made a tree. It grows there still."
> "They used cowhide on you?"
> "And they took my milk."
> "They beat you and you was pregnant?"
> "And they took my milk!" (16–17)

What was lost to Sethe as milk makes its appearance on her surface as "tree," so that this "tree" is always in danger of referencing Sethe's memory of milk, making Sethe ingest shame anew.

For this important reason, "tree" bespeaks the limits of a mental prophylactic (the failure of any surface protection) that seems to be one step behind invasion. Soon other invasive memories start to attach to the sign of the tree on Sethe's back ("it grows there still"). What grows on the tree, as the plot through backward advance unfolds, is the signified "sawing": sawing one's beloved-as-tree.[23] "Milk," again, is hypertextually tied to this relation in *Beloved*'s famous scene of a sawing followed by a milking, since after Sethe has slashed Beloved's neck with a saw (to save her from the approaching slavers), Sethe nurses Denver, "aiming a bloody nipple into the baby's mouth," so that "Denver took her mother's milk right along with the blood of her sister" (152). Here is a nursing blooming with loss. In fact, the lost blooms of *Beloved* are the "doomed roses" planted by a "sawyer"—"something to take the sin out of slicing trees for a living" (47). The "stench" of these dying blooms pervades the scene that precedes Beloved's return, before she comes back to sit on "a [tree] stump" with her "new skin, lineless and smooth" (50).

Beloved may be the ultimate skinflick: a brain content, a clear excitation, projected outside. Readers will likely recall that one of the chief complications of reading *Beloved* is trying to fathom where Beloved, at the point she returns, is portrayed as returning *from*. Should we imagine that she's a projection of Sethe's mind—treated "as though [she] were acting, not from the inside, but . . . the outside"—and thus her mother's mental defense against an invasion of shame from within? Are we to think she's been living lost behind Sethe's eyes as a word or idea or future that desperately wants itself thought? Whatever we, as readers, surmise, some evident break in a shield surrounds Beloved's appearance. A fluids exchange, in all of its strangeness, in front of an outhouse, makes a dangerous breach for a body foreign, and known—as we now see.

Selfish Memes

Beloved's mother-daughter reunion takes its place as an outhouse scene:

A fully dressed woman [Beloved, that is] walked out of the water. . . . Everything hurt but her lungs most of all. Sopping wet and breathing shallow she spent those hours trying to negotiate the weight of her eyelids. . . . "Look," said Denver, "What is that?" And, for some reason she could not immediately account for, the moment she got close enough to see the face, Sethe's bladder filled to capacity. She said, "Oh, excuse me," and ran around to the back of 124. Not since she was a baby girl . . . had she had an emergency that unmanageable. She never made the outhouse. Right in front of its door she had to lift her skirts, and the water she voided was endless. Like a horse, she thought, but as it went on and on she thought, No, more like flooding the boat when Denver was born. So much water Amy said, "Hold on . . . you going to sink us you keep that up." But there was no stopping water breaking from a breaking womb and there was no stopping now. . . . [She was] squatting in front of her . . . privy making a mudhole too deep to be witnessed without shame. Just about the time she started wondering if the carnival would accept another freak, it stopped. She tidied herself and ran around to the porch. No one was there. All three were inside— Paul D and Denver standing before the stranger, watching her drink cup after cup of water. (50–51)

Only Morrison would imagine the filling of a mother's mind with her dead daughter's face (the waste of a life) as the filling of a mother's bladder to capacity. Such a conception cunningly delays before it delivers its recognition that birthing is voiding. The endless voiding here reminds Sethe of flooding a boat with a newborn's birth, anchoring floating to the cruel joke of sinking. And yet this suggestion of birthing as sadly voiding human life has been brooding in *Beloved* since its inception on the novel's third page. Consider the phrase "knees wide open as any grave" (5). This is a sexual image at the start. (Sethe is trading her body for the tombstone that will mark Beloved's grave.) But this is an image that also imagines a quick path to death, with no middle passage to burial from birth. Here in this later scene of a voiding, the lingering legacy of slavery takes shape as a fluids exchange.

Indeed, throughout *Beloved*, the worry is over stopping the flow of memories in and out of bodies, in and out of brains. (We think of Freud's worries.) And yet, in this scene, when flow is stopped, and all might seem safely at an end, the strange cause—or is it the effect?—of Sethe's voiding is *already inside*, drinking cup after cup of water. The scene of Sethe's voiding that we thought was focused on getting something out is taking something in, for while Sethe has gone around to the back, Beloved has entered from the front. The cause and effect of transmission, in fact, make a temporal smear. Has Sethe's voiding caused Beloved's thirst? Or has Beloved's thirst—her quest to be inside—filled Sethe's bladder to capacity? We are not told, but we do learn this: Beloved is infected with cholera ("All that water. Sure sign," Paul D says [53]). One of her major symptoms is incontinence.[24] Symptoms aside, Sethe herself is memory-positive, infected with the idea of a birthing that led to a voiding of human life.

The spate of *Beloved*'s viral depictions is yet to come. I say "viral" for the sake of my reading. But this is no stretch. It plausibly accommodates scenes of decline from Beloved's entry in the passage above to Sethe's hosting of lethal relations—what I am calling "a mother's autoimmune reaction to (the idea of) her dead daughter." There is an even more uncanny parallel, we will later see, to Sethe's increasingly odd and pleading negotiations with Beloved: the letters written to AIDS by its sufferers, found in the best-selling self-help guide *Immune Power*.

But first, it is time to explore why Beloved's viral agendas (as the baby-teen she is in 1987) lack the giddy, optimistic flavor of those produced by cyber-teen activists of the 1990s—activists who argue for teenage-fostered social progress (of a rather vague sort).[25] Take, for example, Jody Radzik, as cited by viral proponent Douglas Rushkoff:

> Radzik first became aware of the power of viruses in the third grade: "I wanted to be a microbiologist, and I became aware of the T4 bacterio-phage ('a DNA virus'). . . . They use T4 to intentionally infect bacteria—to tag them or even to do gene splicing for them. I was fascinated by that. . . ." Jody developed a viral identity . . . and began in the most grass-roots meme pool he could find in his Oakland neighborhood: graf-fiti. . . . [which] became a conduit for Radzik's technological and viral memes: "One day it just occurred to me to call my posse CIP for Cul-tural Insurgent Phages and to make one of my tags 'virus.' My name became 'Saint Virus' because it was a total juxtaposition of something that sounds good with something that sounds bad. I wanted to show that I was a virus, but that I don't want to hurt anybody. I just want to do whatever I can to help evolution along. . . . [We would be] cultural terrorists who would go around infecting inadequate social complexes with little pieces of information that would then deconstruct that so-cial phenomenon. . . . Everywhere I had a tag, I had a little physic lis-tening post. By having a network of tags in my own geographical area, I sort of drew energy from them." (*Media Virus*, 297–98)

For Rushkoff's Radzik, viral fascination and the microbiological-turned-urban-guerrilla game of "tag" find their roots in childhood. In Radzik's own implicit "evolution," his T4 devotion makes "viral identity" the only identity worthy of "saints" who are packing (not guns but) "memes" (more on these in a moment). In his world, copying is transpersonal growth ("I sort of drew energy from them"), a way of plumping the self who feeds back to the culture at large. In fact, the antiestablishment slant to Radzik's vaguely specified target of "cultural terrorism" ("inadequate social com-plexes," "that social phenomenon") contributes to the ensuing success of his self-growth industry. Rushkoff reports:

> By becoming a "somebody" in the graffiti world, Radzik developed the ability to market himself as an expert on youth culture. He was

scooped up by sportswear designers at companies like Stussy and Gotcha, where he chose to make T-shirts the new canvas for his viral tags and chaos ideology. . . . [First "to put a fractal on a T-shirt"] . . . he was hoping to use all of [his] memes to empower the individuals in youth culture to feed back their own impulses to the culture at large and accept their roles as active promoters of viral iteration. (299–300)

It must be noticed that Beloved-as-memory shares something crucial with Rushkoff's portrait of Jody-as-virus. She, like he, is an icon of protest against restraints. Against the restraints of "inadequate social complexes," to put it mildly. To put it more forcefully, in Beloved's case: against the restraints of government-sponsored forced labor and a kind of censorship of the soul that leads to self-censorship (Sethe holding her past at bay, Paul D locking his heart in a tin). But when Baby Suggs, not just Beloved, tries to fight against suppression, the fervor of her preaching is defeated by invasion. (Several times she repeats the line "I'm saying [the whitefolks] came in my yard.")[26] Here is what Morrison has to engage that Rushkoff, Radzik, and their fellow enthusiasts have to downplay for the sake of their empowerment: invasion can be the other side of restraint. Slavery is invasion as well as restraint. Invasion by the idea of an interval—between the past you once had and the future you have lost. For Sethe, it's the interval between Beloved's death and Sethe's current life in 1873; for the reader, it's the interval between that complex known as "slavery" and the reader's current life. This is an interval very much alive, but, only rarely, vitally spoken.

Actually, invasion—invasive ideas—should be grasped by youthful hackers and their activist cohort as potentially oppressive, not just liberating. For this idea of invasive ideas underlies renowned zoologist Richard Dawkins's idea of ideas, or what he calls "memes"; an idea of ideas so compelling, evidently, that hacker activists pepper their writings with mention of "memes" and ground their views with Dawkins's theory of viral transfer. A meme, we learn, is "a complex idea" that (1) forms a memorable unit; and (2) replicates itself, reliably, with fecundity. Memes, for example, can range from "tunes, catch-phrases . . . clothes fashions," to inventions, academic ideas, and symphonies.[27] In Dawkins's book *The Selfish Gene* (1976), a best-seller in thirteen languages, he coins "meme" to sound like "gene"; it refers, moreover, to the Greek root of imitation, "mimeme," and is meant to call up "memory" and "même," the French word for "self" or "same." Daniel Dennett, a cognitive philosopher, has given wide play to the theory of "memes" in his well-known book *Consciousness Explained* (1991). These theorists together offer what they claim are stranger-than-fiction actualities of cultural evolution, for what interests both of these authors is how cultural transmission is analogous to genetic transmission. Dawkins writes:

> Just as genes propagate themselves in the gene pool by leaping from body to body via sperms or eggs, so memes propagate themselves in the meme pool by leaping from brain to brain via a process which, in the broad sense, can be called imitation. . . . As my colleague N. K. Humphrey neatly [sums] up . . . "memes should be regarded as living structures. . . . When you plant a fertile meme in my mind you literally parasitize my brain. . . . [T]he meme for, say, 'belief in life after death' is actually realized physically, millions of times over, as a structure in the nervous systems of individual men the world over." (192)

Fifteen years later, when Dennett summarizes Dawkins's views in 1991, AIDS-related memes emerge. Now memes "leap promiscuously," prove "unquarantinable," are sometimes "pernicious invaders" that prove as deadly and as "hard to eradicate" as "the AIDS virus, for instance."[28]

Dennett, even more than Dawkins, stresses the debasement of the mind by memes that "distract us, burden our memories, derange our judgment" (*Consciousness Explained*, 204). In a passage that Dennett seems to mean as partly comical, he magnifies this point: "I don't know about you, but I'm not initially attracted by the idea of my brain as a sort of dung heap in which the larvae of other people's ideas renew themselves, before sending out copies of themselves in an informational Diaspora. It does seem to rob my mind of its importance as both author and critic. Who's in charge, according to this vision—we or our memes?" (202).

Memes, in Dawkins's view, do not spread because they are good for human populations; they spread because they are good at replicating. Dennett adds: "Memes, like genes, are *potentially* immortal, but, like genes, they depend on the existence of a continuous chain of physical vehicles" (205; his emphasis). Books and even monuments can disappear with time, but thousands or millions of copies of a single meme or meme-complex will account for a meme's "penetrance," its "infective power." And yet, aside from promiscuous travel, a meme's fate depends on the nature of the vehicles that carry the meme into its future. Dennett specifies each meme's ultimate destination as the very kind of place from which it spreads: "The haven all memes depend on reaching is the human mind, but a human mind is itself an artifact created when memes restructure a human brain in order to make it a better habitat for memes" (207). We should not forget that memes are dependent. Like attention-seeking infants, they seek the mind's nurture (its "nest," its "haven" [206–07]). But they also change the structure of a brain to make of the mind their own "habitat." In what he calls his "Pandemonium model" (241), alluding to Milton's *Paradise Lost*, Dennett explains "what words do with us." They are on the alert, he says, to get "incorporated," "ingested," but "when we let [them] in" they "tend to take over, creating us out of the raw materials they find in our brains" (417).

Clearly, this forced ingestion of memes is not the heady rush of control one discovers in Rushkoff, Radzik, R. U. Sirius, or Timothy Leary. Dawkins and Dennett are hardly optimistic in any grand sense—hence they are sometimes tagged "sociobiological" by their critics. In fact, ironically, it is their very discourse on equipping the mind in its defensive fight *against* memes that has lent an insurrectionary edge to their views—an edge hacker activists have appropriated for their call to rebellion. Here, for example, is how Dawkins ends *The Selfish Gene*: "We have the power to defy ['our creators'] the selfish genes of our birth and, if necessary, the selfish memes of our indoctrination. . . . . We, alone on earth, can rebel against the tyranny of the selfish replicators" (200–201).[29] This voice of defiance echoes Milton's Satan via Blake and Shelley, offering a kind of Romantic view of rebellion's allure. (No wonder Dawkins, in July '95, appeared on the cover of *Wired* magazine, touted as a "bad-boy evolutionist.") From this Promethean ledge, hacker optimists leap past the issue of memes in our minds, invading our brains, to focus solely on our manufacture of memes that attack established views.[30]

By dramatic contrast, the wary tone one finds in Dawkins (and Dennett, too) clearly emerges in Morrison's novel. With its fear of mental invasion to the fore, *Beloved*, too, runs with a point seen implicitly in Saussure, in his stress on "the physiological transmission of the sound-image" out of someone's brain into someone else's ear.[31] The point is this: a sign, in order to be a sign to you, must get inside your body. Actually, it must enter your body through an orifice, usually ear or eye. In *Beloved*, it even enters the body through the gullet. Ingestion, that is, is the site of a struggle where a daughter restructures her mother's brain. For her part, Beloved, her own head nearly sawed off by Sethe, would likely depend on reaching the haven of a human mind. For just like a meme, though she evokes the clear language of purpose, she clearly has no mind of her own. Hungry for a haven—"Sethe was licked, tasted, eaten by Beloved's eyes" (57)—Beloved makes Sethe memory-ingestive, as if Sethe eats in accordance with an appetite foreign to her own.

One particular memory fest appears in the guise of a force-feeding. Paul D has just told Sethe that Halle—Sethe's husband—saw the boys hold her down and take her milk (Halle watched from the loft in the barn). In terms of narrative technique, it's a highly stylized scene. Eleven times in two pages the phrase "he saw" (a replicative meme) is repeated in seesaw conversation. ("He saw?"; "He saw"; "whatever he saw go on in that barn . . . broke him like a twig"; "He saw them boys do that to me and let them keep on breathing air? He saw? He saw? He saw?"; "I never knew he saw" [68–69].) The phrase is actually making a slit in the reader's mind that will later allow linked saws to seep in (the sawyer and his doomed roses; Sawyer's restaurant, where Sethe works; Beloved's sawed neck; Paul D's fright that Sethe "talked about safety with a hand-saw" [164]). Structurally even, the meme's repetition is stalling for time, making a short interval between itself ("he saw") and something Sethe will see of Halle as she eats a new memory. For unbeknown to Sethe, there's more for her to learn: "'You may as well know it all [Paul D announces to Sethe]. Last time I saw him he was sitting by the churn. He had butter all over his face.' Nothing happened, and she was grateful for that. Usually she could see the picture right away of what she heard. But she could not picture what Paul D said. Nothing came to mind" (69).

In this context, interval is thematized as the structure of a latent trauma. For when the meaning finally hits, Sethe's delayed recognition suddenly sinks with a vengeance, and the opening of her mind is displayed as the unwilled opening of an orifice:

> She shook her head from side to side, resigned to her rebellious brain.
> . . . Like a greedy child it snatched up everything. Just once, could it
> say, No thank you? I just ate and can't hold another bite? I am full God
> damn it of two boys with mossy teeth, one sucking on my breast the
> other holding me down. . . . Add my husband to it, watching, above me
> in the loft. . . . But my greedy brain says, Oh thanks, I'd love more—
> so I add more. And no sooner than I do, there is no stopping. There is
> also my husband squatting by the churn smearing the butter as well as
> the clabber all over his face because the milk they took is on his mind.
> And as far as he is concerned, the world may as well know it. (70)

As if restructured, Sethe's brain resembles Beloved: "like a greedy child it snatched up everything." Here is an eating disorder equivalent to Sethe's bladder filling to capacity, again with "no stopping." But something more than the brain's involuntary bingeing is revealing. Notice how Halle projects the contents of his mind to his face, wearing them as visible waste for the world to see. He smears the butter "because the milk they took is on his mind"; and this action, Sethe imagines, is Halle's way of stopping his brain ("what a relief to stop it right there"). As for Sethe, "her brain was not interested in the future." "Loaded with the past and hungry for more, it left her no room to imagine, let alone plan for, the next day" (70).

Sethe's gorging appears to be a skewing, a reprise in minor key, of a feast from her short twenty-eight-day period of maternal bliss, between her escape from the slave plantation and her killing of Beloved. That charmed period (the length of a woman's menstrual cycle) was characterized by what Sethe can only remember as "a kind of selfishness," which she renders, rather fittingly, as a kind of bigness and width: "I birthed them and I got them out. . . . It felt good. . . . I was big . . . and wide" (162). In celebration of her joy, she and Baby Suggs had thrown a feast for ninety people, "who ate so well, and laughed so much, it made them angry" (136). This was deemed a "reckless generosity" (137) (a nice phrase for maternal indulgence), which "offended . . . by excess" (138). Meanness was the result of this feast—the kind of meanness that slants across nearly all the book's depicted relations. No one warned Sethe a white man was coming to take her and her children back to slavery; the result was Beloved's death at Sethe's hands.

In a thought to linger on, Morrison makes a maternal hedonism (not a sexual hedonism) the innocent cause of untimely death and dangerous transmissions. Yet, when it all comes back in memory, that is to say when Beloved comes back, the innocence and generosity of the feasting, along with Sethe's width ("I was big . . . and wide"), becomes the gorging of a hedonistic memory—the gorging of Beloved (herself a selfish meme) that grows fat on Sethe's stories and sends Sethe into symptoms. By the end, sickness is a solitude of two, who are locked inside their house. Of course, it is cunning of Morrison to make us wonder—as many readers do—if Beloved is pregnant with Paul D's child.[32] Cunning, I say, since there is a more compelling explanation: Beloved is "pregnant" from "eating" her mother. What can this mean? And how does it bring us, finally, to symptoms?

In *Beloved*'s last third, Sethe and Beloved (with Denver more as witness than participant) are trying to reinhabit Sethe's hedonistic interval, the twenty-eight days between her escape and her murder of Beloved:

> The thirty-eight dollars of life savings went to feed themselves with fancy food and decorate themselves with ribbon and dress goods, which Sethe cut and sewed like they were going somewhere in a hurry. Bright clothes—with blue stripes and sassy prints. . . . Sethe played all the harder with Beloved, who never got enough of anything: lullabies, new stitches, the bottom of the cake bowl, the top of the milk. . . . It was as though her mother had lost her mind.[33]

Feasting, festival, and play reemerge here, but illness finally overtakes this interval. (Like the magical twenty-eight days, it lasts "a whole month.") At first, the two (Beloved and Sethe) are interchangeable: "they changed beds and exchanged clothes. Walked arm and arm and smiled all the time. . . . It was difficult for Denver to tell who was who" (240–41). Then, Beloved becomes the mother, Sethe the teething child, with eyes "fever bright": "Then it seemed to Denver the thing was done: Beloved bending over Sethe looked the mother, Sethe the teething child. . . . The bigger Beloved got, the smaller Sethe became; the brighter Beloved's eyes, the more those eyes that used never to look away became slits of sleeplessness. Sethe no longer combed her hair or splashed her face with water. She sat in the chair licking her lips like a chastised child while Beloved ate up her life, took it, swelled up with it, grew taller on it. . . . her belly protruding like a winning watermelon. . . . [T]he older woman yielded up [her life]."[34]

Here is a form of what AIDS watchers know as autoimmunity, where the body mistakes its "invader" for its "self" and thus lets it in. Consider this explanation given in *Discover* magazine: "Some researchers suspect that the virus . . . trick[s] [the immune system] into an assault on itself . . . causing the T cells to commit suicide. . . . Think about it: to the body, a key part of the AIDS virus looks like—of all things—the 'self' badge on a crucial subset of its own cells."[35] In current cyber-lingo, the virus is a cyberpunk: "I can get in and I can be you." *Rolling Stone* adds to this picture: "Like any virus, the sole mission of HIV is to reproduce. . . . [The virus] twists its genes into the [T-helper's] genes, then, with the host as its commandeered factory, goes about all the work it takes to make new viral packages."[36] Sethe is such a commandeered factory, offering Beloved ("her belly protruding") a site from which to grow and spread.

In *Beloved*, the pertinent confusion turns out to be meme for même, memory for self, so that Sethe wastes at the hands of a memory—a material idea in her own brain—that wears her self-badge. (In fact, Beloved is the age Sethe was when she birthed Denver and killed Beloved.) To grasp just how odd an understanding of the body's borders can be, consider the following attempts at self-help: elaborate efforts that shed some light on Sethe's communicative attempts with her daughter: "the more [Beloved] took, the more Sethe began to talk, explain. . . . listing again and again her reasons" (242). In a *Harper's* essay, "Making Kitsch from AIDS," we learn of patients writing letters to their virus, anthropomorphizing it as a loved one, a pen pal with whom one corresponds. "In the self-help treatment guide *Immune Power*, Dr. Jon D. Kaiser even advises his clients to open up a regular correspondence with their virus. The patient, playing the role of the disease, writes back like a pen pal or a well-bred guest to thank its 'hosts' 'for sharing your feelings with me' '[that I] have overstayed [my] welcome,' adding that 'I appreciate your thoughts and I am not offended by the bluntness of your attitude toward me.'"[37] The patient pretends to swap its self for its invader, attempting to embody a kinder, gentler virus who will find the patient's good wishes, not to mention good manners, infectious. Kaiser even proffers that if letters to the virus indicate "the way you truly feel about yourself," ("since it is within you"), letters from the virus reflect one's "beliefs" about "what . . . will happen" (103–04)— as if the HIV disease, channeled by oneself, were a set of beliefs about the future. What Kaiser sees for the future of AIDS is "viral dormancy," by means of which patients continue to carry HIV while they "revert back to [an] original asymptomatic status" (7). As support for his views, Kaiser cites Harvard's William Haseltine: "HIV can lie dormant indefinitely, inextricable from the cell but hidden from the victim's immune system" (3).[38]

Some form of hiding by the end of the novel, one that is both uneasy and sad—accompanied by a communal forgetting—attends Beloved's dramatic disappearance and Sethe's apparent "rever[sion] back to asymptomatic status."[39] True, it may seem like Beloved is ousted, evacuated, exorcised, disappeared at the end of the book, but the last two pages of *Beloved* suggest a restless dormancy: "There is a loneliness that can be rocked. . . . It's an inside kind—wrapped tight like skin. Then there is a loneliness that roams. No rocking can hold it down. It is alive, on its own" (274). Quite surprisingly, the all or nothing, in/out, yes/no model we think the book is backing—has Beloved disappeared or not? are the dead in or out? are you infected, yes or no?—is really a more pressing issue of intensity, threshold, and extent (like measurements that are rendered in T cells), or, in the case of ideas, memic insistence and width. (How wide is my idea of the dead?) In fact, Dennett and other brain theorists suggest that intensity of memic insistence determines which memes win brain competitions, in which the brain's parallel processors offer different candidates for consciousness.[40]

This is simply to say, the question I thought *Beloved* was asking all along—how can we have a mental prophylactic that protects against invasions from the dead?—is not the most urgent query we are left with. *Beloved* leaves us to ponder how memic intensity is tamed, so that it *can* be carried, by the mind's crowded vehicle, into the space of a virtual future.

Tamed Richness

The phrase "tamed richness" is Roland Barthes's, from his essay "Myth Today," in which he laments the way that myth tames the richness of objects, words, and pictures. At one's first glance, myth's operations seem intriguing but benign, as Barthes hangs his first illustration on a tree: "A tree is a tree. Yes, of course. But a tree as expressed by Minou Drouet is no longer quite a tree, it is a tree which is decorated, adapted to a certain type of consumption, laden with literary self-indulgence, revolt, images, in short, with a type of social *usage* which is added to pure matter" (his emphasis).[41] From this example of mythified matter, the tree-as-matter dressed up in myth ("decorated, adapted"), Barthes proceeds to give examples of both words and pictures that also get dressed, emphasizing, as he goes, "a social usage" that is not only additive ("added to . . . matter") but also "parasitical." In this way, Barthes starts to stress how the form of myth feeds off the "meaning[s]" offered by objects, words, or pictures, "emptying" them of their "own values" so that they might "receive" mythical ones.

"And here is now another example," Barthes writes—one as fitting for *Beloved* as the tree. "I am at the barber's, and a copy of *Paris-Match* is offered to me. On the cover, a young Negro in French uniform is saluting, with his eyes uplifted, probably fixed on a fold of the tricolour. All this is the *meaning* of the picture. But, whether naively or not, I see very well what it signifies to me: that France is a great Empire, that all her sons, without any colour discrimination, faithfully serve under her flag, and that there is no better answer to the detractors of an alleged colonialism than the zeal shown by this Negro in serving his so-called oppressors" (116). A myth, says Barthes, signifies something beyond this picture's im-

mediate meaning. In this case, then, the myth of French imperiality emp-
ties the picture's meaning of whatever history and value it has, apart from
myth, on "its own" (who this particular Negro is; the momentary circumstances of his salute on that day). Moreover, myth drains the meaning of
the picture so as to "fill" it with French imperiality. Or, as Barthes puts
it: "one must put the biography of the Negro in parentheses," "put it at a
distance," "if one wants to . . . prepare [the picture] to receive its signified"
(118). As the result of such a "parasitical" action, "the *meaning* of the picture," says Barthes, "becomes impoverished, history evaporates, only the
letter remains" (117).

Taking just this much from Barthes, we may now understand a signal aspect of *Beloved*, which, to this point, I have been producing as a
tale of parasitical relations (Beloved feeding off of Sethe). Turning the
tables at this juncture, we must broach the possibility that Beloved's parasitical invasion of her mother may be seen as her struggle against the
greater, and greatly parasitical, force of *myth*. To put it succinctly, Beloved
is the victim of a tamed richness and, therefore, she returns to protest
her reduction. On the surface of it, this view does not surprise. It squares
rather neatly with what we know of Morrison's intentions in writing *Beloved*, since in American myths of slavery (historical ones, as much as any
others) the (particular, individual) meaning of the slave has been emptied
and distanced, in order to prepare it to receive a signified, the signified of
Slavery. Morrison, by contrast, would restore the slave to richness.[42] So,
no surprise. And yet, on further view, what does stun is the realization
that Morrison makes the myth-making persons of *Beloved* not just figures
like the white slavers, with their obvious racist beliefs, but, in some ways
more dramatically, the loving black community, the "mothers" (and later,
other folk) who tame Beloved's meaning—rich, historical, full, even pregnant—into decorations lacking memic intensity (which "[made] it easy for
the chewing laughter to swallow her all away"). For "after they made up
their tales, shaped and decorated them, those that saw [Beloved] that day
[pregnant and disappearing] on the porch quickly and deliberately forgot
her. . . . [T]hey realized they couldn't remember or repeat a single thing
she said, and began to believe that, other than what they themselves were
thinking, she hadn't said anything at all" (274).

But Beloved did speak. Even as a structural oddity, a resistance to the
narrative flow. Beloved's narration is five pages long. There we encounter
Beloved awash on the sea of the dead in a time that threatens to be only
now: "All of it is now   it is always now   there will never be a

time when I am not crouching and watching others who are crouching too I am always crouching   the man on my face is dead   his face is not mine   his mouth smells sweet but his eyes are locked" (210). Passages such as these hyperlink us, as *Beloved*'s readers, to where we cannot follow. Carefully crafted to tease us with meaning so rich in its own values and history that it is opaque (the basket, the bridge, the men without skin, even "a hot thing"), *Beloved*'s narration evokes the terrible memory of a slave ship sunk (at least according to *Beloved*) to any operation other than myth. More to the point, Beloved, we learn, has come back to Sethe in search of her face, her own self-badge: "my face is coming I have to have it. . . . she knows I want to join   she chews and swallows me   I see me swim away   a hot thing   I see the bottoms of my feet   I am alone   I want to be the two of us   I want the join" (213). These lines tender a sympathetic view, a *meme's-eye view*, of memic insistence. Beloved is left insistently to follow the trail to where she can be thought. She lies among the dead; but whatever face may be saved for the dead is gained through those who eat them in memory, taking the name (and meanings attached to it) inside the body so that it may lie (sometimes dormant, sometimes active) behind living eyes in the boat of the brain.

Importantly, Morrison does not put Beloved's narration anywhere near the book's beginning, where it might have functioned as a tale of origins, an explanation of where Beloved is returning from. Rather, it appears at the end of part 2, just before Sethe starts to decline. This pointed placement reminds us to read the marauding Beloved as herself a victim, just as the outhouse scene prepared us to understand her gulping as a symptom of Sethe's prior voiding of Beloved, when she killed her. Moreover, as much as Sethe is menaced by Beloved's meaning, as if this mother were taking a sensory dose of her daughter (through her eyes, ears, and mouth), Sethe is also by the novel's end complicit in her daughter's dormancy, one achieved by myth and by those who enable it. In fact, Barthes's take on myth inadvertently provides a canny reading of *Beloved*'s final pages: "One believes that the meaning [here, the meaning of Beloved] is going to die, but it is a death with reprieve; the meaning loses its value, but keeps its life, from which the form of the myth [of Beloved, of the slave dead] will draw its nourishment" (118).

It would be nice to end with a set of neatly understood relations: American myths of American slavery as a way to tame (on behalf of the nation) slavery's virtual and viral remains; Morrison's tale of tamed richness as a way to criticize these national myths. But something would still be hidden by this frame: the fact that Morrison, who slips the particularized face of early death (Emmett Till or Beloved) back into public view, tames richness, too—however much she might wish for a novel that restores but does not simultaneously reduce. That is to say, working from the historical record, Morrison makes a story such as Margaret Garner's (the kernel of her novel), and even the specificity of Beloved (plumped to bursting with lyric effort), "recede a great deal," in the words of Barthes, "in order to make room" (118) for her own myth. Her *myth* of tamed richness.[43]

For this reason, we must raise a final issue so crucial to *Beloved*'s multiple tamings, by raising it first to Roland Barthes. In his example of the meaning of the picture of the Negro soldier, Barthes rather imprecisely slides among "the meaning of the picture," "the picture [of the Negro]," and "the Negro-giving-the-salute" (not to mention "the biography of the Negro") as the object of a taming. Is it different, we may wonder, to tame a body rather than its picture? to tame a dead body rather than a living one? to tame a biography rather than a tree? Notice that, on one level, the novel *Beloved* must engage the problem of how we carry living bodies in our heads. One's beloved is a kind of location from which linguistic and pictorial signs spill forth, offering a rich and steady stream of meanings. Inevitably, however, we build a model (in Barthes's sense, a myth) of this issuing object, taking individual signs as instances meant "to illustrate" our "beloved." (Exactly what signs and images do I call up in my head when I speak the name of my beloved to myself?) The tremendous richness of our relations—a dense web of image, word, idea, and sensation (often daily renewed)—is always tamed, reduced, miniaturized, summarized by signs, often organized as myths, that will fit in our heads, so that we may carry them wrapped inside our skins. This is how we take our beloved with us, also in us, through the day, and what we use, or what uses us, to produce the beloved in the brain. Clearly related to this necessity, *Beloved*, on another level, shows us that the dead present us with a similar opportunity for a taming, since they must also be reduced, miniaturized, and organized as myths, for the sake of our grasp. Without feeding back in the ways of the living, the dead renew themselves as code that travels "alive" inside our brains, capable of invading conscious space when network chains allow their "wish" to speak.

But what about another level still? What, finally, could it mean to carry a chain of human bodies linked by a common cause of death (for example, by cause of state aggression or neglect)? The AIDS Quilt (inaugurated

1987) stands beside *Beloved* as one of the most ingenious attempts to fight tamed richness while employing it: one quilt square for each dead body, each quilt square the size of a grave, the life reduced (even if embroidered) to a set of signs the community can, in some measure, carry. The goal of the quilt—one goal, at least—was to help us see the extent of the dead, all laid out, in brilliant fashion, for the orifice of the eye. Now your eye can't take it in. To receive the visual assault of EXTENT, you would have to consult a miniature copy of an aerial view, reducing the size of the image to get it into your head. But this reduction is exactly how we account for its "spread."[44] For the myth of the quilt, like *Beloved*, is "a call," which, in the words of Barthes, "in order to be more imperious, has agreed to all manner of impoverishments" (125).

Forty to one hundred twenty million bodies infected were being predicted for this past millennium. *Beloved*, too, offers a count—"Sixty Million and more"—in its dedication. These, like the scores of Holocaust dead, are inconceivable extensions of meaning, along with lost futures. Which means, in the case of chain-linked death (and slavery was surely always that), we are forced to tame a richness we may have never seen.[45] How does one regulate an epistemic hunger for bodies that haven't been around to feed it? The task, according to *Beloved* and the quilt, brainchildren both of 1987, is to hold a set of files that are empty and full, mourning while taming the untimely dead. For they remain, in the mind's keep, virtually beloved.

Conclusion

DARK CAMP

BEHIND AND AHEAD

The intricacies of beautiful shame, beloved shame, have surfaced and insisted themselves in this study. They have linked two signs that have no linguistic tie. They have revealed how "black" and "queer" have swapped associations in a vast social game of (de)valuations. They have shown the nature of debasement as blended: there is no black shame, or queer shame per se; only kinds of shame where blacks and queers (not to mention other groups) contribute something crucial, at the level of signs, to each other's debasements. They have shown shame's operations as composite, for every form of shame this book has considered works at a surface, bores to a depth, and then has a life, at the level of signs, in the human brain, whether flickering or intense. Shame's operations have also lit up values, surprising values attached to debasements: sexual attraction, adornment, fascination, bodily pleasures, odd communal solace, and creative mourning.

As for depictions of beautiful debasements, they have emerged on the backs of details extravagant, decorative (even when bloody), lyrical, passionate, highly ambitious, and strangely attractive (even when cruel). And they have borne absurdity's trace. Or, to put it differently, the details in this study link shame to camp. And yet, to a dark camp that keeps the violent edge of debasement visibly wedded to camp caprice. This large question of dark camp bears further study, I suggest, perhaps in future studies, which I will begin to touch on now as I conclude. Here, then, in the final pages of this book, is a speculative prompt for the work ahead.

First, we should note where dark camp has emerged in this book. We have seen the features of dark camp surface in Radclyffe Hall's depiction of her heroine, who plays at being a carpet-cleaning martyr for her housemaid crush ("Please, Jesus, give me a housemaid's knee instead of Collins"), all for the purpose of escaping from the dresses she hates to wear but longs to see on the women she loves ("She wrenched off the dress and hurled it from her, longing intensely to rend it, to hurt it, longing to hurt herself in the process. . . . Going over to the dress she smoothed it out slowly; it seemed to have acquired an enormous importance; it seemed to have acquired the importance of prayer, the poor, crumpled thing lying crushed and dejected"). Such pathetically funny scenes, with over-the-top religiosity and anguish, are dark camp played for a sense of moral earnestness—and for a history of lesbian suffering. In Genet's novel *Querelle*, dark camp clings to the lieutenant's act of lying down (in hopes of having sex) on top of human waste (on top of moistened grass), staining his coat, which makes him see, in the instance of this staining, the glamorous golden braids on his cuffs as a sign of his own divine humiliation. (Both of these figures, from Hall and Genet, act as martyrs to clothes, which both of their authors connect to black skin.)

Dark camp features also grace Toni Morrison's lyrical but almost purple scenes that capture the absurdity of communal trauma—of a neighborhood, for instance, nearly put to death by appearing together "at the mouth of [a] tunnel excavation, in a fever . . . of excitement and joy," an excavation they attempt "to kill"; they attempt to kill a tunnel they're forbidden to build by penetrating dirt—leading to Morrison's signature use of almost laughable details for death ("Mrs. Jackson [at the tunnel], weighing less than 100 pounds . . . slid down the [earthen] bank and met with an open mouth the ice she had craved all her life").[1] In *Beloved*, we encounter an extravagant rendering of Sethe's ambitious murder of her daughter, so as to defeat the death-grip of slavery, a rendering that imagines an absurd exchange of fluids as conveying (the idea of) early death: "Sethe reached up for [her other] baby without letting the dead one go . . . aiming a bloody nipple into the baby's mouth. Baby Suggs slammed her fist on the table and shouted . . . 'Clean yourself up!' They fought then. . . . Each struggling for the nursing child. Baby Suggs lost when she slipped in a red puddle and fell. So Denver took her mother's milk right along with the blood of her sister."[2]

Of course, there are wonderfully exaggerated, decorated sights in Tarantino (as we have seen) that are at once violent, comic, lurid, and sad in the mode of dark camp: the entire narrative chain of events unfolding from Marsellus and his box of donuts to the eerie, leering chuckle that becomes a muffled scream when The Gimp is "lynched." Even Eldridge Cleaver, especially when he's angry and rants in *Soul on Ice*, is a dark camp writer. Cleaver's ire often spills over into lines so excessive they are comic: "[D]esire for the white woman is like a cancer eating my heart out and devouring my brain. In my dreams I see white women jumping over a fence like dainty little lambs, and every time one of them jumps over, her hair just catches the breeze and splays out behind her like a mane on a Palomino stallion: blondes, redheads, brunettes, strawberry blondes, dirty blondes, drugstore blondes, platinum blondes—all of them. They are the things in my nightmares. . . . Frigid, cold, icy, ice. Arctic. Anarctic. At the end of her flight from her body is a sky-high wall of ice"—a wall Cleaver melts in his nightmares and dreams.[3] Clearly, a thread we have not yet traced runs through several figures who dominate this book, especially Genet, Morrison, Tarantino, and even Cleaver. What we might call "camp," in the form of signs and tones, permeates the details shaping these texts. Certainly, it permeates the details just presented.

In fact, we can check them against the definitions—the detailed list of attributes—Susan Sontag famously gave to the general reading public in her essay "Notes on 'Camp,'" from 1964. "A good taste of bad taste." "A variant of sophistication, but hardly identical with it." "A certain mode of aestheticism." An "art [that] is often decorative art, emphasizing texture, sensuous surface, and style at the expense of content." "Love of the unnatural: of artifice." "A quality discoverable in objects and the behavior of persons." "Love of the exaggerated, the 'off.'" "A relish for the exaggeration of sexual characteristics and personality mannerisms." "Melodramatic absurdities." "Flamboyant mannerisms susceptible of a double interpretation." "Either completely naïve or . . . wholly conscious." "Ambition." "Extreme and irresponsible in fantasy—and therefore touching and quite enjoyable." "The excruciating." "A way to find success in certain passionate failures." "A new, more complex relation to 'the serious.'" "A tender feeling."[4]

For all of this emphasis on universal features, Sontag also provides her readers with a "pocket history of Camp" to consider. Citing "mannerist artists" like Caravaggio, or Georges de la Tour's "extraordinarily theatrical painting," Sontag argues that "still, the soundest starting point seems to be the late 17th and early 18th century, because of that period's extraordinary feeling for artifice, for surface . . . its taste for the picturesque and the thrilling." In the nineteenth century, camp became a special, not a general taste, according to Sontag, "tak[ing] on overtones of the acute, the esoteric, the perverse"—hence its appearance in Art Nouveau and in "wits" such as Oscar Wilde and Ronald Firbank, who may be considered camp's "conscious ideologists" (NC, 282). In fact, Oscar Wilde proves to be Sontag's "transitional figure" from old-style dandies, who "hated vulgarity," to new-style "modern" lovers of camp who "appreciate vulgarity." More than that, Sontag appears to use Wilde ("These notes are for . . . Wilde," she states toward the start) to segue into her understanding of the special connection of camp with "homosexuals." In fact, in a now rather famous claim, Sontag offers her opinion that "an improvised self-elected class, mainly homosexuals, . . . constitute[d] themselves as aristocrats of taste." Which is not to say, Sontag stresses, that all homosexuals possess "Camp taste." "But homosexuals, by and large, constitute the vanguard— and the most articulate audience—of Camp." Then, she adds, problematically, parenthetically: "(Jews and homosexuals are the outstanding creative minorities in contemporary urban culture)" (NC, 291).

As perhaps one could predict, Sontag, over time, has been scorned by gay and lesbian and/or queer critics. In a major volume from 1994 (thirty years after her essay), the contributors to *The Politics and Poetics of Camp* lodge their complaints. Two, in particular. First, the volume's writers— all of whom answer to the sign "queer"—take dramatic issue with Sontag's claim that "to emphasize style is to slight content," so that "it goes without saying," she says, "that the Camp sensibility is disengaged, depoliticized—or at least apolitical" (NC, 279). Moe Meyer, writing the volume's introduction, makes the opposite point. Claiming that "camp, or queer parody" formed the central "activist strategy" for such groups as ACT UP (the AIDS Coalition to Unlease Power) and Queer Nation, Meyer views camp as "political" and "critical," not as "frivolous."[5] Camp is "a suppressed and denied oppositional critique," as Meyer spells it out (PPC, 1). What does camp oppose? The stability of identity, we are not surprised to learn. Camp is "an act of serious transgression against the depth model of identity" (PPC, 19). Or, restated in positive terms, camp, says Meyer, is "the total body of performative practices and strategies used to enact a queer identity," which is itself "a refusal of sexually defined identity" (*PPC*, 5; 3).

And yet, for all this embrace of spreading queerness and refusal of identity, Meyer blasts Sontag (his second complaint) for "downplay[ing]," "sanitiz[ing]," and "mak[ing] safe" the "homosexual connotations" of camp. These are moves, on Sontag's part, that allowed camp to mutate, Meyer says, and thus become "confused and conflated with . . . irony, satire, burlesque, travesty, and . . . Pop" (*PPC*, 7). Taking his investment in (the stability of) queer instability even further, as if he were determined to hold his tiger by the tail, Meyer states emphatically: "the same per-formative gestures executed independently of queer self-reflexivity are unavoidably transformed and no longer qualify as camp." The latter are merely "camp traces" or "residual camp," Meyer says, that are trying to borrow on "the queer aura" (*PPC*, 5). Or, to put it in the terms of my book, Meyer is accusing "pseudo"-camp practitioners of trying to steal a switch-point (in Meyer's wording, "camp traces," "queer aura") that he, for one, and other "self-reflexive" queers, he claims, won't relinquish.

Intriguingly, however, the lead essay in Meyer's volume, Thomas King's "Performing 'Akimbo': Queer Pride and Epistemological Preju-dice," reveals that camp is born of switchpoints—the transfer of certain signs from aristocrats to lower-class sodomites and vice versa—during the time Sontag specifies for camp's emergence (the late seventeenth and early eighteenth centuries). Briefly, King explains how certain bodily gestures of aristocrats at this time—the "(studied) relaxation" of an arm "akimbo" (one arm on the hip) meant to signal aristocratic self-control and *sprezzatura*—came to be read by the bourgeoisie as a sign of aristo-cratic "affectation," "self-display," and thus an "empty gesturing," making "studied casualness" the opposite of naturalness and, therefore, a sign of "perversion," says King (*PPC*, 25; 24; 26). That is to say, drawing on the notion of perversion, bourgeois critics considered "sodomy," in the words of King, "a symptom of the excessive pride of the aristocrats," even as "the bourgeoisie . . . [cast] off onto the concept of homosexuality all the traits associated with the obsolete aristocrats—not only sodomy, but also arbitrariness, excessiveness, and, most emphatically, social impotency" (*PPC*, 31; 40). "To be akimbo" was "to be at odds" with bourgeois culture (*PPC*, 45).

In fairness to Meyer, King's historical argument may explain why Meyer, in his fastidious claims for camp's queerness, insists only on the issue of class. True camp is not bourgeois, he says. But he is open, albeit in rather hazy ways, to camp's "applications for marginal social identities in general" (*PPC*, 3). I say "in hazy ways," because discussions of race, for instance, are absent from Meyer's book, which comprises essays by seven people. Even in Meyer's detection of camp's political nature, in the campaign of Joan Jett Blakk, the first Queer Nation candidate to run for public office (Blakk ran for mayor of the city of Chicago in 1991), Meyer in no way discusses how "Blakk" as a sign interacts with the drag queen's "social agency" signified through queer camp. (The reader discovers Blakk's black skin only in the photograph accompanying the essay.)

My point goes beyond the usual one about the necessary inclusion of race in all politicizing claims. I am more interested, as I have shown throughout, in the role of switchpoints. What would the queer sign of camp, I wonder, lend to our reading of authors rarely if ever read in relation to this sign—Morrison and Cleaver, to take two examples? Let me answer briefly—and also provisionally. In chapter 3, I linked Tarantino to Morrison through their craftings of so-called nigger jokes: aggressive joking about black suffering that involves strange emotional combinations (of laughter, sorrow, outrage, sympathy, cruelty, and attraction) and that produces in each of their texts intensely layered tones. Specifically, I pointed out Morrison's almost signature fashion of undercutting sentiment (after she has amped it) by using acts of violence that lean toward absurdity or cutting acts of humor, allowing her, in this way, to bend back tenderly toward the objects of her cruelty, who are often objects of tender disappointment in some essential way. (Camp, for Sontag, is a "tender feeling" toward failure and frustration and often vulgarity.) Deeming this tonal backbend camp, no matter how dark its provocations prove to be, readers may find comprehensible ways of embracing (and describing) the most shameful scenes in Morrison's fiction, with their often complicated tones. These are scenes I puzzled through in *Sula* and *Beloved* (in chapters 2 and 5): kerosene poured by a mother tenderly killing her son who, "messing up his pants and smiling all the time," was trying to re-enter his mother's womb; the "sifting" of a lover's "soil," during sex, by a hand with a "chisel" that is penetrating depths; Baby Suggs's losing her grip on the ground "when she slipped in a red puddle and fell"; Sethe's bladder overfilling its capacity when she sees the returning Beloved and while Beloved drinks endless cups of water. These scenes are all "a good taste of bad taste," as Sontag would put it—but darkly, since Morrison has claimed that "good taste is out of place in the company of death." In fact, to shape her weird and dark depictions, Morrison uses hallmarks of camp:

a certain sense of "artifice" (Sethe's overflowing), "love of the unnatural" (mothers killing sons), "love of the exaggerated" or "the off" (sons trying to enter their mothers' wombs), "flamboyant mannerisms susceptible of double interpretation" (Sula's hand sifting "soil"), and even "melodramatic absurdities" (Baby Suggs's slip in the puddle of blood). Overall, then, in the case of Morrison, one might discover how her blend of African American folk traditions, magic realism, and Faulknerian Southern "black humor" (to name just a few of the strands in her tonalities) distinctively forges a "sensibility" (in the words of Sontag) or a written "activism" (in the words of Meyer) that seems as campy—and as darkly campy—as works by Genet, Tarantino, and Mapplethorpe.

With regard to Cleaver, reading his essays as camping on American racial relations (and on the farce of desegregation) may best explain how we can find him funny, if also rather frightening, and strangely right even when he's clearly "off." His essays are camp in a way defined by a character (voiced by campy John Waters) on *The Simpsons*: camp as the realm of "the tragically ludicrous, the ludicrously tragic." What else can we call the excessively angry but clearly humorous lines of Cleaver's that I cited earlier?

These wild lines—ludicrously tragic, flamboyant, artificial, exaggerated, and melodramatically absurd ("eating my heart out," "devouring my brain," "dainty little lambs," "strawberry blondes, dirty blondes, drugstores blondes, platinum blondes," "icy, ice")—index something serious about cross-racial desire at the time that Cleaver is writing—as do his fanciful, entertaining, crude, if deeply flawed cultural types of Omnipotent Administrator, Supermasculine Menial, Subfeminine Amazon, and Ultrafeminine (which I discuss in chapter 4). There is a campy "ambition" to these intriguing schemata that demonstrate Cleaver's campy "relish," in Sontag's wording, "for the exaggeration of sexual characteristics and personality mannerisms"—which, as a Panther, he both embraced and likely felt besieged by. Seeing these schemata in the mode of camp, especially through our distance from 1968, may keep us from dismissing them wholesale. In fact, we may see these cultural types, in their campy excess, as indices to fantasies still quite alive and powerfully circulating in cultural texts (more on this phenomenon in just a moment). Read as camp, Cleaver's essays on these matters might usefully be regarded as "a variant of sophistication, but hardly identical with it"; "a new, more complex relation to the serious." How these distinctive writers, then, writers as different as Cleaver and Morrison, use camp features in their imaginings is rather telling: telling of (the fantasies of) racial histories and telling of the still unfolding role of camp.

But is camp evolving or taking a break? Is it exhausted as a cultural form? In an essay for the *New York Times Magazine* (March 2003), Daniel Mendelsohn pleads exhaustion. In fact, in a temporally specific essay (entitled "The Melodramatic Moment"), Mendelsohn argues that, post 9/11, we have witnessed the "exhaust[ion] of the Age of Irony" (the 1980s and 1990s) and seen arise, instead, a new taste for classic melodrama.[6] In other words, films such as Todd Haynes's *Far From Heaven* (2002), Pedro Almodóvar's *Talk to Her* (2002), and Baz Luhrmann's *Moulin Rouge* (2001) indicate, says Mendelsohn, our culture's "radical shift" to "a solemn if not deadly earnestness," which finds its high culture outlets in "the gradual comeback" of a "melodrama" that "is more straight than it first appears," "not an arty riff on melodrama, but melodrama itself" (MM, 43).

To make this argument, Daniel Mendelsohn must do several things. Above all, he must sever this new "straight" melodramatic moment from (what one might otherwise argue are) the continuing and evolving appearances of camp in Euro-American culture. And to do this, to uncouple this "moment" from camp history, he must first confine camp to parody, irony, and a lightness (really, an emptiness, in his words) that cannot encompass "real emotion." For Mendelsohn, apparently, there is no dark camp—no camp at all with a "new, more complex relation to the 'serious'" (in the words of Sontag). This act of separation—which gives him something to claim as "a shift"—is immediately apparent in his essay's first discussion: how to read *Far From Heaven*. "At the time ["before it started appearing on critics' 10-best lists"] I'd dismissed it," he says, "as a clever but ultimately empty exercise in camp: a knowing parody that lovingly, even obsessively, quotes the look, feel and rhythms of the kind of 50's melodramas that featured second-rate actresses in first-rate outfits." "My friend wasn't so sure," he continues: "she was convinced that there was more here than just an uncannily sharp eye for mid-century modern" (MM, 40)—something, as Mendelsohn later describes it, "more . . . than about the cleverness of its own allusive style, something perhaps about women and repression and race" (MM, 43), or something "more straight than it first appears."

Perhaps recognizing how odd this argument sounds in relation to filmmakers Almodóvar and Haynes, Mendelsohn tries to be more precise: "'Straight' may be the crucial word. Both Almodóvar and Haynes are gay directors and emerge from a culture steeped in the traditions of camp—

of knowing parody (and self-parody). . . . What's remarkable about these directors' latest films is, in fact, how utterly unironic they are: they make you realize that camp is just melodrama with the addition of irony (and, conversely, that melodrama is camp minus irony)" (43). Even granting these (blended?) divisions, we may note that Mendelsohn makes no convincing case for a lack of irony in these films by Haynes, Almodóvar, and Luhrmann. Nor does he substantiate a lack of earnestness in these filmmakers' earlier ventures. In fact, *Moulin Rouge*—with its "sheer excessiveness," "the unabashed opulence of its designs," and its "loonily anachronistic song-and-dance routines (as soon as these 19th-century Frenchmen break into an *a cappella* rendering of 'The Sound of Music,'" Mendelsohn argues, "you know you're in the presence of a new kind of film)"—sounds ironic even in its melodramatic earnestness. As for *Far From Heaven*, Mendelsohn seems to concede a mix of tones, for "what fascinates," he writes, "is the tentativeness with which it tiptoes along the line between camp parody and melodrama's effortful self-seriousness . . . as if the film is embarrassed by its own emotional and sociological yearnings" (MM, 42). Of course, "camp" is always the "empty" part of Mendelsohn's perceived mix of modes. And so it goes: camp is light and empty, while melodrama plays for more serious effects.

Obviously, I am wanting someone to write a "pocket history" of dark camp—the kind of camp that includes the earnestness of Radclyffe Hall's *The Well of Loneliness* as well as the much slyer tonal mixes we find in the largely unexamined camp of Morrison's novels. (Neither author, I would note, seems at all "embarrassed by [her] own emotional and sociological yearnings.") I hope my book is a step toward this history, insofar as shame and camp have important, entangled relations with each other. Looking ahead to the future unfolding of dark camp, then—and to its specific engagement of switchpoints between "queer" and "black," which have occupied me here—I will end by showing how my book may help us to read the campy debasements depicted in some recent cultural texts of note.

Let me return to one of Mendelsohn's examples. In *Far From Heaven*, obvious, classic markers of camp (by Susan Sontag's definitions) prove to be melodramatic *and* ironic; earnest *and* dark. Todd Haynes looks at 1957, in 2002, with a tender retro love—the kind of love of *objets démodés* that is a chief attribute of camp in Sontag's view.[7] (1957, we recall, is right around the time that Baldwin's novel *Giovanni's Room*, with its dark homosexual, is first circulating; that Norman Mailer is publishing his "White Negro" essay; and that Eldridge Cleaver is first composing essays about his "sick" attraction to white blonde women, a sickness he compares to homosexuality.) Haynes, for his part, makes 1957 the year in which his heroine, a white suburban housewife, discovers that her husband is a "homosexual," which sends her seeking comfort from her "Negro" gardener—a kind black man. Done in the style of a Douglas Sirk melodrama, circa '57, *Far From Heaven* uses our attraction to its details—the heroine's remarkable fifties' clothes, creamsicle cars, "modern" lamps, and Barbie's-dreamhouse-couches-and-chairs—to notice the astonishing importance of surface, and the shame importantly operating there.

Truly, we could not miss this surface if we tried. Its retro camp, so bad it's good, lends it interest (even love, for certain moviegoers). The scale and artificial color of this surface further lend it intensity. Cathleen's (the heroine's) dresses, with their bottom-heavy taffeta skirts (made even larger for Julianne Moore, who was pregnant while filming), seem to sweep the camera along in their turns. And with every turn, around every corner, there is a full retro field that no contemporary thrift shop could ever create on this scale. The colors of the film are particularly striking with reference to clothes. Cathleen's clique of female friends, campy to the contemporary eye, stand in her yard, at the height of autumn, in autumn colors more vivid than life—colors her gardener repeats in his clothes, doubly linking the issue of color to clothes and cloth. This camp focus on surface is no mere joke, however, though certain props and mannerisms prompt us to chuckle, or laugh out loud, with deep ironic pleasure. Such irony, making for camp, is not empty. Rather, surface, with its eye-popping color, is the center of *Far From Heaven's* drama. The film makes its highly intentional bridge between queers and blacks by having the woman who personifies clothes (artifice, surface) be the one to notice—finally, dramatically—the wound of black skin (shades of chapter 1). In fact, Cathleen, the suburban housewife, unwittingly wed to a homosexual, is the only point of contact between the black man and the queer man, who never appear in a single scene together. In this way, the film crafts dramatic switchpoints, between its black and queer melodramas, through the surface of the housewife (who points to cloth and skin). At one point, she is even hit by her husband when he is distraught, a blow that leaves a wound on her skin (below her hairline), something the gardener and others notice. This skin wound is the sign of her husband's homosexuality (he hits her when he fails in his attempt to make love to her); and it clearly signals her immersion in his pain, which makes her highly vulnerable. Indeed, we see how her marvelous surface (to which our eyes are attracted, riveted) has proven to be a kind of faulty prophy-lactic, a failed protective skin (an issue I pursue in chapter 5). Her aqua gloves and lavender matching skirt and bag (not to mention her matching mustard phone and kitchen cabinets) cannot envelope her. She is suscep-tible to the dramatically rendered rip her husband makes in this beauti-ful surface when she finds him kissing a man. In light of Todd Haynes's earlier films—*Poison*, with a narrative strand on AIDS, followed by *Safe*, with Julianne Moore, on household toxins plaguing a housewife—domes-tic prophylaxis seems a likely conscious theme.[8]

Racial mixing is also a threat to the heroine's, and her household's, safety. Once Cathleen begins to seek her gardener—who finds her lost purple scarf on a tree and remarks on its color—the film enters into its own Cleaver plot (see chapter 4). As if Eldridge Cleaver had sketched the protagonists, we find that the drama has the four major players that so ob-sessed Cleaver: the Omnipotent Administrator white suburban husband (here homosexual, just as Cleaver claimed he was); the Supermasculine Menial gardener (beautiful, black, physically strong, and a source of at-traction for our heroine); the Ultrafeminine blond Cathleen (whom the Supermasculine Menial seeks and who seeks him); and the black female Subfeminine Amazon (Cathleen's maid and the gardener's little girl).[9]

What interests me is how Todd Haynes succeeds in suggesting some-thing already implicit and hiding in Cleaver's sexual semiotics. We have explored Cleaver's presumption of a "homo" problem (a problem of a sexual sameness) between black men and women. (By Cleaver's reckon-ing, they are too alike in class and gender codings—strong in body, ag-gressive in spirit, and menial in labor—to be "hetero" for each other.) What we have not yet explored is the underlying "homo" potential of the two most excessive (the campiest?) actors in Eldridge Cleaver's social play: the "Super" masculine Menial and the "Ultra" feminine. Though his possession of the penis (sought by her) marks his difference from her, along with his skin color, Cleaver also shows them ("Super" and "Ultra") as coded alike. That is to say, for Cleaver both are coded as "beautiful" and lacking in (what Cleaver deems) "mental sovereignty"; and both are dependent financially on white men.[10] In *Far From Heaven*, the house-wife and gardener are both portrayed as beautiful: his clothes are as color-ful and matching to his context as hers are. (She matches her walls, he matches her yard.) And Cathleen calls him "beautiful" at a crucial mo-ment.[11] Further, they are both depicted as having intellectual ambitions beyond their job descriptions (as mother and gardener), as having common interests (in modern art, for instance), and as failing their bourgeois potential by the end. He gives up his fledgling garden store when he is forced to move out of her town, and she prepares to fall from suburban bourgeois grace, since she and her husband, who's divorcing her, "have no savings to speak of."

This unusual "homo" sexual relationship—a miscegenation resisted so dramatically by the friends and neighbors of the gardener and the housewife[12]—comes to a halt when the needs of a black girl seem to trump all others. (This is a sort of 2002 Morrisonian twist to a Cleaver plot.) The gardener's little girl—who is dressed to look like Norman Rockwell's Little Rock schoolgirl—has (the idea of) a future to uphold. This future is in question because of her Negro father's interest in Cathleen—this in a world as unprepared to receive miscegenous relations as homosexual ones. In a crucial scene that solidifies switchpoints, the gardener's little girl (in her Little Rock dress) receives her own skin wound when a group of white boys viciously pitch rocks at her. Hit on her forehead, she suffers a wound in much the same spot where Cathleen received hers. She even wears a band-aid, announcing her skin wound, in the scene where Raymond (her father) tells Cathleen that he has to move for his daughter's safety. This plot climax is melodramatic, as we would expect in a Sirkian melodrama. Its camp brilliance, in dark camp mode, suggests the melodramatic nature of the prejudice against blacks and queers—and the melodrama one is made to embrace when responding to "oppression."

David Fincher's *Fight Club* (1999), which might seem light years removed from *Far From Heaven*, crosses through even more issues from this book: the dark play of surface (cloth wounds and skin wounds), along with sacrifice as a central strategy for dealing with "problems" surrounding beauty, from chapter 1; the role of bottom life and bottom economics from chapter 2; the viewer's attractions to dirty details and scenes of shame from chapter 3; the logic of Cleaver, featuring exaggerated, racialized actors who are "extreme and irresponsible in fantasy," from chapter 4; and the aggressive life of a sign that plagues the mind, from chapter 5: all of these appear in this campy text. Indeed, its dark camp, aimed, it appears, at the holy demographic of young (straight) males age eighteen to twenty-four, lies, it seems, at the other end of the gender spectrum from the "women's weepies" of the Sirk melodramas. Here, however, as in *Far From Heaven*, the logic of a cloth wound—primarily attached to white women and only secondarily to dark and light men—forms the central symptom of interlocking traumas and cultural ills, as it does in Haynes's film. And here in Fincher's *Fight Club*, too, an Eldridge Cleaver plot of attractions, replete with queer tensions, becomes the "inevitable" thrust of how the alienations of American class culture (here the corporate culture of the 1990s) drive dark and light, physically and psychically, toward each other—although this film, unlike Haynes's, makes direct reference to neither blacks nor queers. Also unlike *Far From Heaven*, the major erotic drive of the film is the tension that Cleaver viewed with greatest scorn (but also fascination): the drive of light men toward dark men. Critics have summarized *Fight Club*'s focus: "The film . . . details the strange relationship between an unnamed narrator [played by Edward Norton] . . . and a mysterious provocateur [played by Brad Pitt]."[13] "After meeting on [a] plane, [these two men] form a secret club. Members meet in a dank basement and beat the daylights out of one another in a kind of religious ritual meant to purify them from the soul-destroying effects of mass society"; "later [they] train an underground militia and terrorize a city" with a "plot to blow up credit-card companies and coffee franchises."[14]

To put the matter in terms I've made familiar throughout this book: the crisis for the film's unnamed white and white-collar narrator is the entire cloth-wounded life of American middle-class consumer domesticity. In this world, professional men are forced to know something about duvets, designer colors, and business ties of "cornflower blue." "What kind of dining set defines me as a person?" the narrator wonders. "I became a slave to the Ikea nesting instinct"; "we used to read pornography, now it was the Horchow collection." Mind-numbing, even insomniac, concern with commercialized beauty (a shameful harridan) is like some kind of domestic disease, some kind of shameful vanity, that "men" have caught from "women," or at least from things feminine. As the narrator's provocateur explains: "We're a generation of men raised by women. I'm wondering whether another woman is really the answer we need." Resistance to these psychic wounds of cloth and consumer domesticity ("you're not your fucking khakis!" he shouts out at one point) requires the sort of transfer that we encountered in *Stone Butch Blues* (1993) in chapter 1. This is the effort to move the wound from the surface of cloth to the surface of skin, where, for masculine women and men, this wound can look like a form of bold resistance. In *Stone Butch Blues*, this resistance, this refusal, is signaled, we recall, by the butch lesbian's gashes, bruises, and cigarette burns on her skin, from her fights with the cops. In *Fight Club*, we notice, refusal likewise requires facial wounds, bloody noses, battered limbs, resulting from hand-to-hand man-to-man fighting

—the queerness of men's calling arms on themselves, as we saw in Jean Genet's *Querelle* (also chapter 1). This fighting is a queerness the critics have noted: "All these guys masochistically lining up to be beaten by Brad Pitt. . . . The homoeroticism is off the charts, but 'Fight Club' can't bring itself to account for it."[15] Along with this fighting, as we're about to see, the look of refusal requires just as crucially (black) bottom values (see chapter 2) and (black) bottom codes, which allow beauty, but only bottom beauty (blackened, beaten), through the backdoor.

Hence, Tyler Durden: superfly, groovy, hip-hoppish bottom man. When we initially meet him on the plane, he wears an ensemble of burgundy suit-jacket, checked pants, slick shades, and retro 1970s shirt. (Later, he sports a red leather coat, muskcrat jacket, red pants, and starred shirt. In the final scene, the film's climactic scene, Tyler sports a tank top with the words "Black Sugar.")[16] Dressed in garish colors, in flamboyant outfits that give him the look of something between a pimp and a homeless Versace model, Tyler Durden, played by the beautiful Brad Pitt, lives in an "inner city" all his own, in a blasted urban setting, in a filthy crumbling mansion. Did Tyler own this mansion, or was he squatting, the narrator wonders? It was "a shit-hole," he proceeds to tell us, in a part of town with "the fart smell of steam." Tyler works from time to time as a rebel waiter, urinating (also putting other body fluids) in the food he serves. When Tyler works as a film projectionist, he splices dirty details into family films by hiding these details—naked penises—inside the film cuts he makes just barely visible.[17] To schematize Tyler, we could aptly say that through his body's beauty (the Pitt sixpack and beautiful face) and his bottom credentials (the goal of "hitting bottom" is a phrase he repeats), Tyler is a Supermasculine Menial who draws Omnipotent Administrators, like the film's protagonist, to himself (see chapter 4). Indeed, Tyler's fondness for bottom values is repeatedly underscored by his pronouncements: "It's only after we've lost everything that we are free to do anything." "Congratulations: you are one step closer to hitting bottom." Tyler later on: "Hitting bottom is not a weekend retreat." "We are the all-singing, all-dancing crap of the world"; "we are part of the same compost heap." And though he may hold the key to the penis (by being the narrator's fantasy penis)—just as Cleaver's Supermasculine Menial holds the key to the white man's dick—the film makes Tyler's embrace of an economic bottom even bolder, and more telling, than the film's phallic logic (with its dildo jokes). It is to this bottom, in several different senses, that the narrator must go.

And so Tyler and the unnamed white-collar narrator come to squat together (in the crumbling mansion) after their first affectionate fist-fight:

Tyler: "Just ask man; cut the foreplay and just ask."

Narrator: "Can I stay at your place?"

Tyler: "I want you to do me a favor. I want you to hit me as hard as you can."

Narrator: "What? Why?"

Tyler: "How much can you know about yourself if you've never been in a fight? I don't want to die without any scars."

[Smoking a cigarette post-fight; the faces of both men are bruised]

Narrator: "We should do this again sometime."

Lest this attraction to Tyler seem too directly queer to *Fight Club*'s audience (though flirtation with queerness seems flaunted), Tyler is eventually, grandly revealed as the narrator's fantasy-projection of himself, the man he would most like to be in life. Shades of Genet, in this campy twist, Tyler is a Querelle for straight men—men who themselves like a coating of dirt as they fight in the basement. (We recall the beautiful coat of coal dust on Querelle, which Genet depicts as his "playing at blackface.") Here these dirty details at the visual level—blood, grime, and violent brawling—are part of the viewers' invitation to assess (their own) attractions, as we found in chapter 3. Making martyrdom part of this assessment as we saw queer novelists do in chapter 1, the film invites its viewers to rethink beauty—at least its whitened, feminized forms. For sacrificing beauty, throwing it (even one's own beauty) out from the body, in a way remarkably close to what Georges Bataille theorized in his writings on sacrifice, is the bold engine of *Fight Club*'s plot. In a brutal, funny scene, Tyler (Pitt in a Sock-It-To-Me T-shirt) eggs on a mobster to beat him into a bloody pulp, as a result of which his beautiful face is blackened by blood. In another scene, the most beautiful man in the film, a platinum blond named Billy ("you're too blond" a fighter tells him), is smashed in the face until his beauty crumbles. "I felt like destroying something beautiful," the narrator says after thrashing him. Tyler even recuperates soap from its roles of aiding beauty and promoting cleanliness by linking it to grimy destruction and sacrifice. He makes bombs from homemade soap, soap he makes from women's fat (fat he has stolen from liposuction clinics). "You skim off a layer of glycerin," Tyler explains to the narrator; "if you were to add nitric acid you'd get nitroglycerin; if you were then to add sodium nitrate and a dash of sawdust you'd then have dynamite." And while he is burning lye on the narrator's (his own) hand, making a dramatic and permanent skin wound, Tyler explains how soap was originally made from the lye derived from the pulpy remains of human sacrifice. What an elaborate address to beauty (its class and gender problems) through a combination of martyrdom, blackened bottom values, violent attractions, and Cleaver personae.

Because of such scenes, critics have remarked: "[This] is the most incendiary movie to come out of Hollywood in a long time"; it is "a film so harrowingly brutal and unabashedly out there it makes that elephant-dung art at the Brooklyn Museum of Art look about as disturbing as a big-eyed Walter Keane pixie."[18] Fincher answers: "I've always thought people would think the film was *funny*. . . . A dark comedy."[19] Edward Norton adds: "[*Fight Club*] is a highly stylized, comic surrealism where you're . . . sort of winking at the audience."[20] Indeed, the movie's campiness keeps the level of absurdity high, "emphasizing texture [and] sensuous surface," as Sontag would put it, while, she would say, showing "a relish for the exaggeration of sexual characteristics and personality mannerisms," thus turning "the excruciating" toward a "tender feeling." Viewers may well feel tender toward the narrator in his zany fight against corporate domination—especially as he starts to fight his projection of himself-as-Tyler, too.

It is not surprising that something akin to *Beloved*'s depictions of a mental takeover (see chapter 5) seems echoed here. Slavery to the Ikea nest—and what to do about it—is the film's major theme. Speaking and feeding back to state-sponsored and/or corporate forms of aggression—via myths such as Tyler or Beloved—are the means of fighting back explored. These attempts, however, are shown as too ambitious. In both *Fight Club* and *Beloved*, these attempts must be tamed. And so they are corralled, Tyler and Beloved, and made to hang suspended in dark camp's tender feelings toward their failed ambitions. For though the narrator thinks up Tyler, births him in his mind, Tyler is inside him, a sign on a romp (he is "Planet Tyler," in the narrator's words), controlling his thoughts. The film, for its part, seems finally unable to think how to keep the destructions of Tyler's "Project Mayhem" (think of Beloved's rampant undoings) from turning into a kind of fascism—though this may be its point.[21] "In Project Mayhem, there are no questions," only the spread of Fight Club franchises, making Tyler's name bigger and bigger. In this respect, *Fight Club*'s bottom values seem every bit as tricky as *Sula*'s, not just *Beloved*'s, prove to be. How does one negotiate, foster, and preserve the values of a bottom while not succumbing to full-on self-destruction?

Ultimately, there is only one thing the narrator (and, through him, the film) can hold securely. When the narrator sacrifices Tyler, his beloved, by shooting Tyler/himself in the head (since he is in him), he, the narrator, turns back around to embrace the somewhat more domesticated beauty standing beside him—Marla, his girlfriend. Marla is Tyler's more domesticated, far less violent, counterpart, and, in the terms of the film, she is real, not a fantasy. She shares the narrator's sense of malaise (his boredom, his insomnia, his lack of a life), but not his strategy of moving wounds to skin. That is to say, she does not attend Fight Club; the narrator makes no place for her there. His refusals are not hers; and, as a woman, she is deemed to be part of the overarching problem. Even so, she dresses in many ways like Tyler (the narrator's fantasy of himself): she is thrift-shop funky.[22] She also appears to be unemployed and is surely not corporate in any way. A return to Marla, then, is thus a return to domesticated Tyleresque bottom beauty. And she can be embraced because of Tyler's bottom—his sense of "hitting bottom," his having hit bottom—which allows the narrator to turn back to beauty, as through a b(l)ackdoor. Not by accident do Marla and the narrator, holding hands in the film's final frames, look like some odd Adam and Eve at the destruction, which is the new creation, of a brave new world.

This roundabout, through a bottom back to beauty—that is, through Tyler's beautiful bottom—is the narrator's social self-debasement. It truly takes himself and his fantasy self (Edward Norton and Brad Pitt) to get himself debased. It surely makes for holdings—in the sense of property, ideas, and attractions—we have seen as dark and strange.[23] And it is part of the film's long journey to (what it implies is) a new, improved white heterosexuality forged in the (de)basements of "blackness" and "queerness."

Apparently, even straight white folks need beautiful bottoms.

NOTES

INTRODUCTION *Embracing Shame*

1 Benoit Denizet-Lewis, "Living (and Dying) on the Down Low."
2 I mean this "you" to point in two directions: toward the protagonist being seduced and, at the same time, toward the spectator viewing the screen.
3 All definitions in this chapter are from the *American Heritage Dictionary*, College Edition, unless otherwise specified.
4 Fanon, *Black Skin, White Masks*, 7.
5 hooks, *Salvation*, 72.
6 Bataille, *Visions of Excess*, 20.
7 There is also a wing of theorizing on debasement that follows upon the work of Bakhtin: namely, famous works by the critics Mary Russo, Peter Stallybrass, and Allon White, and the many critics influenced by them. Debasement as a form of political, social, and cultural transgression is central to these works — a vein I am not directly working in, as I will explain.
8 Kristeva, *Powers of Horror: An Essay on Abjection*, 16.
9 Taussig, *Defacement*, 5.
10 Bersani, "Is the Rectum a Grave?," in *AIDS: Cultural Analysis/Cultural Activism*, ed. Douglas Crimp, 212.
11 Leo Bersani, *Homos*, 168, 169; Bersani, "Is the Rectum a Grave?," 215.
12 Eve Kosofsky Sedgwick, *Touching Feeling*, 54.
13 Edelman, *Homographesis*, 161.
14 See Lee Edelman, "*Rear Window's* Glasshole," in *Out Takes: Essays on Queer Theory and Film*, ed. Ellis Hanson, 72–96; "*Sinthom*-osexuality," in *Aesthetic Subjects*, 230–50; *No Future*.

15 Litvak, *Strange Gourmets*, book jacket.

16 Kennedy, *Nigger*, xv.

17 Muñoz, *Disidentifications*, 11.

18 Holland, *Raising the Dead*, 4.

19 Reid-Pharr, *Black Gay Man*, 15.

20 Koolhaas, *Delirious New York*.

21 Sedgwick, *Touching Feeling*, 28, 31. See, for example, J. L. King and Karen Hunter, *On the Down Low*.

22 Muñoz, *Disidentifications*, 11.

23 For myself, I still embrace the question-asking side of "theory": theory as "speculation," "hypothesis or supposition" (Late Latin *theoria*, from Greek, contemplation, theory; from *theoros*, spectator; from *theasthai*, to observe; from *thea*, a viewing).

24 Sedgwick lodges a different but highly compelling complaint about current critical thought, along with her sense of how to address it. See her introduction ("Paranoid Reading and Reparative Reading; or, You're So Paranoid, You Probably Think This Introduction is About You") to the volume *Novel Gazing*.

25 Largely, these foci have stemmed from (mis)readings of Judith Butler's *Bodies That Matter*; see, particularly, "Gender Is Burning: Questions of Appropriation and Subversion"—and *Gender Trouble*. This is not to say these dynamics could not be traced in the texts I address throughout this book, but that they are not the dynamics that interest me.

26 I began crafting these views in the first two chapters I wrote for *Beautiful Bottom, Beautiful Shame* (a version of chapter 2 in 1989, a version of chapter 5 in 1995). However, if Bersani's remarks in *Homos* are to be read as corrective—at least, partially so—of his views in his earlier essay "Is the Rectum a Grave?," his views and mine may intersect. Specifically, he and I may agree that the concept to explore is "an anticommunal mode of connectedness we might all share, or a new way of coming together"—"not assimilation into already constituted communities" (*Homos*, 10). Bersani further states: "I will be exploring . . . a redefinition of sociality so radical that it may appear to require a provisional withdrawal from relationality itself" (*Homos*, 7). I invite the reader to compare our views (Bersani's and mine) as I lay out my communal model of disconnectedness.

27 For a sample of other critical projects that bring "black" and "queer" (or "black" and "homosexual") into conversation, see Kobena Mercer, *Welcome to the Jungle*; Kendall Thomas, "Ain't Nothin' Like the Real Thing," in Blount and Cunningham, eds., *Representing Black Men*, 55–70; Phillip Brian Harper, "Eloquence and Epitaph," in Abelove et al., eds., *The Lesbian and Gay Studies Reader*; Lee Edelman, "The Part for the (W)hole," in *Homographesis*; Sioban B. Somerville, *Queering the Color Line*; and Roderick A. Ferguson, *Aberrations in Black*.

28 For a fascinating instance of this strategy—also a highly entertaining one—see Quentin Crisp, *The Naked Civil Servant*.

29 Sedgwick, *Epistemology of the Closet*, 23.

30 Barthes, *Camera Lucida*, 8.

31 Halley, " 'Like Race' Arguments," in Butler, Guillory, and Thomas, eds., *What's Left of Theory?*

32 For a longer take on the matter of mantras in current criticism, especially the reign of "instability" as a critical destination in many studies, see my essay "Reading Details, Teaching Politics."

33 John Lancaster, "Why the Military Supports the Ban on Gays; Arguments Ranging from Privacy to AIDS Offered against Clinton's Rights Pledge," *Washington Post*, January 28, 1993, A8, quoted in Halley, " 'Like Race' Arguments," 54, in the service of a different important point.

ONE *Cloth Wounds*

This chapter started as a talk written for the Interdisciplinary Group in the Humanities at Texas A & M University in April 1998. A different version of it appears in the volume that issued from that conference, *Aesthetic Subjects*, ed. Pamela Matthews and David McWhirter (Minneapolis: University of Minnesota Press, 2003). Warm thanks to Dave and Pam for their advice and also to the faculty and students at Yale University Divinity School, Queen's College, Ontario, and Trent University, Ontario, for their attentive questions about this chapter in talk form.

1 Ironically, it is precisely this nonelective nature of black skin color that is dramatized in a famous book—John Howard Griffin's *Black Like Me*—in which a white man elects to "put on" black skin and to wear it, as if it were his own, as a social experiment. Struggles and prejudice he in no way seeks come upon him as a consequence.

2 Spike Lee's *Jungle Fever* (1991), for example, seeks to untangle the rather intricate strands of pride, aesthetic investment, political value, and sexual attractiveness associated with a range of skin colors, both inside and outside black communities.

3 Even so, my third chapter will engage complaints made by black gay critics about Robert Mapplethorpe's "objectification" and "fetishization" of black men's beauty in his famous photographs of black male nudes.

4 Though made up of highly impermanent skin cells that die every day, skin and skin color are perceived as being far more permanent than the clothes we daily change—even though we may wear different items of the same kind of clothes each day for many years. One could just as well, then, emphasize clothing's relative permanence vis-à-vis the highly changeable nature of our skin.

5 The case of Michael Jackson aside, women (especially, but not only, professional women) in many African countries are targeted by cosmetic companies advertising skin-lightening products. According to a *National Geographic* special, the number of women who routinely use these products—putting their skin and their health in jeopardy—is remarkably high.

6 These and subsequent definitions are taken from *Webster's New World Dictionary*, Third College Edition.

7   For a brief discussion of "social holding" and social self-debasement, particularly their difference from Leo Bersani's stress on the anticommunal nature of self-shattering pleasures, see my introduction.

8   Malcolm Gladwell, "Listening to Khakis," *The New Yorker* (July 28, 1997): 54–65. 56, 57, 62.

9   Michael Brick. "Guy in Skirt Seeks Sensitivity in Brooklyn," *New York Times*, November 2, 2003.

10 Without losing my stress here on "remarkably various," which I ask the reader at all times to keep in mind, I am clearly interested to trace a continuity no one has examined: the use of martyr logic in three such different novels by three crucial authors read by queer critics.

11 By definition, showing one's colors is often a matter of showing cloth. Although "color" in the singular refers to "complexion, skin tone," or "a reddening of the face; a blush," or "the complexion of a person not classed as a Caucasian, especially that of a Negro," "colors" in the plural means "a flag or banner, as of a country, organization, or military unit"; or "any distinguishing symbol, badge, ribbon, or mark": *the colors of a college.* "Colors" may even refer to "one's opinion or position"—as in *Stick to your colors.*

12 Jean Genet, *Querelle*, 88.

13 The modesty/protection/decoration trinity (with varying emphases placed on each) is the single greatest theme in the voluminous history of commenting on clothes. Nearly all studies relate themselves to these three "fundamental motives" (as J. C. Flugel deems them) for human clothing; see J. C. Flugel, *The Psychology of Clothes*. Studies of clothing in the context of consumption (Veblen, most obviously), and even of fashion as a system, also route themselves along this axis, though "decoration" is the category they expand in any number of social, political, and semiotic ways. As one would expect, commentary on the fashion system comes the closest to claiming that we are damaged by clothes. For a sampling of the range of texts that address the meanings and the motives behind human clothing, consider: Thomas Carlyle, *Sartor Resartus*; Herbert Spencer, *Principles of Sociology*, vol. 2, part 4; Thorstein Veblen, *The Theory of the Leisure Class*; Georg Simmel, *Fashion*, in *Georg Simmel: On Individuality and Social Forms*, ed. Donald Levine; Louis Flaccus, "Remarks on the Psychology of Clothes"; Knight Dunlap, "The Development and the Function of Clothing," *Journal of General Psychology* 1 (1928): 64; Hilaire Hiler, *From Nudity to Raiment*; Bernard Rudofsky, *Are Clothes Modern?*; Lawrence Langner, *The Importance of Wearing Clothes*; Roland Barthes, *The Fashion System*; Elizabeth Wilson, *Adorned in Dreams*; Pearl Binder, *Dressing Up, Dressing Down*; Ruth P. Rubinstein, *Dress Codes*; Elizabeth Wilson and Juliet Ash, eds., *Chic Thrills*; Charlotte Herzog and Jane Gaines, eds., *Fabrications*.

14 Sigmund Freud, "Femininity," trans. and ed. James Strachey, *New Introductory Lectures on Psychoanalysis*, Lecture 33, 132. All further references to Freud are from the same page.

15 We are lucky now to have Laura Doan's excellent study, *Fashioning Sapphism: The Origins of a Modern English Lesbian Culture*, which was published while

a version of this chapter (the first version of it) was in press. Revising my chapter for this publication, I take Doan's study as important confirmation of my claim that Hall, in her novelistic discourse, was saying something different, or at least more strongly, about women's clothes than were her contemporaries. Reading Doan's study, carefully based on a range of sources, one could conclude, as I do here, that there was very little public discourse on a woman's *wounding* (especially psychic wounding) owing to clothes. Rather, what comes up overwhelmingly in Doan's book are women's feelings of freedom when they moved toward masculine tailoring during or after World War I (here, Vita Sackville-West: "I had just got clothes like the women-on-the-land were wearing, and in the accustomed freedom of breeches and gaiters I went into wild spirits; I ran, I shouted, I jumped . . . I felt like a schoolboy let out on a holiday," 64). "At worst," says Doan, women in this period could find themselves accused of "inappropriate appropriation of masculine power" (67) as they took on mannish uniforms (see the third chapter of *Fashioning Sapphism*). The closest Doan comes to citing public discourse on psychic debasement (though Doan herself doesn't use these terms) is when she discusses two mannish women from the 1920s (one, Mary Allen, a commandant in the Women's Police Service in London, and Colonel Victoria Barker, who passed "as an ex-soldier until she was found out"). Doan quotes another writer, Joan Lock (author of *The British Policewoman*), who says that Allen "'had the utmost aversion from dresses'" (83) and Doan herself adds "how utterly natural Allen felt in a uniform devoid of the trappings of 'pink satin'" (84). As for Barker, she too "had an aversion to feminine clothing" (84). This is as strong as it gets in Doan.

One more critical point from this study for my essay here. Doan meticulously documents (and aims to restore to our view) the range of masculine dress for women in the 1920s before *Well* was banned, and the striking reduction to a single image of female masculinity that occurred post-banning. Doan: "British culture at this time was familiar with an astonishing range of masculine and feminine dress for women. The styles of the twenties extended to fashion-conscious and 'masculine' women alike an irresistible invitation to experiment—in terms of dress and manner—with near impunity. . . . All this open-endedness of the 1920s began to wane slowly with the introduction of the 'new feminine look' in 1928 that coincided with the obscenity trial of *The Well of Loneliness*. . . . The trial of *The Well of Loneliness* no doubt hastened the demise of the Modern Girl and the 'severely masculine' look. . . . Hall's fashionably masculine appearance became inextricably connected with female homosexuality—a development Hall seems to have encouraged. . . . The presence of Hall's novel and photograph in newspaper reports encouraged the reading public to associate a particular clothing style with a particular sexual preference, hitherto the knowledge of a discreet, private circle" (xviii–xiv, 120, 122–23). Struck by the "dramatic" nature of her claim for such a sharp shift, especially in a study so scrupulous in its reading of historical documents, Doan herself is later led to comment: "An explanatory model based on a dramatic 'before' and 'after' seems almost too seductive in its simplicity, but the simple—if, for some, lamentable—fact of the matter is that after the obscenity trial of *The Well* life changed utterly for *all* women who lived with other women, or *all* women drawn to masculine styles of dress, whether lesbian or not" (193). Now I want to put into critical view a different feature of Hall's public discourse—talk about the ways in which women's clothes wound—which may be a feature more of her novel's rhetoric than of her own experience, since, as we know from Doan and others, Hall did participate in the women's fashions of her own day.

16 For the atmosphere and events surrounding the banning of *The Well of Loneliness*, see Vera Brittain, *Radclyffe Hall: A Case of Obscenity?* Laura Doan richly adds to our knowledge as she reexamines the journalistic scene leading up to the banning. See her chapter "The Mythic Moral Panic: Radclyffe Hall and the New Genealogy" in *Fashioning Sapphism*.

17 Flugel, *Psychology of Clothes*, 20–21. From reading Flugel, one is reminded that the great majority of clothes commentators address themselves to "shame" generally. That is to say, though they all recognize sex and gender differences as critical to the meaning of clothes and to the development of fashion systems, they do not assign differential shame to the fact of men's or women's wearing clothes or to men's and women's clothing. Flugel, for example, discusses "modesty" and "decoration" (in Freud, "shame" and "vanity") as a compromise made by both sexes: "Clothes serve to cover the body, and thus gratify the impulse to modesty. But, at the same time, they may enhance the beauty of the body, and, indeed, as we have seen, this was probably their most primitive function. When the exhibitionistic tendency to display is thus lured away from the naked to the clothed body, it can gratify itself with far less opposition from the tendencies connected with modesty than it could when it was concentrated on the body in the state of Nature. It is as though both parties were contented with the new development, the compromise involved becoming in consequence a relatively stable one.... In fact, the whole psychology of clothes undergoes at once a great clarification and a great simplification, if this fundamental ambivalence in our attitude be fully grasped and continually held in mind" (21, 22). Even where Flugel comes close to implying differential shame—for example, where he addresses men's removal of their hats in church, in contrast to women's keeping theirs on ("the assumption is that clothes are a sign of disrespect in man, but nakedness a sign of disrespect in woman," 104)—his discussion veers off towards a different kind of point about exhibitionism. And though he invokes at several points "the castration complex," at times in ways that indicate he must be assuming differential shame, his mentions of it never break out in the direction of a wounding attached to or worn on clothes (see 28, 30, 42, 102, 105, 120, 121). The closest he comes to direct statement is in his chapter "Individual Differences." Discussing the type of person who seems supremely overconfident in his choice of clothes, Flugel comments: "Such little evidence as I possess points to the excessive satisfaction with clothes being a compensa-

tion for an extreme intolerance of the naked body, an intolerance that is itself founded on a strong castration complex. If this should prove to be generally true, it would seem that persons of this type (all that I have so far met are of the male sex) cling desperately to a satisfaction in clothes, because these, in virtue of their phallic symbolism, give reassurance against the fear of phallic loss" (102).

18 For starters, one could consult writings by Jane Addams, Charlotte Perkins Gilman, Gertrude Stein, Virginia Woolf, Djuna Barnes, and Natalie Barney. See also Laura Doan's *Fashioning Sapphism*.

19 A famous pair of articles may be taken as an index to these debates. See Carroll Smith-Rosenberg, "Discourses of Sexuality and Subjectivity: The New Woman, 1870–1936," in Martin Duberman et al., eds., *Hidden from History*, a revision of her final chapter to *Disorderly Conduct* (1985), and Esther Newton, "The Mythic Mannish Lesbian: Radclyffe Hall and the New Woman" in the same volume (a revision of her essay in *Signs* from 1984). What makes this pair of essays especially intriguing in their split views is their common origin: a paper coauthored by these women in 1981, which itself appeared in French under the title "Le Myth de la lesbienne et la femme nouvelle," in *Strategies des femmes*.

20 Smith-Rosenberg, "Discourses of Sexuality and Subjectivity," 276, 279.

21 Newton, "The Mythic Mannish Lesbian," 283.

22 It is important to keep in mind the public's collapse of their image of Hall into the image of *Well's* protagonist—a character from a novel that was not straightforwardly autobiographical.

23 For commentary on the largely antagonistic relationship between Bataille and Genet, see Edmund White, *Genet*: 360, 397–98, 565. Especially germane is this observation: "Sadly, he [Bataille] and Genet had so much in common (a love of Sade, Gilles de Rais, Nietzsche, a taste for violence, steely eroticism and Catholic pomp) that they *should* have appreciated one another, but there is evidence of personal animus" (398).

24 Georges Bataille, *Theory of Religion*, 57. This is a later work in the corpus of Bataille (compared to his essay "Sacrificial Mutilation," which I discuss below). It was published in 1973, eleven years after his death in 1962.

25 Bataille, "Sacrificial Mutilation and the Severed Ear of Vincent Van Gogh," in *Visions of Excess*, 67. The madman's automutilation boldly illustrates the elements of sacrifice previously mentioned, especially those that link to fantasy: one's destruction of real ties, one's link to unreality, one's withdrawal from utility, and one's participation in a clearly unintelligible caprice. Bataille furnishes this example in his essay: "In the days that preceded the automutilation, ["Gaston F . . . embroidery designer"] drank several glasses of rum or cognac. He still suspects that he was influenced by the biography of Van Gogh, in which he had read that the painter, during a spell of madness, had cut off his ear and sent it to a girl in a house of prostitution. It was then that, walking along the Boulevard de Menilmontant on December 11, he 'asked the sun for advice, got an idea into his head, stared at the sun to hypnotize him-

self, guessing that its answer was yes.' He thereby seemed to receive approval. 'Lazy man, get out of your sorry state' it seemed to be telling him, through thought transmission. 'It did not seem very hard,' he added, 'after contemplating suicide, to bite off a finger. I told myself: I can always do that'" (61–62).

26 I intend the doubleness of meanings here in the phrases "self-betrayal" and "give yourself away." Both should be taken as pointing to self-shattering (Bataille's strong sense of disrupting the self) *and* revelation of what you wish (here, a wish to throw yourself out to a surface that is not your own).

27 Radclyffe Hall, *The Well of Loneliness*, 246.

28 Of course, these portraits (a historical portrait of a New Woman, a portrait of a butch woman now) can operate for some commentators as overlapping categories. Esther Newton, in her essay on Hall ("The Mythic Mannish Lesbian"), may be bridging these views. Consider these statements: "Cross-dressing for Hall is not a masquerade. It stands for the New Woman's rebellion against the male order and, at the same time, for the lesbian's desperate struggle to be and express her true self" (290). "*The Well* has continued to have meaning to lesbians because it confronts the stigma of lesbianism—as most lesbians have had to live it. . . . [The] reason for *The Well's* continuing impact . . . is that Stephen Gordon articulated a gender orientation with which an important minority of lesbians still actively identify, and toward which another minority is erotically attracted" (282–83). For an important reminder of the range of female masculinities in the twentieth century—even "the multiple and contradictory models of female masculinity produced not only by John [Radclyffe Hall] but also her many inverted friends and contemporaries"—see Judith Halberstam's excellent study *Female Masculinity*. This being said, Halberstam states that "*The Well of Loneliness*, by Radclyffe Hall, is the best record we have of masculine inversion in women" (95).

29 See Elizabeth Lapovsky Kennedy and Madeline D. Davis, *Boots of Leather, Slippers of Gold: The History of a Lesbian Community*, 9, 34, 328–31. For a witty reading of how *The Well of Loneliness* has been sold by publishers, over the years, to a mainstream audience via its book-covers, see Michèle Aina Barale, "Below the Belt: (Un)Covering *The Well of Loneliness*," in *Inside/Out*, ed. Diana Fuss, 235–57. For a delightful investigation of the mutual ferment between Radclyffe Hall and Noel Coward, see Terry Castle's *Noel Coward and Radclyffe Hall*, in which she claims that "Hall [in *Well*] established the standard tropes—moral and descriptive—on which other writers would draw obsessively for the next fifty years" (60).

30 Halberstam notes: "[Hall's] life, as critics have noted, was far from lonely and isolated, and she and Una knew other masculine women as well as many other same-sex couples. They frequented lesbian bars, which were not the vile places she describes in the novel but provided a lively base for a rather flourishing community" (*Female Masculinity*, 96).

31 Onto "elegant" cloth, moreover. Interestingly, in another passage, after she has already been dressing in "tailor-made clothes" (129), Stephen indulges herself in what look like beautiful clothes, though they are still manly: "py-

jamas made of white crêpe de Chine which she spotted in Bond Street" and "a man's dressing-gown of brocade—an amazingly ornate garment" (186). Two paragraphs later, we encounter the famous passage in *Well*, in which Stephen, in front of the mirror, expresses "hate" for her naked body, with its oddly configured masculine femininity (186–87). I find suggestive the close proximity of this famous passage to mention of the "amazingly ornate" man's dressing-gown, with its show of masculine femininity; also the way in which the terms of Stephen's "hate" for her naked body ("she longed to maim it," "so poor and unhappy a thing") so clearly echo Hall's words in the earlier passage on Stephen's wrenching off of her dress ("longing intensely to rend it, to hurt it," "the poor crumpled thing lying crushed and dejected"). For very different readings of this passage, see Halberstam, *Female Masculinity*, 100–106; and Teresa De Lauretis, *The Practice of Love*, 209–13 and 239–43.

32 The novel ends, of course, with Stephen's grandest sacrifice. Concerned to preserve Mary's future as a potentially normal woman, Stephen fakes her unfaithfulness to Mary, which sends Mary off, as Stephen plans, to the arms of Martin. (As another character puts it: "Aren't you being absurdly self-sacrificing?" 433.) Hall's novel closes not with the assurance of salvation, however, but with a kind of demon possession: "Oh, but there were many, these unbidden guests. . . . The quick, the dead, and the yet unborn—all calling her. . . . Aye, and those lost and terrible brothers from Alec's [bar], they were here, and they also were calling: 'Stephen, Stephen, speak with your God and ask Him why He has left us forsaken!' She could see their marred and reproachful faces with the haunted, melancholy eyes of the invert" (436). The novel concludes with Stephen's unanswered plea to God: "We believe . . . We have not denied you . . . Acknowledge us, oh God . . . Give us also the right to our existence!"

33 Leslie Feinberg, *Stone Butch Blues*, 5.

34 This circumstance, and this narrative structure, makes the novel curled at the start, contained in a letter that the novel is seeking to send itself at length. Tellingly, this letter is so self-sustaining that it appears in an edited volume (Joan Nestle, *The Persistent Desire*) as (what looks like) an archival document, presented with the title "Letter to a fifties femme from a stone butch," by Leslie Feinberg—a document I assumed *was* archival until the publication of *Stone Butch Blues*. Ann Cvetkovich (see note below) has noticed this oddity, too. The phrase "fifties femme" in the title is confusing, since the protagonist of the novel, Jess Goldberg, is born in 1949 and thus frequents lesbian bars in the 1960s and 1970s.

35 On femme/butch as an erotic system (with a variety of butches and femmes), see the essays in Sally R. Munt and Cherry Smith, eds., *Butch/Femme*, especially the essay by Ann Cvetkovich, "Untouchability and Vulnerability: Stone Butchness as Emotional Style." See also Judith Halberstam, *Female Masculinity*; Sue-Ellen Case, "Toward a Butch-Femme Aesthetic," *Discourse* 11, no. 1 (Fall 1988/Winter 1989): 55–73; Joan Nestle, ed., *The Persistent Desire*; Teresa De Lauretis, *The Practice of Love*; and Sally R. Munt, *Heroic Desire*.

36 As it happens, it is not at all clear there was any such rule. Elizabeth Kennedy and Madeline Davis: "According to Professor Nan Hunter of the Brooklyn College Law School, no such law exists (personal communication, January 1992). It is her guess that a judge in a particular case made a ruling that two or three pieces of clothing of the 'correct' sex negated male or female impersonation and that set a precedent used by law enforcement agencies" (*Boots of Leather*, 411).

37 For example, as a girl, before she routinely dresses in men's clothes, Jess "fights" girls' clothes "tooth and nail" (18). When she is hospitalized by her parents for getting caught in her father's clothes, a stated rule on the ward is that "I must wear a dress" (21), later followed by the enforced "humiliation of charm school" ("I might have killed myself," 23). By age 16, "I promised myself I would never wear a dress again" (50). (See also the dramatic scene, 116–17.) By contrast, Jess finds fully alluring "women in tight dresses and high heels" (28) or "jeans too tight for words" (6) ("Just watching made me ache with need," 28).

38 About my words, "clichés" and "failures": I hope it is obvious that I am not critiquing the fascinating work of gendered attraction between butch and femme as depicted by Feinberg. This pair's creativity comes from their surprising use of available signs: their idiosyncratic embrace of clichés and their commitment to a failed authenticity. (Otherwise, the butch would seek to fully pass as a man, which is a major topic and a different kind of stance in *Stone Butch Blues*.)

39 See Kennedy and Davis, *Boots of Leather, Slippers of Gold*, 41, 42, 46, 56, 63, 74, 90, 92–98, 127–28, 145–47, 149. Here, we read: "In the 1950s there were even fewer raids on lesbian and gay bars than in the 1940s. Not one narrator can remember a raid during the 1950s. . . . Only the Canadians remember any harassment in the bars, and this was from the border patrol, who would come in and check for IDs. Whitney had a male friend who spent the night in jail because he didn't have proper identification" (74). "Since the police did not generally exert their authority in the bars . . . arrests rarely occurred in the bars themselves. They were more likely to occur on the streets, especially in the area around the bars. Black lesbians in particular were targets of police harassment even in their own neighborhoods" (92). "Black narrators, unlike white narrators, recall the police as vicious during the 1950s. Racial prejudice seems to have magnified hostility toward lesbians and gays to the extent that Black lesbians risked arrest for 'disorderly conduct' just by walking in their own neighborhoods" (127). Finally, "all the bars that were important hangouts for lesbians in Buffalo during the 1950s closed at the end of the decade or the beginning of the next, and were not easily replaced. . . . Within a twenty-one-month period between 1960 and 1961, we have been able to document at least six license revocations for bars frequented by homosexuals" (145). Feinberg might counter that at least for her depictions post-1968, she is representing, as her narrator states, that "the police really stepped up their harassment after the birth of gay pride"; "cops scribbled down our license plate numbers

and photographed us as we entered the bars. We held regular dances at a gay-owned bar, using police radios to alert everyone when the cops were about to raid us" (Feinberg, *Stone Butch Blues*, 135).

40 Edmund White explains that the French publisher Gaston Gallimard first brought out *Querelle* in 1947 without a publisher's name attached; then Gallimard, in 1951, "[began] to publish the *Complete Works* of Genet in several volumes" (294).

41 Though the novel's setting is named as Brest—and Genet wants us to know of this location—the novel, hung quite literally in a fog, gives no clue to historical setting or event. Even so, given the fact of Brest's wartime destruction, along with the novel's date of publication (1947; 1953), one can imagine that Genet's first readers could better appreciate that the novel's setting is a fantasy Brest. On the circumstances surrounding Genet's composition of *Querelle*, see White, *Genet*, 288–94. For a discussion of *Fight Club* (1999), see my conclusion, "Dark Camp: Behind and Ahead."

42 One could regard this narratorial "we" as the royal "we" of a singular narrator; I am purposely deciding to take the "we" more literally—as a plurality.

43 For dramatic contrast, see Malcolm Gladwell's "Listening to Khakis" on Dockers-logic and Haggar-speak. "In the best of the [Haggar] ads," writes Gladwell, "entitled, 'I Am,' a thirtyish man wakes up, his hair all mussed, pulls on a pair of white khakis, and half sleepwalks outside to get the paper. '*I am not what I wear. I'm not a pair of pants, or a shirt . . . I'm just a guy, and I don't have time to think about what I wear, because I've got a lot of important guy things to do.*' All he has left now is the sports section and, gripping it purposefully, he heads for the bathroom. '*One-hundred-per-cent-cotton-wrinkle-free khaki pants that don't require a lot of thought. Haggar. Stuff you can wear*'" (56).

44 We read in the novel: "The fact that the cop had recognized his generosity spurred the Lieutenant on to further sacrifices. It elated him. . . . He [the Lieutenant] became more and more attached to the young mason, in a mystical and specific way" (209, 210). As a matter of fact, this young mason, named Gil, who has murdered his co-worker, is, quite dramatically, the victim of a cloth wound. He is the object of a cruel joke, perpetrated by the queer bully, Theo, whom he later kills in rage. The joke is this: Theo has gone through Gil's laundry bag and found a pair of his dirty briefs ("slightly soiled with shit and blood at the back"); when he lays them out on Gil's bed, they attract flies, along with the attention of all the other masons who have gathered round to taunt. They use the cloth wound to suggest to Gil that he is open at the back.

TWO *Bottom Values*

This chapter originated as a talk sponsored by the Humanities Center at the University of Utah, February 1989. It subsequently appeared in *Cultural Critique* 24 (Spring 1993): 81–118 and is reprinted here, with major revisions, by permission of Oxford University Press. I gratefully acknowledge criticisms generously offered by Peggy Pascoe, Barry Weller, Stephanie Pace, Gillian Brown, Henry Staten, and Melanee Cherry.

1 See my initial discussion in my introduction to this book, 34–35.

2 On anal penetration as this central focus for homophobic hate, see Leo Bersani, "Is the Rectum a Grave?"

3 *American Heritage Dictionary*, College Edition.

4 See Sigmund Freud, "Anal Erotism and the Castration Complex," in *Standard Edition of the Complete Psychological Works of Sigmund Freud* (SE) 17:72–88; "Aspects of Development and Regression: Aetiology," in *General Introduction to Psychoanalysis* (GI), 348–66; "Character and Anal Erotism," SE 9: 167–75; "Development of the Libido and Sexual Organizations," GI, 329–47; "The Excretory Functions in Psychoanalysis and Folklore," in *Character and Culture*, 219–22; *Jokes and Their Relation to the Unconscious*; "Obsessive Actions and Religious Practices," SE 9:117–27; "On Transformations of Instinct as Exemplified in Anal Erotism," SE 17:125–33; "The Paths of Symptom-Formation," GI, 367–85; "The Sexual Life of Man," GI, 312–28; and *Three Case Histories*.

5 Toni Morrison, *Sula*, 4.

6 Clearly, Morrison uses the congealed terms "blacks" and "whites." I will follow her practice, using these terms to refer to those people whom she depicts as (being read by the people around them as) "white" or "black."

7 The attentive reader will notice that these are different kinds of questions: (1) Can the metaphor of the Bottom receive a different tenor (mean something other than an economic basement)? (2) Can the tenor (economic basement) itself take on new meanings? The phrasings of these questions ("unhinge a metaphor"; "partially redirect") suggest, in any case, that there can be no wholesale correction of the Bottom's metaphorical meaning, which throughout the novel bears a dreadful force. One last question: Are the novel's characters unhinging metaphor (depicted as fighting to make other meanings of their neighborhood seen) or is Toni Morrison? It is hard to tell. Readers should keep this question before them.

8 Despite the burgeoning critical attention focused on Morrison, critics have not addressed *Sula*'s anal focus. For major collections on Morrison, see Gates and Appiah, *Toni Morrison*; McKay, *Critical Essays on Toni Morrison* (with essays by Robert Grand and Deborah McDowell on *Sula*); and Bloom, *Toni Morrison* (esp. the essays by Cynthia Davis and Melvin Dixon). In addition, see Samuels and Hudson-Weems, *Toni Morrison*; Awkward, *Inspiring Influences*; Butler-Evans, *Race, Gender, and Desire*; and Willis, *Specifying*.

9 Realize, these debates have generally understood "black" fictions to mean literature written by African Americans, not, as I am claiming in this book, texts that substantially engage the sign "black." For a sample of these critical, theoretical debates, see notes 18 and 19 below.

10 See Roland Barthes, "The Death of the Author," in *Image/Music/Text*.

11 In "Missionary Positions," Simon Watney, in 1989, smartly analyzed how, in the 1980s, Western media were bastardizing these complex links. Wat-

ney showed how, at that time, Western journalists' extreme focus on "promiscuity" in Africa led to their "regarding black Africans and gay men as effectively interchangeable"; thus "Africa," he writes, "becomes a 'deviant' continent, just as Western gay men are effectively Africanized" (88). More specifically, since the symptoms of "African AIDS disease" correspond to familiar Western images of (African) famine ("lassitude, extreme weight loss, huge staring eyes"), AIDS became in these journalists' descriptions "a virus which eventually kills by transforming all its 'victims' into 'Africans,' and which threatens to 'Africanize' the entire world" (91–92).

12　The word "medallion," which shares its etymological roots with "medal," traces back to the Vulgar Latin *medalia*, meaning "a small coin" (*Webster's New World Dictionary*).

13　In "The Motives of Jokes: Jokes as a Social Process," Freud claims that jokes may be used by a person who "finds criticism or aggressiveness difficult so long as they are direct, and possible only along circuitous paths" (*Jokes*, 142). As we will see, Morrison, along with several of her characters (Sula, most especially) has good reason to be both aggressive and sadistic in the face of what must be told about the beautiful Bottom.

14　The narrator tells us: "Just like that ["rich white folks"] had changed their minds and instead of keeping the valley floor to themselves, now they wanted a hilltop house with a river view and a ring of elms" (166).

15　Morrison herself, in an interview with *Time*, pointed to the unique economic placement of blacks in relation to European immigrants: "But in becoming an American from Europe, what one has in common with that other immigrant is contempt for me—it's nothing else but color . . . Every immigrant knew he would not come as the very bottom. He had to come above at least one group—and that was us" ("Pain" 120).

16　Philip Sheldon Foner, *Organized Labor and the Black Worker*, 130. Foner quotes from a leaflet distributed throughout Alabama: "Are you happy with your pay envelope? Would you like to go North where the laboring man shares the profits with the Boss? . . . Let's Go Back North. Where no trouble . . . exists, no strikes, no lock outs, large coal, good wages, fair treatment, two weeks pay, good houses. If you haven't got all these things you had better see us. Will send you where you can have all these things. . . . Will advance you money if necessary. Go now. While you have the chance" (130). "In April 1919, the Division of Negro Economics announced that 99% of Chicago's black veterans were still unemployed, with little prospect of work in the immediate future" (132).

17　Bersani, 222.

18　We are now familiar with many black critics' deep hesitancy toward what we have come to call "critical theories." (See, for example, the debate in *New Literary History*: Joyce, "Black Canon" and "Who the Cap Fit"; Gates, "What's Love"; and Baker, "In Dubious Battle.") Even critics who use these theories, such as those forged by Freud, Marx, Lacan, Althusser, Foucault, Derrida, Irigaray, Kristeva, Sedgwick, and Butler, caution against (the specifically Western European limitations to) their analytical presumptions and historical perspectives as applied to African American texts and contexts. See also Robinson, *Black Marxism*, 2–5; and Gates, *"Race," Writing, and Difference*, 13–15.

19 See Barbara Christian, "The Race for Theory," 52.

20 Perhaps things changed faster than Christian could have imagined when she published her article in 1987, for Morrison (by the time I published the first version of this essay in 1993) was already becoming canonical on English department syllabi and exam lists. My caveat, however, does not change the force of Christian's complaint, since how these fictions are ultimately valued in relation to older, established canonical works and "theories" remains to be seen. The likelihood remains that critics, in making a case for these novels' canonical status, will tame what is most aggressive in these fictions—a situation that occasions my book.

21 In chapter 3, "When Are Dirty Details and Scenes Compelling?: Tucked in the Cuts of Interracial Anal Rape," I work out this issue at much greater length. In the present chapter, I'm discussing "context," which could be taken to mean social context, though clearly the context I mean most directly is Morrison's novel—her imaginative construction of the social. How does the context she provides make trouble for Freud? In the next chapter, I trouble Barthes's views on visual pleasure and visual power by tucking his claims into *Pulp Fiction*.

22 Freud, "Development," 336.

23 Freud, "Sexual Life," 324.

24 See Freud, "Aspects." There he notes: "The ego may countenance the fixation and will then be perverse to that extent"; for "regression of libido without repression would never give rise to a neurosis, but would result in a perversion" (360, 353).

25 See Davis, *Women, Race, and Class*. Though more directly focused on "the African female in captivity," Spillers's essay "Mama's Baby, Papa's Maybe" also provides a crucial discussion of the black woman's differential relation to domesticity.

26 Clearly, it is the bourgeois, not the working-class, woman our culture has traditionally linked most directly with passivity, since working-class women may not be privatized and may work outside the home in the capitalist economy (even as domestic workers). And yet this scheme clearly begs the question of white bourgeois women who themselves work in the capitalist economy. Many women (especially since *Sula*'s publication, and even since I first wrote a version of this essay in 1989) have become petit bourgeois or bourgeois "in their own right" (that is, not by marriage). This circumstance is precisely their problem at certain times. Since these women cannot be labeled passive or privatized, they sometimes bear a troubled relation to their gender sign as figured according to dominant codes. The copious advertisements and women's magazine articles devoted to helping "professional" women maintain their femininity (and, as well, their maternal overtones) surely indicate this problematic status.

27 "Black and White in America," *Newsweek*, March 7, 1988, 20.

28 One gets a lesson in public racial discourse and mainstream analysis by read-
    ing *Newsweek*'s self-proclaimed "pioneering race coverage," launched in their
    cover-story series that began in 1963. Among the most instructive essays for
    the issues I uncover in this chapter are "The Negro in America: What Must Be
    Done" (*Newsweek*, November 20, 1967), "Black and White in America" (*News-
    week*, March 7, 1988), "Can the Children Be Saved?" (*Newsweek*, September 11,
    1989), "The New Politics of Race" (*Newsweek*, May 6, 1991), "The Hidden
    Rage of Successful Blacks" (*Newsweek*, November 15, 1993), "A World with-
    out Fathers: The Struggle to Save the Black Family" (*Newsweek*, August 30,
    1993), and "The Good News about Black America (And Why Many Blacks
    Aren't Celebrating)" (*Newsweek*, June 7, 1999). This last-named essay, from
    1999, is particularly provocative in its mixed messages (signaled in its title
    and its statistics, which themselves are titled "Moving Forward, But Still Be-
    hind"). This cover story shifts away from the full-on discourse of "impasse"
    and "shattered dreams" still so apparent in the coverage of the early 1990s.
    ("The problem today," *Newsweek* wrote in 1991, "is shattered dreams. After
    all the high hopes and genuine progress of the past 30 years, people on both
    sides of the color line feel they've reached an impasse, and that things are get-
    ting worse," May 6, 1991, 29.) In the essay from 1999, *Newsweek* tells us that
    "never before has black been quite so beautiful" (31), since African Americans
    "are no longer relegated" to what King called "'a lonely island of poverty'"
    (30). Citing poverty-line statistics (lowest ever), job rates (up), the clear rise
    in home ownership, and the renewal of "once desolate inner-city neighbor-
    hoods" (one case-study describes "a community coming back from the dead,"
    31–32), *Newsweek* explains that "today's upswing in black fortune is unfold-
    ing in a singular context, against the backdrop of a superheated economy that
    has been booming since April 1991" (31). And yet. . . . First, "there is the
    fear—deeply felt. . . . What happens . . . when the economy hits the bottom?"
    (38). Then, "there is the cold reality: for every upbeat statistic that engen-
    ders joy, there is a dismal number . . . that invites alarm" (38). "The prob-
    lem is that although certain blacks are thriving, others are not. Many of those
    'beneath the surface of socioeconomic viability,' as sociologist Elijah Ander-
    son describes them, are worse off than ever. Many blighted, black neighbor-
    hoods . . . are dying slow, painful deaths" (36). Though "black income . . . is at
    its highest level ever," "black unemployment (at 8.9 percent) remains more
    than twice the rate for whites (3.9 percent). Among workers 20 to 24, the un-
    employment numbers are even more lopsided (16.8 percent for blacks, 6.5
    percent for whites). Such high unemployment among blacks 'in a virtually
    full-employment economy says there's still something wrong,' observes Wade
    Henderson, executive director of the Leadership Conference on Civil Rights"
    (40). Add to that "intense segregation" and the circumstance that "more black
    men than ever languish in [American] prisons"; also "suicides among young
    black men have risen sharply, reflecting a deep 'sense of hopelessness,' says
    Jewelle Taylor Gibbs, a psychologist and University of California, Berkeley,
    professor" (40, 31). *Newsweek* even ends on a down note, which explains their

choice of cover title, "The Good News About Black America (and Why Many Blacks Aren't Celebrating)": "We look with equanimity, even pride, upon a statistical profile of black Americans that, were it of whites, would be a source of horror and consternation. That is not likely to change soon" (40).

29 For a remarkable indication of the persistence of the Moynihan perspective ("today the situation has only grown worse," 18), see its newfangled version in *Newsweek*'s essay "A World without Fathers: The Struggle to Save the Black Family" (August 30, 1993), in which we learn that "for blacks, the institution of marriage has been devastated" (17). Particularly striking to the *Newsweek* writers is their observation that this is not "solely a problem of the entrenched underclass": "Among the poor a staggering 65 percent of never-married black women have children, double the number for whites. But even among the well-to-do, the differences are striking" (17). In a boxed feature within the larger essay ("Three Generations of Single Mothers"), some kind of version of the matriarchy thesis even appears in a *Newsweek* paraphrase: "When they get together [mother and daughter] debate whether there are no men because the women in her family are so strong, or whether the women are so strong because there are no men" (25). Though they state emphatically that "the evidence comes down solidly on the side of marriage," the *Newsweek* writers do concede, in a second essay attached to the main one, that "as the nation grapples with this latest social crisis, it's worth keeping two other facts in mind. One is that for all the hand-wringing over unmarried mothers, single parenthood is not necessarily dysfunctional" (though the words "devastating," "staggering," "perilous," "endangered" keep appearing in their essays); "the other fact is that nothing anyone is likely to do will return America to the 1950s" (29). Solution? "Even if we cannot return to a simpler time, we should be able to come up with social policies that work better than those now in place" (29).

30 My mention of "hailing" makes obvious reference to Althusser's notion of subjectivity-formation, which takes place, he argues, "by that very precise operation which I have called interpellation or hailing, and which can be imagined along the lines of the most commonplace everyday police (or other) hailing: 'Hey, you there!'" (*Lenin and Philosophy*, 174). That Althusser imagines here a hailing by police may lead us to connect hailing with "arresting" in the latter's double sense of stopping and being placed under the law. In the passage where "blackness greeted [Shadrack] with its indisputable presence," Morrison seems to imagine a moment of interpellation that, while certainly not located outside the law, takes the character toward a positioning from which he can arrest himself—literally, for a moment, stop his trauma.

31 These definitions are from *Webster's New World Dictionary*. The last sense of "tuck" as linked "to pierce" comes by way of Old French (*estoquier*) and Middle Dutch (*stocken*)—"to stick, pierce, poke"—giving rise to the archaic noun form of "tuck" that means "a thin sword."

32 The "vast back-of-the-head that [God] had turned on them in death" is not a simple image of a turning away. In fact, the revelation of God's back parts is in-

vested with extraordinary richness—even tenderness—in the story of Moses, where, as a sign of his favor, God agrees to reveal his glory—backward (Exodus 33:20–23).

33 In his analysis of the Wolf Man, Freud refers to the belief "that sexual intercourse takes place at the anus" as "an older notion, and one which in any case completely contradicts the dread of castration" ("Anal Erotism," 78).

THREE *Dirty Details and Scenes*

1 José Muñoz, *Disidentifications*, 57.

2 Eve Kosofsky Sedgwick, *Touching Feeling*, 116. See my introduction for further discussion.

3 Of course, we are generally encouraged not to focus our attention on film cuts. This is an old saw in film history. Textbooks as late as the late 1980s describe this editing—"invisible editing or découpage"—as "unobtrusive editing": "not so much unseen as disregarded" (Thomas and Vivian C. Sobchack, *An Introduction to Film*, 117). In fact, we are told that "although this kind of editing was perfected in Hollywood, it is probably accurate to say that today the vast majority of narrative films—no matter where they are made—are edited this way" (117). "The best praise an editor can ask for is that no one noticed the shifts from shot to shot" (118). Even so, despite these assertions in praise of seamlessness, some experimental filmmakers have made "their cuts highly visible" (118). The term "jump cut" was coined after Jean-Luc Godard's *Breathless* was released in 1959, in order to describe the "abrupt editing used in this film" (118). In discussing cuts, one could further distinguish among the cuts made by writers (in a screenplay, marked "CUT TO"); the cuts produced by the cinematographer or the director (made by virtue of camera angles, camera movements, or the director's yelling "cut"); and those made in post-production editing. For my purposes, more important than these last distinctions (among the cuts made by various filmmaking participants) are those between visible and invisible cuts.

4 It is helpful to remember that our view of this band-aid is neither short nor subtle. When we see Marsellus for the first time in the film, the camera holds a shot on the back of his head for several minutes while he delivers a speech to Butch.

5 Male-to-male anal rape was the shock of John Boorman's *Deliverance* (1972), to which Tarantino makes obvious reference in this scene. It appears that Tarantino ratchets up the shock—or decides to add a twist?—by putting a black man (with an imposing physical form) in the place of the timid white Bobby from *Deliverance*. Although Tarantino clearly states the name of the pawnshop in his script ("Butch cuts across traffic and dashes into a business with a sign that reads: MASON-DIXON PAWNSHOP"), he makes the sign much harder to read in the finished film. Instead, he spreads a Confederate flag just inside the pawnshop door. Whether these moves, for most spectators, would convey a historical sense of this rape, I can't fully tell. Nevertheless, I assume

that many viewers of this scene make a conscious or unconscious link to the history of Southern (or simply American) white-on-black violence, which includes a range of sexual injuries (rape and genital wounding, for example). Marsellus drops through the trapdoor of codes (all too familiar) that take a black boss to a racial (de)basement.

6 Obviously, this is Tarantino *thematizing* our placement in his cuts, making us feel in these later scenes (through his formal play with interrupting scenes and reordering scenes) that we are "in" his cuts. It is unlikely (to say the least) that he shot the footage of the earlier scenes in one piece; then made cuts; then directly used this cut material in the later "restored" scenes.

7 Pat Dowell, "Pulp Friction," 4, 5.

8 Anthony Lane, "Degrees of Cool," 96.

9 Thomas M. Leitch, "Know-Nothing Entertainment," 9.

10 Michael Rogin, "The Two Declarations of American Independence," 25.

11 Sharon Willis, "Borrowed 'Style': Quentin Tarantino's Figures of Masculinity," in *High Contrast*, 189, 211.

12 Carolyn Dinshaw, "Getting Medieval," in Frese and O'Keeffe, *The Book and the Body*, xx, 117, 126.

13 See D. A. Miller, "Anal *Rope*," in *Inside/Out*, ed. Diana Fuss, 119–41; and Lee Edelman, "*Rear Window's* Glasshole," in *Out Takes*, ed. Ellis Hanson, 72–96.

14 Susan Stryker, *Queer Pulp*, book jacket, 8. Needless to say, Stryker's book is a gold mine for the kind of titles I have listed in this section.

15 Muñoz, *Disidentifications*, 59.

16 Kobena Mercer and Isaac Julien, "Race, Sexual Politics and Black Masculinity: A Dossier," in *Male Order*, ed. Rowena Chapman and Jonathan Rutherford, 141, 143.

17 Kobena Mercer, "Skin Head Sex Thing: Racial Difference and the Homoerotic Imaginary," in *How Do I Look?*, ed. Bad Object-Choices, 169.

18 Kobena Mercer, "Looking for Trouble," in *The Lesbian and Gay Studies Reader*, ed. Abelove et al., 356.

19 Mercer, "Skin Head Sex Thing," 184.

20 Muñoz, *Disidentifications*, 73, 74.

21 Roland Barthes, *Camera Lucida*, 7.

22 This issue finds a succinct formulation in this familiar postmodern dictum: all meaning is context-bound, but context is boundless. In the context of his own historical moment, if reviews and essays are any indication, the optical shocks that Tarantino plans largely succeed: viewers have been boldly and consistently struck by Marsellus's rape, Mia's resurrection, and Marvin's sudden shot to the face. How future viewers will be struck by (what I am calling here) these arrows to the eye remains unclear.

23 Obviously, we do not know with any certainty that this photograph existed. Barthes could be working from the fiction of a photograph such as this one. For the purposes of my discussion that follows, it doesn't really matter. What concerns me are the theories he produces around it.

24 Clearly, I assume that Barthes's theory of *punctum/studium* has wider applica-

tion than to the photograph. There is no reason that the sometimes idiosyncratic immediacy of the *punctum*'s unstudied "arrow" must be solely photographic (or visual). Nor does it seem convincing to argue that there cannot be *punctum* in the cinema because the images come too quickly—don't stay still. "That accident which pricks me" seems, to my mind, to need little time to launch to the eye, as I think many cinema viewers would admit. In fact, it is precisely the time it takes a viewer to ponder the detail, even after it has vanished from the screen, that makes a cut in a film's flow.

25 As I explain in chapter 2, "the revelation of God's back parts is invested with extraordinary richness . . . in the story of Moses, where, as a sign of his favor, God agrees to reveal his glory—backwards."

26 Obviously, I am not claiming to know whether or not Tarantino intends (what I am calling) "the brilliant effect" of his *punctual* rape. I only know that this rape seems calculated to offer its viewers an optical shock.

27 It may seem that the *studium* that this *punctum* punctures (the narrative of Butch's escape and his redemption of his sins against Marsellus) is a different one than that which draws the *punctum* out (American history and the politics of race). However, I am on my way to showing that these two *studia* are crucially related through the larger question of redeeming history.

28 Quoted in Marriott, *On Black Men*, 1, 2, 9.

29 These dynamics are explored in Vito Russo's *The Celluloid Closet*.

30 Robert F. Reid-Pharr, *Black Gay Man*, 87.

31 Quoted in Reid-Pharr, 138–39.

32 Lane, "Degrees of Cool," 96.

33 In spite of copious commentaries on the racialized rape in *Pulp Fiction* (and on Tarantino's use of "nigger"), I have not discovered any discussion of Captain Koons's name as a racial slur. Nor do critics link the watch up the ass to the trope of hiding time or history.

34 Tarantino says the band-aid was simply meant to cover an ugly wart on Ving Rhames's head. I must say, however, that until *Mission Impossible Two*, I had never seen this wart on his head. It was strangely missing, without aid of band-aid, in the film *Rosewood*, in which Rhames starred and in which he was prominently shown from the back.

FOUR *Erotic Corpse*

The core of this chapter was given as a talk at the Society for the Study of Narrative Literature, April 1996. I am grateful to the late Barbara Christian, who was in my audience and who discussed my arguments with me (along with Cleaver's views) later that evening.

1 For three different takes on this grand antagonism, see David Bergman, "The African and the Pagan in Gay Black Literature," in *Sexual Sameness*, ed. Joseph Bristow, 148–69; Marlon B. Ross, "White Fantasies of Desire: Baldwin and the Racial Identities of Sexuality" in *James Baldwin Now*, ed. Dwight A. McBride, 13–55; and Robert F. Reid-Pharr, "Tearing the Goat's Flesh." Reid-

Pharr's essay is the only one I know of, other than my own—indeed, they were written around the same time—that imagines intersections between the writings of Baldwin and Cleaver.

2 It will become apparent why I use the term "homosexual" in this essay, even in reference to Baldwin himself who claimed to represent "bisexuals" in his fiction and who did not like the terms "gay" or "homosexual." ("I feel like a stranger in America," he wrote, "from almost every conceivable angle except, oddly enough, as a black person. The word 'gay' has always rubbed me the wrong way. . . . I simply feel it's a world that has very little to do with me, with where I did my growing up. I was never at home in it." Richard Goldstein, " 'Go the Way Your Blood Beats': An Interview with James Baldwin," in Quincy Troupe, ed., *James Baldwin: The Legacy,* 174.) Specifically, I would like to underscore the notion of a "homosexuality" (a so-called sameness) built on a logic of opposites attracting, which I examine in this chapter. Readers may wish to keep the term "bisexual" attached to "homosexual" throughout this essay as a reminder of the doubled logic of race-attached-to-sex that adheres to my purposely jarring designation of "homosexual miscegenation." For an attempt to restore the bisexual signification of Baldwin's fictional representations, see Marjorie Garber, *Vice Versa,* 126–34.

3 Detailed views of historical contexts surrounding the decision in *Brown v. Board of Education* and their sociopolitical effects can be found in James T. Patterson, *Brown v. Board of Education*; Richard Kluger, *Simple Justice*; Austin Sarat, ed., *Race, Law, and Culture*; and Mark Tushnet, with Katya Levin, "What Really Happened in *Brown v. Board of Education*."

4 Surely, it is always tricky to prove the absence of any concept in a culture. By this claim, I am not saying that there was no discourse on or fear of interracial sexual relations between men. I simply mean to point to the oddity of any concept of men interbreeding with each other, which would seem impossible. For his paradigmatic example of discourse on miscegenation, James T. Patterson offers the following: "For many whites the very idea of desegregated schools prompted the ugliest imaginable images of racial mixing. No one expressed this feeling more clearly than Herbert Ravenel Sass, a South Carolinian, in the *Atlantic Monthly* in 1956: 'To suppose that . . . we can promote all other degrees of race mixing but stop short of interracial mating is . . . like going over Niagara Falls in a barrel in the expectation of stopping three fourths of the way down. The South is now the great bulwark against intermarriage. A very few years of thoroughly integrated schools would produce larger numbers of young Southerners free from all "prejudice" against mixed matings' " (6). Notice that "mating," in a context such as this one, does the double-duty work of signifying both "intermarriage" and "interracial" reproduction.

5 Some critics have famously claimed that Baldwin "identified with young, handsome, blond males" (Calvin C. Hernton, *White Papers for White Americans,* 114). Making no judgment on Baldwin if he did, I do not profess to know.

6 James Baldwin, *Giovanni's Room,* 59.

7 We will see to what extent Cleaver and Baldwin, as they perform their re-
spective analyses, use an *image* of decomposition in order to perform it. As
for Picasso, in his (de)compositions from his phase of analytical cubism (for
example, *A Man Playing a Clarinet*), we can see the analysis of a particular
relation (a clarinet being played by a man) visually broken out into horizon-
tal planes. These layers, as it were, produce the complications of the cubist
image—what I am calling here a "thick" or "thickened" sight. Even deconstruction (in spite of its prefix "de-" that suggests a pulling apart of linguistic
constructions) is a form of analyzing that layers on linguistic meanings.

8 For a popular media index to this issue, see James S. Kunen, "Back to Segregation," *Time*, April 29, 1996, 39–45, in which we are told that "after two de-
cades of progress of integration, the separation of black children in America's
schools is on the rise and is in fact approaching the levels of 1970, before the
first school bus rolled at the order of a court" (39). For scholarly analyses of the
enduring nature of American segregation, see Gary Orfield and Susan Eaton,
Dismantling Desegregation; Orfield and John Yun, Civil Rights Project, Harvard
University, *Resegregation in American Schools*; Orlando Patterson, *The Ordeal
of Integration*; Douglas Massey and Nancy Denton, *American Apartheid*.

9 Norman Mailer, "The White Negro" in *Advertisements for Myself*, 340.

10 Eldridge Cleaver, *Soul on Ice*, 98, 99.

11 "White Negro," 340. One should notice, in what follows, how Hemingway's
"Good" becomes, must be, an urban good for Mailer.

12 The intricacies of the Mailer-Baldwin relation have still not been much analyzed, beyond those discussions provided by biographers (though Gerald
Early, in his book of essays [*Tuxedo Junction*, 183–95], provides a sharp perspective on Mailer-Baldwin differences with regard to their writing on boxing). The well-known biographical discussions are David Leeming, *James
Baldwin*, 183–86; James Campbell, *Talking at the Gates*, 137–44; W. J. Weatherby, *Squaring Off*.

13 James Baldwin, "The Black Boy Looks at the White Boy" in *Nobody Knows My
Name*, 216–41.

14 Two other critics make single-sentence references to miscegenation in this
context. Marlon Ross comments: "[Houston] Baker wants to rescue Baldwin's
seminal place in the canon of African American literature and culture, as opposed to the inseminated position in a miscegenated relation to white culture
given him by some of the late 1960s militants" ("White Fantasies," 18). Garber: "In this passage the black man becomes the bottom, the white man the
top; the white man is the inserter, the black man the insertee, the 'passive'
recipient of white sex and white culture" (*Vice Versa*, 133).

15 David Bergman, Marlon Ross, and William J. Spurlin (in "Culture, Rhetoric, and Queer Identity: James Baldwin and the Identity Politics of Race
and Sexuality," in *James Baldwin Now*, ed. Dwight McBride) all briefly point
out Cleaver's siding with Norman Mailer against James Baldwin. Important
for my purposes, Ross, in this context, makes a telling comment and provides a helpful hint when he concludes: "the complexities of Cleaver's cross-

identifications are too entangled to unravel here" (18). These are precisely the complexities to which I turn. For a helpful presentation of the biographical contexts of Cleaver's work, see Kathleen Rout, *Eldridge Cleaver*.

16 Notice Cleaver's doubled phrase "bisexual homosexual," which seems to imply that, in Cleaver's view, bisexuals are simply a subset of the more telling category "homosexual."

17 W. J. Weatherby, in his biography, *James Baldwin: Artist on Fire*, relates Baldwin's reactions to Cleaver's vitriolic commentary: " 'Well [Baldwin wrote] I certainly hope I know more about myself, and the intentions of my work than that, but I *am* an odd quantity. So is Eldridge, so are we all . . .' Artists and revolutionaries, he warned Cleaver, are both odd and disreputable, but seldom in the same way; they were both driven by a vision and needed each other 'and have much to learn from each other' " (292). Even so, "the Cleaver attack came like a slap in the face bringing Baldwin to attention, making him reexamine his own situation"—so much so that "Cleaver helped to shape [Baldwin's] racial attitudes in middle age" (293).

18 Cleaver rather dramatically imagines that "all black women" share his investment in the restoration of his masculine prowess. In this final essay in *Soul on Ice*, Cleaver writes: "Across the naked abyss of negated masculinity, of four hundred years minus my Balls, we face each other today, my Queen. I feel a deep, terrifying hurt, the pain of humiliation of the vanquished warrior. . . . I feared to look into your eyes because I knew I would find reflected there a merciless Indictment of my impotence and a compelling challenge to redeem my conquered manhood. . . . [I]t is in your eyes, before you, that my need is to be justified" (206–07).

19 The only problem is: we don't know when, exactly, Cleaver sees this picture, though it would have to be between 1955 (the date of the picture's publication) and 1965 (the date by which he had written this essay).

20 Juan Williams, with the Eyes on the Prize Production Team, *Eyes on the Prize*, 43.

21 In *Emmett Till*, Clenora Hudson-Weems makes a cogent case for the Till lynching (which took place before Rosa Parks made her resistance) as the beginning of the civil rights movement. She even argues that the undertreatment of the Till case in the historiography of civil rights owes to "factors [that] made the Till case somewhat embarrassing for civil rights' leaders." "After all," writes Hudson-Weems, "Till . . . had failed to conduct himself properly according to the rules of southern etiquette. . . . Even the well-intentioned have felt more comfortable venerating a mature woman [Rosa Parks] who refused to surrender her seat on a bus to a white man rather than a young black man who was murdered for whistling at a white woman. . . . [Parks's] deliberate and courageous stand has simply proven more palatable than the horrible image of a mutilated Till" (4–5). David Marriott, in *On Black Men*, mentions the Till photo in a footnote, where he gives Muhammad Ali's account of his sight of this famous photograph: "A week after [Till] was murdered. . . . I stood on a corner with a gang of boys, looking at pictures of him in the black news-

papers and magazines. In one, he was laughing and happy. In the other, his head was swollen and bashed in, his eyes bulging out of their sockets, and his mouth twisted and broken. . . . I felt a deep kinship to him when I learned he was born the same year and day I was. I couldn't get Emmett Till out of my mind, until one evening I thought of a way to get back at white people for his death" (22).

22 We should remember, as Siobhan Somerville reminds us in her essay "Scientific Racism and the Emergence of the Homosexual Body" (in *Journal of the History of Sexuality* 5, no. 2 [1994]: 243–66), that in the minds of some racist commentators in the antebellum period there was a crucial link between blacks in general and homosexuality, since in these commentators' views "the descendents of Ham had overdeveloped sexual organs and were the original Sodomites of the Old Testament" (260).

23 Kaja Silverman, glossing Lacan, explains it this way: "Lacan suggests . . . that the male subject . . . 'mortgages' the penis for the phallus. In other words, during his entry into the symbolic order he gains direct access to those privileges which constitute the phallus, but forfeits direct access to his own sexuality, a forfeiture of which the penis is representative." See *The Subject of Semiotics*, 185–86. The statement Silverman is glossing is this: "What by its very nature remains concealed from the subject [is] [this] self-sacrifice, that pound of flesh which is mortgaged in his relationship to the signifier," Jacques Lacan, "Desire and the Interpretation of Desire in *Hamlet*," 28. I have discussed this line of thought in feminist theory in my book *God Between Their Lips*, 29–30. See also Jane Gallop, "Of Phallic Proportions: Lacanian Conceit," in *The Daughter's Seduction* and Jacqueline Rose, "Introduction-II," in Jacques Lacan, *Feminine Sexuality*.

24 Lacan writes: "Paradoxical as this formulation might seem, I would say that it is in order to be the phallus, that is to say, the signifier of the desire of the Other, that the woman will reject an essential part of her femininity, notably all its attributes through masquerade. It is for what she is not that she expects to be desired as well as loved. But she finds the signifier of her own desire in the body of the one to whom she addresses her demand for love" (*Feminine Sexuality*, 84).

25 Judith Butler, *Gender Trouble*, 44, my emphasis.

26 Craftily, Cleaver puts some of his most scandalous comments in the voice of an old black man, in a chapter he titles "The Allegory of the Black Eunuchs." This ploy allows him to say the kinds of things that even Cleaver might hesitate to state in his own voice. And yet, these views are remarkably consistent with his views in the chapter that follows this one, "The Primeval Mitosis," where no such narrative device is used.

27 Ross provides a helpful genealogy of Baldwin criticism in his essay and also in his footnotes (47n16, 48n17, 51n27, 52n30). For a listing and short synopses of the contemporary reviews of *Giovanni's Room*, see Fred L. Standley and Nancy V. Standley, *James Baldwin*. See also Emmanuel Nelson, "Critical Deviance: Homophobia and the Reception of James Baldwin's Fiction," *Jour-*

nal of American Culture 14, no. 3 (1991): 91–96. For an illuminating analysis that suggests Baldwin's influence on the queer black writer Randall Kenan, see Sharon Holland's essay on *Giovanni's Room* and Kenan's *A Visitation of Spirits* in her *Raising the Dead*. See also the article by Robert F. Reid-Pharr, "Tearing the Goat's Flesh," and the essay by Lee Edelman, "The Part for the (W)hole: Baldwin, Homophobia, and the Fantasmatics of 'Race'" in his book *Homographesis*.

28 For a reading of the novel that views "difference" as the culprit and that stresses "David's history of attempting . . . to transcend race boundaries and gender-role expectations," see Donald H. Mengay, "The Failed Copy: *Giovanni's Room* and the (Re)Contextualization of Difference," *Genders* (Fall 1993): 59–70.

29 Baldwin, *Giovanni's Room*, 118.

30 Cora Kaplan makes a wonderfully distinctive contribution to Baldwin criticism by exploring "the significance of Baldwin's early fiction for women readers [including herself] in the fifties and early sixties." See "'A Cavern Opened in My Mind': The Poetics of Homosexuality and the Politics of Masculinity in James Baldwin," in *Representing Black Men*, ed. Marcellus Blount and George P. Cunningham, 31.

31 Leslie Fiedler's comments on *Giovanni's Room* ("The Homosexual Dilemma," in *Critical Essays on James Baldwin*, ed. Fred L. Standley and Nancy V. Burt) offer the most interesting example of those early readings that did not interpret the novel as engaging racial issues.

32 In this respect, *Giovanni's Room* resembles *Heart of Darkness*, a novel in which the only present unfolding action is Marlow's reflection on his adventures. For the length of the novel, he sits on a boat, talking aloud to a group of men who are falling asleep.

33 GR, 17–18. For detailed readings of (the complications of) Baldwin's misogyny in *Giovanni's Room*, see Kaplan, Garber, Mengay, and Drowne, "'An Irrevocable Condition': Constructions of Home and the Writing of Place in *Giovanni's Room*," in *Reviewing James Baldwin*, ed. D. Quentin Miller, 72–87. I would suggest that the mirroring corpses of David's mother and the Joey relation (which we'll see in a moment) echo how Hella and Giovanni (the Ultrafeminine and the Supermasculine Menial, in Cleaver's semiotic codings) bend around to meet each other on the plane of the body-once-attractive that haunts the mind with its decay. In Cleaver's semiotics, the Ultrafeminine and the Supermasculine Menial share the codes of beauty and lack of mental sovereignty.

34 In a striking passage, after the narrator has described in scathing terms those gay men who "always dressed in the most improbable combinations, screaming like parrots the details of their latest love affairs"—and one boy in particular "wearing makeup and earrings and . . . his heavy blond hair piled high"—he betrays his worry of the threat of resemblance: "[B]ut I confess that his utter grotesqueness made me uneasy; perhaps in the same way that the sight of monkeys eating their own excrement turns some people's stom-

achs. They might not mind so much if monkeys did not—so grotesquely—resemble human beings" (38–39).

FIVE *Prophylactics and Brains*

I gratefully acknowledge a chain of help in writing this essay. It was first composed as a public lecture sponsored by the Humanities Center at Wesleyan University in February 1995. I benefited greatly from criticisms offered by Henry Abelove, William Cohen, Christina Crosby, Ellen Feder, Patricia Hill, Eric Jarvis, Indira Karamcheti, Danielle Langston, Tavia Nyong'o, James Scott, Duffield White, Sandra Wong, and center director Elizabeth Traube. An informal group of critical legal theorists, some formerly and some currently of Harvard Law School (David Kennedy, Karen Engle, Mitchell Lasser, Ileana Poras, Nathaniel Berman, Jorge Esquirol, and Susan Keller), raised indispensable questions for the talk's transformation into this longer essay. Finally, many Utah colleagues generously offered comments on my final drafts: Karen Brennan, Rebecca Horn, Dorothee Kocks, Kim Lau, Colleen McDannell, Jacqueline Osherow, Henry Staten, and especially Barry Weller. Warm thanks also to Shelley White, Nicole Stansbury, Grant Sperry, and Constance Merritt for their attentive readings.

1 Gail Caldwell, "Author Toni Morrison Discusses Her Latest Novel *Beloved*," in *Conversations with Toni Morrison*, 241.

2 Caldwell reports: "Morrison spent two years thinking about the story of *Beloved* and another three writing it; she says now that she was so frightened by the effort that she hit a writing impasse in 1985," 240.

3 Margaret Croyden, "Toni Morrison Tries Her Hand at Playwriting," in *Conversations with Toni Morrison*, 219.

4 Croyden, "Toni Morrison Tries her Hand," 221, 220.

5 Croyden reports in the *New York Times* in 1985: "[Morrison's] drama, *Dreaming Emmett*, commissioned by the New York State Writers Institute at SUNY-Albany and directed by Gilbert Moses, will have its world premiere Saturday at the Market Theater there," 218.

6 For a particularly striking exception to this silence, one that confirms that there has been a silence, see the article I mention at the start of my book: Benoit Denizet-Lewis, "Living (and Dying) on the Down Low: Double Lives, AIDS and the Black Homosexual Underground," *New York Times Magazine*, August 3, 2003, 28–53.

7 See, for example, Michael Specter, "The Vaccine," in *The New Yorker*, February 3, 2003.

8 There's even one instance—in a largely Hispanic community—of using an AIDS-like quilt to commemorate the victims of teen homicides (teens gunned down by other teens, along with parents and infant siblings who were crossfire victims). *People* magazine (November 15, 1993, 93–98), which reported the story, has referred to it as "the Killing Quilt."

9 "Cloning: Where Do We Draw the Line?," *Time*, November 8, 1993, 68.

10 Ibid., 69.

11 "Cyberspace: The Software That Will Take You There," *Business Week*, February 27, 1995, 82.

12 In *Newsweek's* special issue "TechnoMania: The Future Isn't What You Think" (February 27, 1995), Paul Saffo, director of the Institute for the Future in Menlo Park, California, exclaims: "The problem is that so far only half the information revolution has been delivered to us: the access and the volume. . . . The people who make the money are going to be the ones who make the filters and the 'off' switches" ("Have Your Agent Call My Agent," 76).

13 Citations are from "Stop! Cyberthief!" *Newsweek*, February 6, 1995, 37; *Business Week's* "Cyberspace," 80; and *60 Minutes*, February 26, 1995. The good and bad news of *60 Minutes'* sample hacker is all too obvious: the remarkably fresh portrait of a black hacker youth, a portrait that breaks the stereotype of the white male suburban geek, unwittingly (one says generously) solidifies the stereotype of the black male criminal. By contrast, the paradigmatic media portrait of a hacker can be found in thirty-one-year-old Kevin Mitnick, the "superhacker" who "started out in the early 1980s, pulling pranks as a teenage 'phone phreak' before moving on to more serious computer crime" ("A Superhacker Meets His Match," *Newsweek*, February 27, 1995, 61).The study *Cyberpunk* by Katie Hafner and John Markoff explains the shift from the 1960s and 1970s, the time of hacker "honor" and the Hacker Ethic, to the 1980s when hackers, through media- and even self-portrayal, "were no longer seen as benign explorers but malicious intruders," who because they "are comfortable with a new technology that intimidates their elders" have given rise to a "hacker hysteria . . . sweeping the nation" (11).

14 Douglas Rushkoff, *Media Virus!*, 10.

15 Aside from these claims for unresolvability, *Johnny Mnemonic* (a film released in 1995, starring pre-*Matrix* Keanu Reeves), bears out Rushkoff's optimistic views, even amid the darkest of landscapes. The Johnny of the title can stop the spread of a fatal disease (NAS: information-overload) if he can extract the cure for this plague from his own head (where it is stuffed to a deadly extent). The good guys would cure the disease at hand; the bad guys would "treat" it, making it a renewable source of a need for pharmaceutical drugs. The tale thus pits the corporation Pharmakon (a self-conscious Derridean pun?) against the little people (here represented by Johnny, a macho babe-for-hire, and, most intriguingly, kids and teens who follow the recycling guerilla played by Ice-T). Fascinating for *Beloved*, the latter live on a bridge called "Heaven," fashioned from junk but fitted with a tower of TV screens from which they feedback to (whatever is left of) the culture at large. Their goal is democratic resistance: recontextualizing and sharing information. At the end, they broadcast "the cure," literally changing what's on the screen, even as they blow up the Pharmakon complex.

16 "Is There a Case for Viruses?" *Newsweek*, February 27, 1995, 65.

17 Toni Morrison, *Beloved*, 213.

18 Obviously, in a bold anachronism, I impose the word "teen" on *Beloved*, which

in its portrayals does not use the word, even though Morrison, pointedly for her contemporary readers (or so I believe), makes Beloved nineteen and Denver eighteen. That is to say, some carryover of contemporary understandings of adolescence and its threat of an alien consciousness may be expected on the part of the reader. At the very least, the book does nothing to protect against it. A reading that would honor 1987, of course, demands it.

19 *Webster's New World Dictionary* traces "latent" back to the Latin *latere*, "to lie hidden, to lurk," and to the Old Norse *lomr*, "betrayal, deception."

20 For a speculative discussion of the different injunctions to remember in Jewish Holocaust memorials and black writers' invocations of slavery, see the earlier published versions of this essay in *Studies in the Novel* 28 (Fall 1996) and *Novel Gazing*, ed. Eve Kosofsky Sedgwick. Specifically, I contrast Cynthia Ozick's novella *The Shawl* (1983, published when Morrison was writing *Beloved*) with Morrison's novel, showing how in Ozick, so different from what we find in Morrison, the effort is to guard against any memories escaping from the living, rather than guarding against their lethal entry.

21 In this passage we start out suspended, as if we were watching the reenactment of a hypothetical ("she might be hurrying across a field. . . . . [n]othing else would be in her mind"); then, it seems, by the fifth sentence ("[t]he picture of the men . . . was as lifeless as the nerves") that the hypothetical is a memory of something that has happened in the past; finally, however, we realize this scene (in spite of its floating, commemorative quality) occurs, somehow, in narrative time as a present, unfolding action, for Paul D is sitting on Sethe's porch as she rounds the front of her house "collecting her shoes and stockings on the way" (6). Other memory passages perform a stricter suspension of the plot, beginning with a hyperlink that carries the reader away on the crest of the character's thoughts and ending with a repetition of the hyperlink, returning the reader to narrative flow. An excellent example of this pattern occurs in the novel's second chapter. As Paul D and Sethe lie in bed, disappointed and resentful after sex, each is successively carried away (for several paragraphs) by a hyperlink. Paul D's is "tree"; Sethe's is the phrase "maybe a man was nothing but a man" (21–22).

22 Sigmund Freud, *Beyond the Pleasure Principle*, vol. 18 of *The Standard Edition*, 30, 33.

23 Obviously, the tree as a sign of sacrifice—of one's beloved, in particular—has its precedents, to put it mildly. Christianity founds itself on the tree as the site (and later sign) of such a loss.

24 "Four days she slept, waking and sitting up only for water. Denver tended her . . . and . . . hid like a personal blemish Beloved's incontinence. . . . She boiled the underwear and soaked it in bluing, praying the fever would pass without damage" (54).

25 For a strong dose of adult cyberoptimistic manifestos ("The PC is the LSD of the 1990s"), see Timothy Leary, *Chaos and Cyber Culture*. For a more academic optimism, run through the filters of theory, see Mark C. Taylor and Esa Saarinen, *Imagologies*.

26 *Beloved*, 179. Baby Suggs's name, by dint of which she is often simply desig-
nated "Baby" in the text, seems to hint at her connection to Beloved over what,
early on, she protests against. For her "feedback" sermons in the Clearing,
see 87–89, where Baby commands a series of expressive actions: " 'Let your
mothers hear you laugh. . . . Let your wives and children see you dance. . . .
Cry . . . [f]or the living and the dead. . . . [Y]onder, hear me, they do not love
your neck unnoosed and straight. So love your neck; put a hand on it, grace it,
stroke it and hold it up' " (87–88). It is the invasion of her life by "whitefolks"
that eventually shuts down Baby Suggs's protest.

27 Richard Dawkins, *The Selfish Gene*, 192. Dawkins is aware that it is not always
"obvious what a single unit-meme consist[s] of": "I have said a tune is one
meme, but what about a symphony: how many memes is that?" (195). Ap-
pealing to the "same verbal trick" he used to define "gene" ("a unit of conve-
nience, a length of chromosome with just sufficient copying-fidelity to serve
as a viable unit of natural selection"), Dawkins answers his own question: "If
a single phrase of Beethoven's ninth symphony is sufficiently distinctive and
memorable to be abstracted . . . and used as the call-sign of a maddeningly
intrusive European broadcasting station, then to that extent it deserves to be
called one meme" (195). Beloved, by this reasoning, could be regarded as a
single meme or as what Dawkins calls "a co-adapted stable set of mutually-
assisting memes" (197). For his discussion of "copying-fidelity," "continuous
mutation," and "blending," see 194–96.

28 Daniel Dennett, *Consciousness Explained*, 205, 204. One could say that the
word "meme" itself has spread promiscuously since I wrote this essay in
1995. Aside from its lively life on the Internet, the notion of memes grounds
several major studies. See, for example, Richard Brodie, *Virus of the Mind*;
J. M. Balkin, *Cultural Software*; Susan Blackmore, *The Meme Machine*; Aaron
Lynch, *Thought Contagion*; and Robert Aunger, *The Electric Meme*. There is
also now a *Journal of Memetics*.

29 Perhaps because the defense one makes is against a "replicator," Dawkins
brings a decidedly prophylactic slant to bear on his defiance. Prophylaxis as
rebellion. Thus Dawkins: "We, that is our brains, are separate and independent enough from our genes to rebel against them. As already noted, we do
so in a small way every time we use contraception. There is no reason why we
should not rebel in a large way [against memes], too" (332).

30 Dawkins and Dennett are both hard to classify. Criticized in the left antisocio-
biological treatise *Not in Our Genes* by Lewontin, Kamin, and Rose, Dawkins
is nonetheless praised by the likes of Donna Haraway, the leading poststruc-
turalist feminist historian of biological science. Specifically, Dawkins, along
with E. O. Wilson (author of *Sociobiology*), is criticized by Rose et al. for
being a "reductionist" in his views on genetic determinism *and* a "liberal"
for "invok[ing] free will." Dawkins responds in one of his footnotes: "[I]t is
only in the eyes of Rose and his colleagues that we are 'genetic determin-
ists.' What they don't understand . . . is that it is perfectly possible to hold
that genes exert a statistical influence on human behavior while at the same

time believing that this influence can be modified, overridden or reversed by other influences" (331). Haraway, for her part, places Dawkins "among the most radical disrupters of cyborg biological holism" ("The Biopolitics of Postmodern Bodies,"24). "[D]eeply informed by a postmodern consciousness . . . [Dawkins] has made the notions of 'organism' or 'individual' extremely problematic." As for Dennett, he bemusedly accepts the appellation of "semiotic materialis[t]" (411), while being accused of naive idealism and extreme materialism.

31 Ferdinand de Saussure, *Course in General Linguistics*, 12.

32 Though Morrison herself seems to imagine Beloved as pregnant by Paul D (see her interview with Marsha Darling, "In the Realm of Responsibility"), her novel depicts more intriguing possibilities, as I will suggest. This odd discrepancy between intention and representation may even support a more striking oddity: the ways in which Paul D and Denver are kept *centrally peripheral* in this novel. That is to say, both are staged—quite intensely so—as characters pushed to the margins by memory (that is, by Beloved), giving them roles as frustrated bystanders, until the very end of *Beloved* when both act to restore Sethe's health. As for Paul D, so many of his movements are moved by Beloved: "She moved him," we read, "and Paul D didn't know how to stop it because it looked like he was moving himself" (114). As a bizarre figuration of these movements, Paul D enters into sexual relations with Beloved, whose demands on him are simple. Offering herself as seductive hyperlink, it is as if she gets him to click on her name: " 'You have to touch me. On the inside part. And you have to call me my name' " (117). The result: the speaking of Paul D's past, by this sexual ventriloquist act, is moved from a place between Beloved's lips.

33 *Beloved*, 240. Denver's desperation for a sibling leads her to measures that look like—at some points—imitations of her mother's bizarre relations with Beloved. Thus, at the start, when Beloved has cholera, Denver takes upon herself the incontinence her mother profoundly embodies in the novel's outhouse scene ("[Denver] hid like a personal blemish Beloved's incontinence," 54). Later, we find that Denver was "nursing Beloved's interest like a lover whose pleasure was to overfeed the loved" (78). Here's that overfeeding relation that Beloved dramatically demands from Sethe. Even a form of fluids exchange, as I argue in the text, has prefigured these connections. On the day Beloved was killed by her mother, Sethe "aim[ed] a bloody nipple into [Denver's] mouth," so that "Denver took her mother's milk right along with the blood of her sister" (152). The bottom line, however, is exclusion: Beloved's exclusive concern with her mother. As she puts it to Denver, " 'You can go but she is the one I have to have' " (76). Of course, Denver's central marginality is hardly an acknowledgment of her unimportance. On the contrary, there are arguments to be made about the intricate unfolding of Denver as a kind of margin or limit to the tale, but these lie beyond the scope of this essay.

34 *Beloved*, 250. Sethe displays four major symptoms listed on the AIDS symp-

toms list: weight loss, dementia, fatigue, and fever. See Jon D. Kaiser, *Immune Power*, 12.

35 "The Long Shot," *Discover*, August 1993, 66–67.

36 Sullivan, "The Search for the Cure for AIDS," 63.

37 Daniel Harris, "Making Kitsch from AIDS," 58.

38 When I wrote a first version of this chapter in 1995, AIDS was still largely considered a death sentence. By this point, it appears that Haseltine's take on viral dormancy has proved to be correct—at least for patients who have physical and financial access to the best drugs and treatment. As we know, this access is the problem for many people of color. The spread of AIDS and its deadly effects on the African continent remains, at this writing, largely unchecked.

39 In fairness, I suppose, it may be hard to say if Sethe is saved from her demise. Though the book remains ambiguous on this point, her slow recovery seems implied by Paul D's willingness to nurse her back to "'some kind of tomorrow'" (273): "'Don't you die on me!'" (271).

40 In this sense, *Beloved* offers a range of cybernetic relations, ones that might interest Eve Kosofsky Sedgwick and Adam Frank, who, in an essay on Silvan Tomkins ("Shame in the Cybernetic Fold") explore "Tomkins's habit of layering digital (on/off) with analog (graduated and/or multiply differentiated) representational models" (505). Clearly, AIDS involves such a layering, for what begins as a digital relation (do you have the virus or not?) immediately gives way to graduated developments, measured in T cells—but also in the P-24 antigen test (reported as a numerical value ranging from 1 to 600 if positive) and the intensity of the patient's symptoms and infections. Dennett, on another landscape, explains how a single spoken phrase is the result of "swift generations of 'wasteful' parallel processing, with hordes of anonymous [word] demons and their hopeful connections never seeing the light of day" (238).

41 Roland Barthes, *Mythologies*, 109.

42 She is particularly intent to restore the slave-ship dead. Morrison: "The gap between Africa and Afro-America and the gap between the living and the dead and the gap between the past and the present does not exist. It's bridged for us by our assuming responsibility for people no one's ever assumed responsibility for. They are those who died en route. Nobody knows their names, and nobody thinks about them. In addition to that, they never survived in the lore" (interview with Darling, "Responsibility").

43 In Gail Caldwell's review of *Beloved* in the *Boston Globe* (October 6, 1987, 67–68), we learn that "unlike her four previous books, the idea of the plot of *Beloved* came from an actual event—gleaned from a 19th-century newspaper story she'd discovered while editing *The Black Book* (an overview of black American history) at Random House. The woman in the news story [Margaret Garner, who killed her child to save it from slavery] became Sethe, and Morrison began to write." On her use of this source, Morrison herself has commented: "I did not do much research on Margaret Garner other than the obvious stuff, because I wanted to invent her life, which is a way of saying I

wanted to be accessible to anything the characters had to say about it. Recording her life as lived would not interest me, and would not make me available to anything that might be pertinent. . . . The point of all this being that my story, my invention, is much, much happier than what really happened" (interview with Darling, "Responsibility").

44 In Peter S. Hawkins's illuminating essay "Naming Names," we learn that "[Cleve] Jones made the first panel of what was to become the NAMES Project Quilt in late February 1987." "In memory of his best friend," Hawkins tells us, "he spray-painted the boldly stenciled name of Marvin Feldman on a white sheet that measured three feet by six feet, the size of a grave; the only adornment was an abstract design of five stars of David, each one dominated by a pink-red triangle. Jones's panel, at once a tombstone and a quilt patch, served as a model for the improvised handiwork of others" (757–58). See Hawkins's essay as well for two photographs: one at ground level from the quilt display in 1987, the other, clearly aerial, from 1992.

We should recall in all of this that *Beloved*, too, has its quilt. It is first associated with Baby Suggs who, when she is on her way to death, becomes "starved for color." "There wasn't any," the novel tells us, "except for two orange squares in a quilt [of "muted" colors] that made the absence [of color] shout"; the "two patches of orange looked wild—like life in the raw" (38). Sethe, at the end, lies under this quilt, in Baby Suggs's bed, in the keeping room.

45 In a cover story, "AIDS and the Arts: A Lost Generation," released on Rudolph Nureyev's death, *Newsweek* (January 18, 1993, 16–20), explains how "a single death creates a cultural chain reaction" (16). Then the writers raise a question: "The average age of death from AIDS in the United States is 35, one study shows. But the preponderance of works that hang in the Museum of Modern Art is by artists older than 35. How many rooms of empty frames would have to be filled to create a museum of unpainted art? Or shelves built for unwritten books?" (18).

CONCLUSION *Dark Camp*

1 Toni Morrison, *Sula*, 161–62.

2 Toni Morrison, *Beloved*, 152.

3 Eldridge Cleaver, *Soul on Ice*, 160, 184.

4 Susan Sontag, "Notes on 'Camp,'" 292, 277, 279, 280, 277, 279, 280, 281, 283, 283, 284, 285, 286, 289, 293, 293; hereafter referred to as NC.

5 Moe Meyer, ed. *The Politics and Poetics of Camp*, 1; hereafter referred to as PPC.

6 Daniel Mendelsohn, "The Melodramatic Moment," *New York Times Magazine*, March 23, 2003, 40–43; hereafter referred to as MM.

7 Sontag writes: "[M]any of the objects prized by Camp taste are old-fashioned, out-of-date, démodé. It's not a love of the old as such. It's simply that the process of aging or deterioration provides the necessary detachment—or arouses a necessary sympathy. . . . What was banal can, with the passage of time, be-

come fantastic. . . . [T]hings are campy . . . when we become less involved in them, and can enjoy, instead of be frustrated by, the failure of the attempt" (NC, 286–87).

8 *Poison*, which appeared in 1990, braids three strands of narrative: a suburban housewife's domestic battering and loss of her son (when, in strange fashion, he flies out the window); a scientist's contraction of a highly contagious, leprous disease, which results from sexual attraction and appears as horrible skin wounds (a narrative done in the campy style of the horror flick); and a weaving together of scenes from Genet.

9 Cathleen's maid is dressed in domestic uniforms that match the dinner table, kitchen cabinets, and phone, outfits that are unlike Cathleen's elegant, feminine dresses, making her seem a Subfeminine character.

10 Black men's similarities (in terms of signs and codes) to both black and white *women*, in different ways, explains why Cleaver at every turn—via his belief that opposites attract—imagines that white men and black men are so strongly driven toward each other.

11 Cathleen's announcement of the black man's beauty occurs in a striking context of shame. Her speaking of his beauty occurs when she is telling him they cannot be friends. For in this scene, he has touched her on the arm, causing something of an uproar among white people walking by them. Haynes here employs the slanted camera angles and sense of threat that accompanies the AIDS strand in his movie *Poison*.

12 Even the homosexual husband rants against her—against the shame she brings upon their family through the rumors surrounding her relationship.

13 Chris Heath, "The Unbearable Bradness of Being," *Rolling Stone*, October 28, 1999, 72.

14 Corie Brown, "Getting Ready to Rumble," *Newsweek*, September 6, 1999; Susan Faludi, "It's 'Thelma and Louise' for Guys," *Newsweek*, October 25, 1999, 89.

15 David Ansen, "A Fistful of Darkness," *Newsweek*, October 18, 1999, 77.

16 Camping it up even more in this respect, Pitt, shortly after he starred in *Fight Club*, appeared on the cover of *Rolling Stone* in a funky mini-dress. The yellow rubber glove on Brad's left hand (a key prop from *Fight Club*) is a link to his character Tyler Durden. *Rolling Stone* reports: "The photographs that accompany this story were taken during this period, at Pitt's instigation, with him wearing a dress. He is extremely reluctant to discuss this." "[Interviewer]: Have you slipped into many frocks before?" "Pitt: No, I can't say I have. . . . Funnily enough I was quite serious about it. I just wanted it to work. . . . We just wanted to create some other world—some alternative to modern living." Heath, "Unbearable Bradness," 72, 74.

17 Actually, he uses the opportunity of changeovers between film reels to insert these details. The "cigarette burn" in the upper corner of the film (marking the point of the changeover) is the sign he's about to do his work—or so the narrator directly tells us. One has to wonder if *Fight Club* is camping on its own erotic drives, visibly hiding its erotic interests inside the men's fights.

18 Ansen, "Fistful," 77; Benjamin Svetkey, "Blood, Sweat and Fears," *Entertainment Weekly*, October 15, 1999, 26.

19 Svetkey, "Blood," 26.

20 Heath, "Unbearable Bradness," 74.

21 Many critics believe the film loses control in the "Project Mayhem" section. David Ansen, for example: "Fincher inflates *Fight Club* with apocalyptic mayhem that's positively Wagnerian in its pretension. There is a major plot twist . . . [that is] clearly meant to spin the movie into a provocative new orbit of meaning, but it reads more as if the story has boxed itself into a corner and can't find a way out. The movie doesn't so much end as self-destruct" (77).

22 Marla has something of her own take on cloth wounds, which clings to her, to a certain extent, as a narrative emerging from her own dress: "I got this dress," she tells the narrator, "at a thrift store for one dollar. It's a bridesmaid's dress. Someone loved it intensely for one day and tossed it like a Christmas tree. . . . Bam! It's on the side of the road . . . like a sex-crime victim, underwear inside out, bound with electrical tape. You can borrow it sometime."

23 There is even a direct scene of a physical holding between Tyler and the narrator. After their climactic car crash, which starts the narrative's turn toward the narrator's self-realization about who Tyler is (namely, himself), Tyler holds the narrator (Pitt holds Norton) in a kind of pietà after he has pulled him from the car. After this scene, Tyler, as the narrator has known him, disappears. The next time we as viewers see Tyler, we know that Tyler is inside the narrator.

BIBLIOGRAPHY

Abelove, Henry, Michèle Aina Barale, and David M. Halperin, eds. *The Lesbian and Gay Studies Reader*. New York: Routledge, 1993.

Althusser, Louis. *Lenin and Philosophy, and Other Essays*. New York: Monthly Review Press, 1972.

Aunger, Robert. *The Electric Meme: A New Theory of How We Think*. New York: Free Press, 2002.

Awkward, Michael. *Inspiriting Influences: Tradition, Revision, and Afro-American Women's Novels*. New York: Columbia University Press, 1989.

Bad Object-Choices. *How do I Look? Queer Film and Video*. Seattle: Bay Press, 1991.

Baker, Houston A. Jr. "In Dubious Battle." *New Literary History* 18, no. 1 (1987): 363–69.

Baldwin, James. *Giovanni's Room*. New York: Dial Press, 1956.

———. *Nobody Knows My Name: More Notes of a Native Son*. New York: Dell, 1961.

Balkin, J. M. *Cultural Software: A Theory of Ideology*. New Haven, Conn.: Yale University Press, 1998.

Barthes, Roland. *Camera Lucida: Reflections on Photography*. Translated by Richard Howard. New York: Hill and Wang, 1981.

———. *The Fashion System*. Translated by Matthew Ward and Richard Howard. Berkeley: University of California Press, 1990.

———. *Image, Music, Text*. Translated by Stephen Heath. New York: Hill and Wang, 1988.

———. *Mythologies*. Translated by Annette Lavers. New York: Hill and Wang, 1972.

Bataille, Georges. *Theory of Religion*. Translated by Robert Hurley. New York: Zone Books, 1992.

———. *Visions of Excess: Selected Writings, 1927–1939*. Translated by Allan Stoekl. Minneapolis: University of Minnesota Press, 1985.

Bersani, Leo. *Homos*. Cambridge, Mass.: Harvard University Press, 1995.

Binder, Pearl. *Dressing Up, Dressing Down*. London: Allen and Unwin, 1986.

Blackmore, Susan. *The Meme Machine*. New York: Oxford University Press, 1999.

Bloom, Harold, ed. *Toni Morrison: Modern Critical Views*. New York: Chelsea House Publishers, 1990.

Blount, Marcellus, and George P. Cunningham, eds. *Representing Black Men*. New York: Routledge, 1996.

Bristow, Joseph, ed. *Sexual Sameness: Textual Differences in Lesbian and Gay Writing*. New York: Routledge, 1992.

Brittain, Vera. *Radclyffe Hall: A Case of Obscenity?* London: Femina, 1968.

Brodie, Richard. *Virus of the Mind: The New Science of the Meme*. Seattle: Integral Press, 1995.

Butler, Judith. *Bodies that Matter: On the Discursive Limits of "Sex."* New York: Routledge, 1993.

———. *Gender Trouble: Feminism and the Subversion of Identity*. New York: Routledge, 1989.

Butler, Judith, John Guillory, and Kendall Thomas, eds. *What's Left of Theory? New Work on the Politics of Literary Theory*. New York: Routledge, 2000.

Butler-Evans, Elliott. *Race, Gender, and Desire: Narrative Strategies in the Fiction of Toni Cade Bambara, Toni Morrison, and Alice Walker*. Philadelphia: Temple University Press, 1989.

Campbell, James. *Talking at the Gates: A Life of James Baldwin*. New York: Viking, 1991.

Carlyle, Thomas. *Sartor Resartus*. Edited by Kerry McSweeney and Peter Sabor. Oxford: Oxford University Press, 1999.

Castle, Terry. *Noel Coward and Radclyffe Hall: Kindred Spirits*. New York: Columbia University Press, 1996.

Chapman, Rowena, and Jonathan Rutherford, eds. *Male Order: Unwrapping Masculinity*. London: Lawrence and Wishart, 1988.

Christian, Barbara. "The Race for Theory." *Cultural Critique* 6, no. 6 (spring 1987): 51–63.

Cleaver, Eldridge. *Soul on Ice*. New York: Dell, 1968.

Crimp, Douglas, ed. AIDS: *Cultural Analysis, Cultural Activism*. Cambridge, Mass.: MIT Press, 1988.

Crisp, Quentin. *The Naked Civil Servant*. New York: Holt, Rinehart, and Winston, 1968.

Darling, Marsha. "In the Realm of Responsibility: A Conversation with Toni Morrison." *Women's Review of Books*, March 5, 1988, 5–6.

Davis, Angela Y. *Women, Race, and Class*. New York: Random House, 1981.

Dawkins, Richard. *The Selfish Gene*. New York: Oxford University Press, 1989.

De Lauretis, Teresa. *The Practice of Love: Lesbian Sexuality and Perverse Desire.* Bloomington: Indiana University Press, 1994.

Delphy, Christine, and Diana Leonard. *Close to Home: A Materialist Analysis of Women's Oppression.* Amherst: University of Massachusetts Press, 1984.

Denizet-Lewis, Benoit. "Living (and Dying) on the Down Low: Double Lives, AIDS and the Black Homosexual Underground," *New York Times Magazine,* August 3, 2003.

Dennett, Daniel C. *Consciousness Explained.* Boston: Little, Brown, 1991.

Doan, Laura L. *Fashioning Sapphism: The Origins of a Modern English Lesbian Culture.* New York: Columbia University Press, 2001.

Dowell, Pat. "Pulp Friction: Two Shots at Quentin Tarantino's *Pulp Fiction.*" *Cineaste* 21, no. 3 (1995): 4–5.

Duberman, Martin B., Martha Vicinus, and George Chauncey, eds. *Hidden from History: Reclaiming the Gay and Lesbian Past.* New York: NAL Books, 1989.

Dunlap, Knight. "The Development and the Function of Clothing." *Journal of General Psychology* 1 (1928): 64.

Early, Gerald Lyn. *Tuxedo Junction: Essays on American Culture.* New York: Ecco Press, 1989.

Edelman, Lee. *Homographesis: Essays in Gay Literary and Cultural Theory.* New York: Routledge, 1994.

———. *No Future: Queer Theory and the Death Drive.* Durham, N.C.: Duke University Press, 2004.

Fanon, Frantz. *Black Skin, White Masks.* Translated by Charles Lam Markmann. New York: Grove Press, 1967.

Feinberg, Leslie. *Stone Butch Blues: A Novel.* Ithaca, N.Y.: Firebrand Books, 1993.

Ferguson, Roderick A. *Aberrations in Black: Toward a Queer of Color Critique.* Minneapolis: University of Minnesota Press, 2004.

Flaccus, Louis. "Remarks on the Psychology of Clothes." *Pedagogical Seminary* 13 (1906).

Flugel, J. C. *The Psychology of Clothes.* London: Hogarth Press, 1930.

Foner, Philip S. *Organized Labor and the Black Worker, 1619–1981.* 2nd ed. New York: International Publishers, 1982.

Franklin, John Hope. *From Slavery to Freedom: A History of Negro Americans.* New York: Knopf, 1980.

Frese, Dolores Warwick, and Katherine O'Brien O'Keeffe, eds. *The Book and the Body.* Notre Dame, Ind.: University of Notre Dame Press, 1997.

Freud, Sigmund. *Character and Culture.* Ed. Philip Rieff. New York: Collier Books, 1963.

———. *A General Introduction to Psychoanalysis.* Ed. Joan Riviere. New York: Pocket Books, 1975.

———. *Jokes and their Relation to the Unconscious.* Ed. James Strachey. New York: Norton, 1963.

———. *New Introductory Lectures on Psycho-Analysis.* Ed. James Strachey. New York: Norton, 1965.

———. *The Standard Edition of the Complete Psychological Works of Sigmund Freud.*

Edited by James Strachey, Anna Freud, and Carrie Lee Rothgeb. London: Hogarth Press: Institute of Psycho-analysis, 1953.

———. *Three Case Histories.* Ed. Philip Rieff. New York: Macmillan, 1963.

Fuss, Diana, ed. *Inside/Out: Lesbian Theories, Gay Theories.* New York: Routledge, 1991.

Gallop, Jane. *The Daughter's Seduction: Feminism and Psychoanalysis.* Ithaca, N.Y.: Cornell University Press, 1982.

Garber, Marjorie B. *Vice Versa: Bisexuality and the Eroticism of Everyday Life.* New York: Simon and Schuster, 1995.

Gates, Henry Louis Jr., ed. *"Race," Writing, and Difference.* Chicago: University of Chicago Press, 1986.

———. " 'What's Love Got to Do with It?': Critical Theory, Integrity, and the Black Idiom." *New Literary History* 18, no. 1 (1987): 345–62.

Gates, Henry Louis Jr., and Anthony Appiah, eds. *Toni Morrison: Critical Perspectives Past and Present.* New York: Amistad, 1993.

Genet, Jean. *Querelle.* Translated by Anselm Hollo. New York: Grove Press, 1974.

Godard, Jean Luc, and James Dudley Andrew. *Breathless.* New Brunswick, N.J.: Rutgers University Press, 1987.

Griffin, John Howard. *Black Like Me.* Boston: Houghton Mifflin, 1961.

Hafner, Katie, and John Markoff. *Cyberpunk: Outlaws and Hackers on the Computer Frontier.* New York: Simon and Schuster, 1995.

Halberstam, Judith. *Female Masculinity.* Durham, N.C.: Duke University Press, 1998.

Hall, Radclyffe. *The Well of Loneliness.* New York: Anchor Books, 1928; 1990.

Hanson, Ellis, ed. *Out Takes: Essays on Queer Theory and Film.* Durham, N.C.: Duke University Press, 1999.

Haraway, Donna. "The Biopolitics of Postmodern Bodies: Determinations of Self in Immune System Discourse." *differences* 1, no. 1 (winter 1989): 24.

Harris, Daniel. "Making Kitsch from AIDS." *Harper's,* July 1994.

Hawkins, Peter S. "Naming Names: The Art of Memory and the NAMES Project AIDS Quilt." *Critical Inquiry* 19, no. 4 (summer 1993): 752–80.

Hernton, Calvin C. *White Papers for White Americans.* Garden City, N.Y.: Doubleday, 1966.

Herzog, Charlotte, and Jane M. Gaines, eds. *Fabrications: Costume and the Female Body.* New York: Routledge, 1989.

Hiler, Hilaire. *From Nudity to Raiment: An Introduction to the Study of Costume.* New York: Educational Press, 1930.

Holland, Sharon Patricia. *Raising the Dead: Readings of Death and (Black) Subjectivity.* Durham, N.C.: Duke University Press, 2000.

hooks, bell. *Salvation: Black People and Love.* New York: William Morrow, 2001.

Hudson-Weems, Clenora. *Emmett Till: The Sacrificial Lamb of the Civil Rights Movement.* Troy, Mich.: Bedford Publishers, 1994.

Hurston, Zora Neale. *Their Eyes Were Watching God.* Urbana: University of Illinois Press, 1978.

Joyce, Joyce A. "The Black Canon: Reconstructing Black American Literary Criticism." *New Literary History* 18, no. 1 (1987): 335–44.

———. "'Who the Cap Fit': Unconsciousness and Unconscionableness in the Criticism of Houston A. Baker, Jr. and Henry Louis Gates, Jr." *New Literary History* 18, no. 1 (1987): 371–84.

Kaiser, Jon D. *Immune Power: A Comprehensive Healing Program for HIV.* New York: St. Martin's Press, 1993.

Kennedy, Randall. *Nigger: The Strange Career of a Troublesome Word.* New York: Vintage, 2002.

Kennedy, Elizabeth Lapovsky, and Madeline D. Davis. *Boots of Leather, Slippers of Gold: The History of a Lesbian Community.* New York: Routledge, 1993.

King, J. L., and Karen Hunter. *On the Down Low: A Journey into the Lives of "Straight" Black Men Who Sleep with Men.* New York: Broadway Books, 2004.

Kluger, Richard. *Simple Justice: The History of Brown v. Board of Education and Black America's Struggle for Equality.* New York: Knopf, 1976.

Koolhaas, Rem. *Delirious New York: A Retroactive Manifesto for Manhattan.* New York: Monacelli, 1978.

Kristeva, Julia. *Powers of Horror: An Essay on Abjection.* Translated by Leon S. Roudiez. New York: Columbia University Press, 1982.

Lacan, Jacques. "Desire and the Interpretation of Desire in *Hamlet.*" *Yale French Studies* 55/56, no. 1 (1977): 11–52.

———. *Feminine Sexuality: Jacques Lacan and the École Freudienne.* Translated by Juliet Mitchell and Jacqueline Rose. New York: Norton and Pantheon Books, 1985.

Lane, Anthony. "Degrees of Cool." *New Yorker,* October 10, 1994.

Langner, Lawrence. *The Importance of Wearing Clothes.* New York: Hastings House, 1959.

Leary, Timothy. *Chaos and Cyber Culture.* Ed. Michael Horowitz and Vicki Marshall. Berkeley, Calif.: Ronin, 1994.

Leeming, David Adams. *James Baldwin: A Biography.* New York: Knopf, 1994.

Leitch, Thomas M. "Know-Nothing Entertainment: What to Say to Your Friends on the Right, and Why it Won't do any Good." *Literature/Film Quarterly* 25, no. 1 (1997): 9.

Lemann, Nicholas. *The Promised Land: The Great Black Migration and How It Changed America.* New York: Knopf, 1991.

Levine, Donald, ed. *Georg Simmel: On Individuality and Social Forms.* Chicago: University of Chicago Press, 1971.

Lewontin, Richard C., Steven P. R. Rose, and Leon J. Kamin. *Not in our Genes: Biology, Ideology, and Human Nature.* New York: Pantheon Books, 1984.

Litvak, Joseph. *Strange Gourmets: Sophistication, Theory, and the Novel.* Durham, N.C.: Duke University Press, 1997.

Lock, Joan. *The British Policewoman: Her Story.* London: R. Hale, 1979.

Lynch, Aaron. *Thought Contagion: How Belief Spreads through Society.* New York: Basic Books, 1999.

Mailer, Norman. *Advertisements for Myself.* New York: Putnam, 1959.

Marriott, David. *On Black Men*. New York: Columbia University Press, 2000.

Massey, Douglas S., and Nancy A. Denton. *American Apartheid: Segregation and the Making of the Underclass*. Cambridge, Mass.: Harvard University Press, 1993.

Matthews, Pamela R., and David McWhirter, eds. *Aesthetic Subjects*. Minneapolis: University of Minnesota Press, 2003.

McBride, Dwight A., ed. *James Baldwin Now*. New York: New York University Press, 1999.

McKay, Nellie Y., ed. *Critical Essays on Toni Morrison*. Boston: G.K. Hall, 1988.

Mercer, Kobena. *Welcome to the Jungle: New Positions in Black Cultural Studies*. New York: Routledge, 1994.

Meyer, Moe, ed. *The Politics and Poetics of Camp*. London: Routledge, 1994.

Miller, D. Quentin, ed. *Re-Viewing James Baldwin: Things Not Seen*. Philadelphia: Temple University Press, 2000.

Morrison, Toni. *Beloved*. New York: Plume, 1988.

———. *Sula*. New York: New American Library, 1973.

Morrison, Toni. *Conversations with Toni Morrison*. Ed. Danille Taylor-Guthrie. Jackson: University Press of Mississippi, 1994.

Muñoz, José Esteban. *Disidentifications: Queers of Color and the Performance of Politics*. Minneapolis: University of Minnesota Press, 1999.

Munt, Sally. *Heroic Desire: Lesbian Identity and Cultural Space*. London: Cassell, 1998.

Munt, Sally, and Cherry Smyth, eds. *Butch/Femme: Inside Lesbian Gender*. London: Cassell, 1998.

Nestle, Joan, ed. *The Persistent Desire: A Femme-Butch Reader*. Boston: Alyson Publications, 1992.

Orfield, Gary, and John Yun. *Resegregation in American Schools*. Cambridge, Mass.: Harvard University Press, 1999.

Orfield, Gary, Susan E. Eaton, and Harvard Project on School Desegregation. *Dismantling Desegregation: The Quiet Reversal of Brown v. Board of Education*. New York: New Press, 1996.

Ozick, Cynthia. *The Shawl*. New York: Knopf, 1989.

Pasquier, Marie-Claire. *Stratégies Des Femmes*. Paris: Tierce, 1984.

Patterson, Orlando. *The Ordeal of Integration: Progress and Resentment in America's "Racial" Crisis*. Washington, D.C.: Counterpoint, 1997.

Patterson, James T. *Brown v. Board of Education: A Civil Rights Milestone and its Troubled Legacy*. New York: Oxford University Press, 2001.

Reid-Pharr, Robert F. *Black Gay Man: Essays*. New York: New York University Press, 2001.

———. "Tearing the Goat's Flesh: Homosexuality, Abjection and the Production of a Late Twentieth-Century Black Masculinity." *Studies in the Novel* 28, no. 3 (fall 1996): 372–94.

Robinson, Cedric J. *Black Marxism: The Making of the Black Radical Tradition*. London: Zed Press, 1983.

Rogin, Michael. "The Two Declarations of American Independence." *Representations* 55 (summer 1996): 25.

Rout, Kathleen. *Eldridge Cleaver*. Boston: Twayne Publishers, 1991.

Rubinstein, Ruth P. *Dress Codes: Meanings and Messages in American Culture*. Boulder: Westview Press, 1995.

Rudofsky, Bernard. *Are Clothes Modern? An Essay on Contemporary Apparel*. Chicago: P. Theobald, 1947.

Rushkoff, Douglas. *Media Virus! Hidden Agendas in Popular Culture*. New York: Ballantine Books, 1994.

Russo, Vito. *The Celluloid Closet: Homosexuality in the Movies*. Rev. ed. New York: Perennial Library, 1987.

Samuels, Wilfred D., and Clenora Hudson-Weems. *Toni Morrison*. Boston: Twayne Publishers, 1990.

Sarat, Austin, ed. *Race, Law, and Culture: Reflections on Brown v. Board of Education*. New York: Oxford University Press, 1997.

Saussure, Ferdinand de. *Course in General Linguistics*. New York: McGraw-Hill, 1966.

Sedgwick, Eve Kosofsky. *Epistemology of the Closet*. Berkeley: University of California Press, 1990.

———, ed. *Novel Gazing: Queer Readings in Fiction*. Durham, N.C.: Duke University Press, 1997.

Sedgwick, Eve Kosofsky, and Adam Frank. "Shame in the Cybernetic Fold." *Critical Inquiry* 1, no. 2 (winter 1995): 496–522.

———. *Touching Feeling: Affect, Pedagogy, Performativity*. Durham, N.C.: Duke University Press, 2003.

Silverman, Kaja. *The Subject of Semiotics*. New York: Oxford University Press, 1983.

Smith-Rosenberg, Carroll. *Disorderly Conduct: Visions of Gender in Victorian America*. New York: Knopf, 1985.

Sobchack, Thomas, and Vivian Carol Sobchack. *An Introduction to Film*. 2nd ed. Boston: Little, Brown, 1987.

Somerville, Siobhan B. *Queering the Color Line: Race and the Invention of Homosexuality in American Culture*. Durham, N.C.: Duke University Press, 2000.

Sontag, Susan. "Notes on 'Camp.'" In *Against Interpretation*. New York: Dell, 1966.

Spencer, Herbert. *Principles of Sociology*. Hamden, Conn.: Archon Books, 1969.

Spillers, Hortense J. "Mama's Baby, Papa's Maybe: An American Grammar Book." *Diacritics* 17, no. 2 (1987): 65–81.

Standley, Fred L., and Nancy V. Burt. *Critical Essays on James Baldwin*. Boston: G.K. Hall, 1988.

Standley, Fred L., and Nancy V. Standley, eds. *James Baldwin: A Reference Guide*. Boston: G.K. Hall, 1980.

Staples, Robert. *Black Masculinity: The Black Male's Role in American Society*. San Francisco: Black Scholar Press, 1982.

Stockton, Kathryn Bond. *God Between Their Lips: Desire Between Women in Irigaray, Brontë, and Eliot*. Stanford, Calif.: Stanford University Press, 1994.

———. "Reading Details, Teaching Politics: Political Mantras and the Politics of Luxury." *College English* 64, no. 1 (2001): 109–21.

Stryker, Susan. *Queer Pulp: Perverted Passions from the Golden Age of the Paperback.* San Francisco: Chronicle Books, 2001.

Sullivan, Robert. "In Search of the Cure for AIDS." *Rolling Stone,* April 7, 1994, 55–64.

Taussig, Michael T. *Defacement: Public Secrecy and the Labor of the Negative.* Stanford, Calif.: Stanford University Press, 1999.

Taylor, Mark C., and Esa Saarinen. *Imagologies: Media Philosophy.* New York: Routledge, 1994.

Troupe, Quincy, ed. *James Baldwin: The Legacy.* New York: Simon and Schuster, 1989.

Tushnet, Mark, and Katya Levin. "What Really Happened in *Brown v. Board of Education.*" *Columbia Law Review* 91, no. 8 (December 1991): 1867–1930.

Watney, Simon. "Missionary Positions: AIDS, 'Africa,' and Race." *differences* 1, no. 1 (winter 1989): 83–100.

Weatherby, William J. *James Baldwin: Artist on Fire: A Portrait.* New York: D.I. Fine, 1989.

———. *Squaring Off: Mailer vs Baldwin.* New York: Mason/Charter, 1977.

White, Edmund. *Genet: A Biography.* New York: Vintage, 1994.

Williams, Juan. *Eyes on the Prize: America's Civil Rights Years, 1954–1965.* New York: Viking, 1987.

Willis, Sharon. *High Contrast: Race and Gender in Contemporary Hollywood Film.* Durham, N.C.: Duke University Press, 1997.

Willis, Susan. *Specifying: Black Women Writing the American Experience.* Madison: University of Wisconsin Press, 1987.

Wilson, Elizabeth. *Adorned in Dreams: Fashion and Modernity.* Berkeley: University of California Press, 1987.

Wilson, Elizabeth, and Juliet Ash, eds. *Chic Thrills: A Fashion Reader.* Berkeley: University of California Press, 1993.

INDEX

Abjection, 7–8, 12, 17, 19, 21–22. *See also* Shame

Aesthetics, 17–18, 24, 40, 42, 64–65, 114, 117–31. *See also* Beauty

AIDS: African AIDS crisis, 177, 179, 234 n. 11; AIDS quilt, 26, 202–3, 247 n. 8, 253 n. 44; American AIDS crisis, 14, 21, 73, 78, 116, 122–23, 177–80, 183–84, 225 n. 33, 251 n. 34, 252 n. 40, 253 n. 45, 254 n. 11; autoimmunity and, 180, 197; blacks and, 73, 122–23; Down Low and, 1–2, 22, 247 n. 6; fluids exchange and, 6, 37, 180, 189–90, 193, 197–98, 251 n. 33; HIV and, 1, 184, 197–98; viral dormancy and, 180, 198–202, 252 n. 38

Althusser, Louis, 238 n. 30

Anality, 14, 35, 67–100, 101–47, 234 n. 8, 239 n. 33, 240 n. 5

Attraction: hidden histories of, 104, 112, 114–16, 119, 136–40, 145–46; shame and, 13, 24–25, 34–36,

149–76; violence and, 40, 102–47, 178–79, 219

Autoimmunity, 180, 197

Bakhtin, Mikhail, 223 n. 5

Baldwin, James, 6, 22, 36, 123, 149–76, 178, 213, 242 n. 2, 242 n. 5; Cleaver and, 151–76; critical studies on, 245 n. 27, 246 n. 28, 246 nn. 30–31; Mailer and, 154–59, 169, 172–75, 243 n. 12, 243 n. 15; theories of attraction in, 149–76

Barthes, Roland, 31, 35, 107, 123–33, 236 n. 21, 240 nn. 23–24; on aesthetic wounding, 107, 123–33, 141–42, 145; "Myth Today," 199–203

Basements, 109–13, 131, 133, 138, 219, 239 n. 5

Bataille, Georges: Genet and, 229 n. 23; on sacrifice, 47–48, 62, 65, 69, 219, 229 n. 24, 229 n. 25, 230 n. 26; on shame, 10–14, 17

Beauty: Bataille on, 10–11, 14; black

Beauty (*continued*)
men and, 118–22, 215, 218–21, 225
n. 3, 254 n. 11; blackness and, 61–
62, 218–21; clothing and, 40–43,
46, 50, 56, 58–66; dirt and, 61, 69,
150, 219; land and, 74, 150; racialized standards of, 9; skin and, 40;
violence and, 69, 71, 107, 123–33,
141–42, 145, 149–50
Beloved (Morrison), 6, 26–27, 37,
177–203, 206, 210–11, 220
Berlant, Lauren, 29
Bersani, Leo, 6, 26, 77–78, 93, 97,
224 n. 26, 226 n. 7
Bible, 133, 238 n. 32, 241 n. 25, 245
n. 22
"Black" and "Queer": defined, 27–33;
as linguistic signs, 2, 5, 68, 103,
107–8, 115–16, 118, 122, 132, 139,
149, 179, 205, 221, 224 n. 27, 234
n. 9. *See also* Black queers
Black Book (Mapplethorpe), 117–23,
176
Black Book (Morrison), 177–78, 252
n. 43
Black gender, 68–100
Black labor history, 68–100
Black leather, 119, 122, 136–39
Black masculinity, 1, 21, 83, 87, 91–
92, 117–23, 133–47, 158–69. *See
also* Cleaver, Eldridge: on theory of
cultural types
Black Nationalism, 21
Black queers, 2, 8, 21–23, 103, 117–
23, 140, 179, 232 n. 39; black gay
critics, 19–23, 117–23, 225 n. 3, 245
n. 27
Black studies, 24–25
Black unemployment, 75–76, 83–88,
93–94, 99, 135, 237 n. 28
Boots of Leather, Slippers of Gold (Kennedy and Davis), 48, 57, 230 n. 29,
232 n. 36, 232 n. 39
Bottom: of body, 7, 66–100, 102, 151;
economic meaning of, 7, 18, 35, 66–

100, 102, 218–21, 234 n. 7, 235 n. 15,
237 n. 28; low-lying land as, 68,
74–75; of mind, 7, 102, 151, 171–76;
Morrison's fictional neighborhood,
25, 33, 35, 67–100, 102, 150, 235
n. 13
Brown v. Board of Education, 152, 160,
162, 167–68, 176, 242 n. 3
Butch–femme relations, 54–57, 65–
66, 69, 231 n. 35
Butler, Judith, 29, 166–67, 224 n. 26

Camera Lucida (Barthes), 107, 123–33,
240 nn. 23–24
Camp: black comedy and, 11, 13, 16,
19, 147, 211; Cleaver and, 207, 210–
12; dark, 37–38, 205–21; defined,
207–10, 253 n. 7; Genet and, 42,
57–66, 69, 108, 206, 211, 219; Hall
and, 206; Morrison and, 69, 108,
132, 135, 206–07, 210–12; Tarantino
and, 108–11, 135, 207, 211
Capitalism, 75, 79, 84–85, 102–3, 135,
236 n. 26
Castle, Terry, 230 n. 29
Castration, 4, 68, 91–92, 114, 228
n. 17, 239 n. 33
Catholicism, 47–48, 55, 65, 229 n. 23
Césaire, Aimé, 8
Christian, Barbara, 78–79, 236 n. 20
Christianity, 13, 47–48, 69, 72, 75,
146, 249 n. 23. *See also* Catholicism
Civil rights, 84–86, 99, 237 n. 28,
244 n. 21. See also *Brown v. Board of
Education*; Desegregation; Segrega-
tion
Cleaver, Eldridge, 36, 38, 149–76,
178, 244 n. 16, 244 n. 18, 244 n. 19;
Baldwin and, 151–76, 243 n. 7, 243
n. 15, 244 n. 17; camp and, 207,
210–12; on theory of cultural types,
164–68, 175–76, 211, 215–21, 246
n. 33, 245 n. 26, 254 nn. 9–10
Cloning, 181–84
Closeting, 2, 17

Clothing: defined, 43; shame and, 34–35, 39–66, 226 n. 13, 228 n. 17, 233 n. 44, 255 n. 22. *See also* Switchpoints: black skin and queer clothes as

Computer hackers, 183, 248 n. 13

Cops, 26, 55–59, 62–64, 233 n. 44

Corpses, 6, 12, 145, 151–54, 161–63, 169–76, 246 n. 33. *See also* Decomposition

Crisp, Quentin, 224 n. 28

Critical legal theory, 32

Cross-dressing, 48–57

Crucifixion, 20, 62, 146

Cvetkovich, Ann, 231 nn. 34–35

Cybernetics, 15, 37, 180–203, 248 nn. 12–13, 249 n. 25, 252 n. 40

Dawkins, Richard, 192–94, 250 n. 27, 250 nn. 29–30

Death, 12, 20–21, 26, 29–30, 89, 93, 96, 144–45, 171, 177–203. *See also* Corpses; Decomposition

Debasement, 7

Decomposition: of attraction, 151–76; defined, 153. *See also* Corpses

Deconstruction, 14, 53–54, 240 n. 22, 243 n. 7

Defacement, 13–14, 123

Deliverance (Boorman), 239 n. 5

Dennett, Daniel, 192–94, 199, 250 n. 28, 250 n. 30, 252 n. 40

Desegregation, 152, 154, 160, 176, 211, 242 n. 4, 243 n. 8. See also *Brown v. Board of Education*; Segregation

Details, theory of, 33, 35, 69–70, 101–23, 131–47, 170, 205, 254 n. 17

Dignity, 8–9, 20. *See also* Pride

Dinshaw, Carolyn, 29, 113

Dirt, 12–13, 61, 68–71, 74–75, 81, 96–98, 150, 219; dirtiness, 10, 12, 13, 18, 36, 68, 170–71; "dirty" defined, 103; dirty details in texts, 101–23, 131–47, 151, 218–19

Doan, Laura, 226 n. 15, 228 n. 16

Domesticity, 236 n. 26

Down Low, 1–2, 22, 247 n. 6

Dreaming Emmett (Morrison), 178–79, 247 n. 5

Edelman, Lee, 6, 17, 19, 29, 114, 224 n. 27

Egan, Beresford, 53–54

Embarrassment, 7, 18. *See also* Shame

Eminem, 19

Fani-Kayode, Rotimi, 103, 117

Fanon, Frantz, 8–9

Far From Heaven (Haynes), 38, 212–16

Feinberg, Leslie, 5, 26, 46, 48–49, 54–57, 64–66, 69, 217, 231 n. 34, 232 nn. 38–39

Female masculinity, 227 n. 15, 230 n. 28. *See also* Femme–Butch relations; Mannish lesbians

Femininity, 13–14, 43–44, 63, 168, 217, 227 n. 15, 236 n. 26, 245 n. 24

Feminism, 118–19, 166–67, 245 n. 23, 250 n. 30; historians of, 45, 83

Femme–butch relations, 54–57, 65–66, 69, 231 n. 35

Fiedler, Leslie, 246 n. 31

Fight Club (Fincher), 38, 58, 216–21, 254 nn. 16–17, 255 nn. 21–23

Film cuts, 106–14, 131–67, 239 n. 3, 240 n. 6, 240 n. 24

Fincher, David. See *Fight Club*

Fisher, Gary, 21–22, 140

Flugel, J. C., 45, 226 n. 13, 228 n. 17

Foner, Philip Sheldon, 75, 235 n. 16

Foucault, Michel, 14, 24, 77

Frank, Adam, 252 n. 40

Franklin, John Hope, 75

Freud, Sigmund, 236 n. 21, 236 n. 24, 239 n. 33; on activity and passivity, 77, 79–80, 82–84, 87, 94, 100, 236 n. 26; Bersani and, 14; on brain's protective shields, 186–90; on clothing, 43–45, 53; Hall and, 44, 53; on jokes, 75, 235 n. 13; Morri-

Freud, Sigmund (*continued*)
son and, 35, 68–82, 88–100; on
obsessional neurosis, 81, 89; on
projection, 186–89; on regression, 80–82, 88–89, 236 n. 24; on
sublimation, 81–82, 89–90, 94–96

Gallop, Jane, 245 n. 23
Gay bars, 49, 54–57, 66, 230 n. 30,
231 n. 32, 231 n. 34, 232 n. 39
Gays in the military, 67, 225 n. 33
Genet, Jean: Bataille and, 229 n. 23;
Black Panthers and, 122; camp and,
42, 57–66, 69, 108, 206, 211, 219;
dirty details and, 101; martyrdom to
clothes and, 42, 46–47, 57–66, 69,
108, 206, 211, 219; Morrison and,
23, 69, 114, 153, 211; *Poison* and,
254 n. 8; *Querelle*, 57–66; Tarantino
and, 23, 114, 141, 153, 211
Giovanni's Room (Baldwin), 6, 149–
76, 213
Gladwell, Malcolm, 41, 233 n. 43
Griffin, John Howard, 225 n. 1
Guilt, 7

Hackers, 183, 248 n. 13
Halberstam, Judith, 230 n. 28, 230
nn. 30–31, 231 n. 35
Hall, Radclyffe, 26, 44–54, 64–66,
206, 227 n. 15, 229 n. 22, 230
nn. 28–31, 231 n. 32
Halley, Janet, 32
Haraway, Donna, 250 n. 30
Hawkins, Peter, 253 n. 44
Haynes, Todd, 38, 212–16, 254 n. 8,
254 n. 1
Hedwig and the Angry Inch (Mitchell),
3–5
Helms, Jesse, 122–23
Hemingway, Ernest, 155–56, 243 n. 11
Heterosexuality: Cleaver and Mailer
on, 154–68, 207; clothing and, 41–
42, 46, 58–62; Down Low and, 1–2;
in *Far From Heaven*, 213–17; in *Fight*

Club, 217–21; Morrison and, 76–
100, 102, 195–96; in *Pulp Fiction*,
138–41; queer pulp and, 115–16;
"straight queers" and, 29
Historicizing: attraction and, 153,
162, 176; Barthes on, 125–31; camp
and, 207–10; clothing and, 41–66,
227 n. 15; Genet and, 233 n. 41;
interlocking histories and, 25–26;
Morrison and, 68–69, 71–76; redemption and, 142–47, 241 n. 27,
241 n. 33; slavery and, 200–203;
Tarantino and, 104–23, 131–47, 239
n. 5. *See also* Jim Crow history
HIV. *See* AIDS
Holland, Sharon Patricia, 6, 20, 29–
30, 245 n. 27
Homophobia, 67–68, 104, 113–14, 118,
132, 234 n. 2, 245 n. 27
Homosexuality. *See* "Black" and
"Queer"; Black queers; Femme–
Butch relations; Homophobia;
Queer theory; Stigma; Switchpoints
hooks, bell, 8–9
Hughes, Langston, 117, 123
Humiliation, 7–8, 15, 22, 26, 43, 59,
63. *See also* Shame
Humility, 13, 60, 63
Hyperlinking, 182–85, 201–3, 249
n. 21, 251 n. 32. *See also* Memory

Instability of meanings and identities,
33, 225 n. 32
Inverts, 58–60, 64, 230 n. 28, 231
n. 32

Jackie Brown (Tarantino), 140
Jews, 167, 208, 249 n. 20
Jim Crow history, 36, 104–15, 132,
138–39, 150
Johnny Mnemonic (Longo), 248 n. 15
Jouissance, 12–13, 15, 77, 97
Julien, Isaac, 35, 117–23, 132, 140, 145
Jungle Fever (Lee), 225 n. 2

Pietà, 42, 62–66, 255 n. 23
Pitt, Brad, 219–21, 254 n. 16
Poison (Haynes), 215, 254 n. 8, 254 n. 11
Pornography: Mapplethorpe and gay
versions of, 118–19, 145; Morrison
and, 186; paperbacks and, 116, 138;
Reid-Pharr on, 21; Tarantino and
gay versions of, 36, 106, 109, 132,
138–39
Powell, Colin, 34–35, 67–68
Pregnancy, teenage, 86–87, 180–81,
238 n. 29
Pride, 9, 30–31. *See also* Dignity
Prophylactics, 6, 37, 177–203, 250
n. 29
Prostitution, 14
Psychoanalysis, 12–15, 31. *See also*
Freud, Sigmund; Lacan, Jacques
Pulp Fiction (Tarantino), 6, 35–36,
101–23, 131–47, 150, 178, 207, 236
n. 21
Pulp fictions: queer, 104–8, 115–16,
131–47; racialized, 104, 106–17,
131–47
Punctum and *Studium*, 125–47, 240
n. 24, 241 nn. 26–27

"Queer" and "Black": defined, 27–33;
as linguistic signs, 2, 5, 68, 103,
107–8, 115–16, 118, 122, 132, 139,
149, 179, 205, 221, 224 n. 27, 234
n. 9. *See also* Black queers
Queer Eye for the Straight Guy, 1, 28,
41–42
Queer Nation, 31, 208, 210
Queer theory, 9, 24–25
Querelle (Genet), 57–66

Racism, 104, 113, 114, 118, 132, 152,
162, 232 n. 39, 245 n. 22
Rape, 6, 102–4, 108–15, 116, 118, 131–
67, 239 n. 5, 240 n. 22, 241 n. 26,
241 n. 33
Redemption, 103, 108, 112, 114, 119,
141–47, 241 n. 27

Reid-Pharr, Robert F., 6, 20–22, 30,
140
Rogin, Michael, 113

Sacrifice: Bataille on, 46–48, 229
n. 25; Christianity and, 249 n. 23;
clothing and, 34–35, 42, 51, 55, 58–
59, 62, 233 n. 44; in *Fight Club*,
219–21; Mapplethorpe and, 119;
murder and, 58–59, 62
Sadism and sadomasochism: Mapplethorpe and, 118–22, 136–38; Morrison and, 70, 75–76, 79–80, 89–93,
95, 100, 235 n. 13; Tarantino and,
109, 113–15, 131, 136–38
Safe (Haynes), 215
Saints, 13; Saint Stephen, 48, 53–54
Saussure, Ferdinand de, 194
Sedgwick, Eve Kosofsky, 6, 15–17, 20,
26, 29, 31, 104, 224 n. 24, 252 n. 40
Segregation, 99, 167–68, 237 n. 28.
See also Desegregation
Sex change, 3–5
Shame: attraction to, 13, 24–25, 34–
36, 149–76; blushing and, 16, 45,
64, 104, 226 n. 11; clothing and,
34–35, 39–66, 226 n. 13, 228 n. 17,
233 n. 44, 255 n. 22; corpses and,
6, 12, 145, 151–54, 161–63, 169–76,
246 n. 33; death and, 12, 20–21,
26, 29–30, 89, 93, 96, 144–45,
171, 177–203; defined, 7; embraced,
1–37; fascination with, 16, 102,
104, 106–7, 114, 122, 145, 147, 150,
162, 184, 186; fighting and, 57–66;
future and, 175–76, 181–84, 198–
99, 216–21; genitals and, 43–44,
53–54, 62, 86–87; law and, 56–57;
loneliness and, 48–54; martyrdom and, 34–35, 39–66, 68–69,
206, 219–21, 226 n. 10; objectification and, 118–24, 145, 177, 225
n. 3; prayer and, 50–52; redemption and, 103, 108, 112, 114, 119,
141–47, 241 n. 27; seduction and,

Kathryn Bond Stockton is a professor of English and
director of Gender Studies at the University of Utah.
She is the author of *God Between Their Lips: Desire
Between Women in Irigaray, Brontë, and Eliot.*

Library of Congress Cataloging-in-Publication Data
Stockton, Kathryn Bond, 1958–
Beautiful bottom, beautiful shame : where "Black"
meets "queer" / Kathryn Bond Stockton.
p. cm. — (Series Q)
Includes bibliographical references and index.
ISBN 0-8223-3783-5 (cloth : alk. paper) —
ISBN 0-8223-3796-7 (pbk. : alk. paper)
1. American fiction—20th century—History and
criticism. 2. Homosexuality in literature.
3. Homosexuality and literature—United States.
4. American fiction—African American authors—
History and criticism. 5. Shame in literature.
6. African Americans in literature. I. Title.
II. Series.
PS374.H63S76 2006
813'.509353—dc22   2005036016